Bounce Back
From
Bankruptcy

New Expanded Fifth Edition

Bounce Back
From
Bankruptcy

*A Step-by-Step Guide to Getting Back
on Your Financial Feet*

Paula Langguth Ryan
Foreword by Herbert Beskin

&
MEDIA

For Michele.
Thanks for asking.

MEDIA

Published 2025 by Gildan Media LLC
aka G&D Media
www.GandDmedia.com

Front cover design by David Rheinhardt of Pyrographx

Interior design by Meghan Day Healey of Story Horse, LLC

Library of Congress Cataloging-in-Publication Data is available upon request

ISBN: 978-1-7225-0715-2

10 9 8 7 6 5 4 3 2 1

Contents

SECTION II
BEFORE NEW CREDIT,
SHED OLD HABITS AND BELIEFS

SECTION IV
IF YOU FIND YOURSELF IN
OVER YOUR HEAD AGAIN

Foreword

Before becoming a Chapter 13 Trustee, I was a consumer bankruptcy attorney for several decades, filing personal Chapter 7 and Chapter 13 cases. I realized early on in my practice that filing a case for you only solved some problems. It allowed you to tie a ribbon around many of the consequences of a difficult time in your life, but it did little or nothing to provide you with guidance for coping with the world after bankruptcy. I looked around for a resource I could give you that would provide that guidance after we'd parted ways.

I found what I was looking for with the first (and later second) edition of Paula Langguth Ryan's *Bounce Back from Bankruptcy*. It was thorough, logically arranged, and written in language that anyone could understand. It explained the credit-obsessed world we all are involuntarily locked into, and contained practical steps, and even forms, to help you successfully navigate that system. It had a myriad of down-to-earth recommendations for reviving your credit and moving toward financial security. No one left my office without this essential guidebook and my urging that they read it.

When a debtor education course became a requirement before your bankruptcy discharge, I welcomed that development. But I still thought that Paula's common-sense, nuts-and-bolts approach provided essential information and a valuable framework for rebuilding after bankruptcy, in a highly usable format. I am pleased Paula has written an expanded and updated fifth edition of this book. I strongly recommend you read it. It gives you an insightful, complete, sensibly organized, and easily readable roadmap for traveling beyond your bankruptcy. It is a resource worth having and sharing.

—Herb Beskin

P.S. When I retired, one of the few books I took home was the second edition; I still have it.

Introduction

When I was fourteen my father, a carpenter, built our home. Two lots away, a giant hole attested to another family's building adventure. Digging out a full basement, they hit an underground spring, which quickly filled the massive hole. They abandoned their homesite without building anything. Seeing what had happened, my father planned ahead.

He requested a water table survey to learn at what depth he was likely to hit water. Finding the water table was high (just 10 feet below the surface), he didn't throw in the towel, declaring a basement wasn't feasible. Instead, he dug down just a few feet—well above the water table—built concrete forms that loomed aboveground and poured our basement walls. Once the concrete set, he backfilled the dirt to the top of the basement walls, sloped it away from the house and turned our little house on the prairie into a home on a knoll.

To me, rebuilding your financial house after bankruptcy is like building your dream home. You could build it fast—at a high cost to you, with low-quality materials, shoddy workmanship, and an unstable foundation. *Or* you could build it using quality materials and the best workmanship, at the lowest possible price, with complete assurance your house sits on a firm foundation—and a sump pump as added insurance should the creek rise.

When I went bankrupt at age twenty-one, my attorney shook my hand outside the courthouse, said "Good luck," and walked away. No guidance, no suggestions. Just a wish for luck and I was on my way . . . to repeating the same financial patterns that led me back into debt. I vowed to break my patterns and started educating myself. Within eight years, with my bankruptcy still clearly listed on my credit reports, I bought my first home with a beautiful view of the Chesapeake Bay—without paying a higher interest rate.

About that time, a friend who was going bankrupt called for advice. As I was babbling on about the steps to take, she stopped me, asking, "Could you please just write all this down so I can remember it?" So I did. Thirty years later, here we are with the fifth edition of *Bounce Back from Bankruptcy*.

I fully recovered from my bankruptcy, with no guidance, within eight years. Another person who went bankrupt wanted a quicker way to get credit after bankruptcy and wrote a book touting what he achieved after eight months . . . only to file for bankruptcy again, with massive debt compared to his first bankruptcy. My deepest hope is that you'll see the sanity in the slow and steady approach to recovering from your bankruptcy. As Navy SEALs say, "Slow is smooth, smooth is fast."

The fast track, laser-focused on getting new *credit* after bankruptcy, isn't a well-rounded or sustainable path. As I often say, "You can't eat your credit score for lunch." Instead, follow the path outlined in this book. Here, you will find practical, strategic financial steps that are legal, ethical and financially sound—combined with tools to transform the way you think and feel about money—so you permanently break the patterns that led to your bankruptcy.

I am living proof that bankruptcy is not the end of the road. My road wasn't without obstacles, by any means. But yours can be.

Within a few years, you can build a firm foundation of financial security, establish a positive net worth, and learn to use credit in ways that serve *you* and not creditors. From this day forward, *you* determine the financial course of your life.

The truth is, your credit score is a piece of paper. It doesn't determine your self-worth or your ability to repay your debts. Raising your credit score in ways that are meaningful to lenders will happen naturally once you change your financial focus.

How to Use This Book

This book is arranged in five sections. Section I focuses on immediate steps to take after bankruptcy—or after you discover this book! It's like cleaning up after a party once all the guests are gone. You'll discover the best ways to review and update your credit reports, handle debt collectors, create a savings plan, and decide what to do with any remaining debts, including debt you may have reaffirmed.

Section II is where you start laying a foundation for financial success. Where you've *been* is essential to knowing where you're *going* if you want to break the debt cycle for good. Your financial well-being is at stake here, and I don't want old money habits to ruin all your hard work. Together, we'll create strategies so you can set and meet your financial (and life) goals and explore credit-savvy moves to help you reach those goals faster, without incurring debt.

Section III is all about rebuilding—putting new, positive credit information in front of your old, negative information. Step by step you'll discover how to get credit after bankruptcy the right way, including the best strategies for getting credit cards, car loans and buying a home after bankruptcy. You'll even learn ways to travel without a credit card. And, to protect your hard-earned credit, I've included steps to help you avoid, recognize and recover from identity theft.

Life isn't always a straightforward path, so in Section IV I detail the immediate steps to take if you find yourself in over your head again financially. I've also included the best strategies if you are considering credit counseling, dealing with habits that derail your financial progress, and ways to save your home if you're falling behind on your mortgage. You'll also find some sage advice on what to do if it seems another bankruptcy may be your only option.

Finally, in Section V, it's time to move beyond recovery and making ends meet, so you can truly *thrive*, with or without credit. Here's where you'll learn to make thoughtful choices about what to do with your income and your life in order to maximize your true worth—far beyond your finances.

No matter where you are in your bankruptcy recovery I encourage you to start with Section I so you have a clear picture of your current financial situation. A picture that's based on facts, not feelings. Taking the steps in Section I gives you a stable foundation to build on. If you're already struggling financially again, use the strategies in Section IV to give yourself some financial breathing room. Then go back to Section I and take each step in order.

Work with Money's Natural Ebb and Flow

Even if your financial situation looks bleak, remind yourself of the progress you're making simply by learning this material. Baby steps can build a positive net worth, where you *own* more than you *owe*. Temporary setbacks will happen. It's part of money's ebb and flow. Do not despair. You're about to discover how to even out those financial ups and downs. Whenever you get anxious or fearful, sit quietly for 20 minutes, review your current finances, and ask yourself these four questions:

1. What am I already doing (or have I done) to create a more *positive* financial future?

2. Where in my spending can I *temporarily* cut back to increase my cash flow?

3. Where am I out of integrity financially, and what one step can I take *today* to set things right?

4. What *one* action can I take today to reduce my spending and increase my income?

Promise Yourself a True Fresh Start

You have an opportunity to create what you truly want in your life. It doesn't matter whether you mentally struggled with your decision to declare bankruptcy or rejoiced at being out from under your debt. It doesn't matter whether you have sworn off credit forever or have gotten yourself back into debt again.

What matters is that you have found your way here, today. Right now, promise yourself you are going to start fresh today. Instead of being angry, worried, or frustrated about your financial situation, promise yourself you're going to choose to move forward, creating true financial freedom. Promise yourself, you will take time to ask questions about money—and will keep asking questions—until you get answers you understand so you can make the best, informed financial decisions for your life.

These strategies have worked for me and countless others who have declared bankruptcy and were determined to create financial security and solvency. Let them work for you.

SECTION I

FIRST STEPS TO REBUILD AFTER BANKRUPTCY

Chapter 1

Understand Your Credit Reports

Let's start with the nuts and bolts of your current financial situation. Your bankruptcy will be listed on your credit reports for up to ten years. This doesn't mean your credit is ruined for ten years or that *you* are financially ruined for ten years. It simply means this *information* will be listed where future creditors will see it. Bankruptcy does *not* automatically make you a bad credit risk. With other positive credit information on your credit report, your bankruptcy may show you in a better financial light.

What Current and Future Creditors See

Creditors subscribe to services from four major credit bureaus: Equifax, Experian, and TransUnion, and the lesser known Innovis. These companies compile all our financial data into files known as *credit reports*. You are legally entitled to know what your credit reports tell creditors, to request and receive a free copy of each credit report at least annually, and to dispute errors on your reports.

What Your Credit Reports Say About You

Your credit reports list current and past creditors, how much you borrowed from them, and whether you pay your bills on time. Each report is divided into sections to show your payment history for all revolving accounts (like credit cards), mortgages, and installment accounts (including car and personal loans). Each should also confirm that your bankruptcy has been discharged and lists other public records, including liens and judgments against you.

Many creditors report information to credit bureaus only when your account becomes 90 days or more past due or if your account is sent to a collection agency. Other creditors (especially credit cards) report your payment history monthly. Your payment history is usually reported in 30-day increments and, for each creditor, will show how many times you paid 30, 60, 90, 120 or 150 days late. The credit bureau's coding system is usually explained right under the payment history for each account.

It's important to understand *every* piece of information on *each* credit report. Otherwise, you could overlook an error. When a future creditor sees that error, they might turn you down for a car loan or mortgage and you will have no idea why. If anything on any credit report is unclear after you read this section, call the credit bureau at the number listed on the report and ask a representative to walk you through the information.

Order Your Free Annual Credit Reports by Mail

It takes up to 90 days after a bankruptcy discharge for your credit files to be updated. If your bankruptcy wasn't discharged at least 90 days ago, write that 90-day date on your calendar, skip ahead to Section II, and come back to this step once your bankruptcy has been discharged at least 90 days. You want your credit reports to show your most up-to-date credit information.

To order your Experian, TransUnion, and Equifax credit reports by mail, you'll need a copy of their combined official request form.

You can print out the form from The Central Source website (annual creditreport.com). It's hard to find the form on their site, so I've also included a downloadable pdf at rebuildafterbankruptcy.com.

Print the form, carefully follow the instructions, fill out the form, fold it and place it in a business-size #10 envelope (do not staple or tape the form), and send it via certified mail, return receipt requested to:

Annual Credit Report Request Service
P.O. Box 105281
Atlanta, GA 30348-5281

This way you have a dated document showing when your request was received. You should receive your credit report from each credit bureau within 30 days. If you haven't received your three reports by then, call 877-322-8228 to request assistance. If you still have a challenge getting your credit reports, submit a complaint to the Consumer Financial Protection Bureau (consumerfinance.gov/complaint).

Although my preference is to request these three credit reports by mail for safety reasons, you can also call The Central Source's automated help line (877-322-8228) to order these reports. The process takes about seven minutes of your time. This is an automated phone call that is activated by voice recognition, so speak slowly and clearly. If you have an accent or get frustrated easily, you may be better off ordering your report by mail.

The phone system will ask for your name, address, Social Security number, and date of birth. The system will also prompt you for your previous address if you've moved in the past two years. Follow the directions. When the system asks which report you want, say, "All three."

Order Your Free Innovis Credit Report

Innovis (innovis.com/personal/creditreport) recommends you order your credit report via mail for security reasons. You can print and complete the mail-in form or provide your information by phone (866-712-0021) or online to have a form mailed to you. Innovis responds quickly; if you mail the form in you will likely get your Innovis credit report before your other reports.

The Innovis credit report is also generally more in-depth than reports from the other three credit bureaus. When you submit your mail-in form, you'll need to include specific documentation showing proof of your current address and proof of your identity. You should receive your report within 10 days after they receive your form. Mail your completed form and copies of requested documents via certified mail, return receipt requested to:

Innovis Consumer Assistance
P.O. Box 530088
Atlanta, GA 30353-0088

Order Check Reporting Service Reports

You may have difficulty opening a new checking account if you bounced checks before your bankruptcy. Just like creditors, who subscribe to the credit reporting bureaus, banks subscribe to special *check reporting services*. Hopefully, any checks you bounced were included in your bankruptcy, and would be listed in these reports as *discharged under bankruptcy*.

Request your free reports from the four main check reporting services (listed below) to confirm bounced checks listed on your bankruptcy are reported as discharged. And double-check for any outstanding bounced checks you might have forgotten to list in your bankruptcy. Before applying for a new checking account, tell the banker about your bankruptcy. Follow each agency's instructions on how to submit your report request by mail and how to properly dispute any information on your report. Send each request via certified mail, return receipt requested. The top four check reporting services are:

ChexSystems (chexsystems.com; 800-428-9623). Scroll down the home page to the Requesting Reports section. You can submit your request online, by phone via the 24/7 automated system, or by mail. Download the Consumer Request for Disclosure Form and mail it to the address provided on the form.

TeleCheck (telecheck.com; 800-366-2425). Click the Consumer File Report link on the upper right side of the home page. Complete the online form and click Submit or scroll down below the form for instructions on submitting your request by mail. To submit your request by phone, call the number above.

Early Warning (earlywarning.com; 800-745-1560). Click on Your File Disclosure in the upper right corner of the home page, then click the How to Request Your Report button for details on how to order your report, including a link to a form you can print, fill out and mail in with a copy of your identification. You can also submit your request on weekdays by phone and they'll send your report by mail.

CrossCheck (cross-check.com; 800-843-0760). The Consumer Request Forms are under the Consumers & Privacy tab. Select Consumer Request Forms, then click the box indicating you're requesting an Annual Report to reveal the online request form. Fill in the information and they'll mail your report to you. To get the mail-in address or phone instructions, select the FAQs under that same Consumer & Privacy tab and then select "How can I request an annual file report disclosure?"

Declined for a Checking Account?

If you've already been declined for a checking account, the banker is required to let you know, either in person or through the mail. Once you know which screening service the bank used, follow the instructions above to get your report from the service that turned you down. Just like with your credit report, you must show the check reporting service if any checks they show as outstanding were discharged under your bankruptcy. If there are truly any outstanding checks that weren't listed on your bankruptcy, you'll need to pay those checks before you can open a new checking account.

Avoid Having Your New Checking Account Flagged

Instead of accepting the standard starting check number of 101, order your checks and select a four-digit starting number, like 1251. Low check numbers indicate a checking account is new, and some businesses won't accept those checks as payment.

While You Wait for Your Credit and Checking Reports . . .

If you've followed my advice and mailed the requests for your credit reports, you'll have a few weeks to wait for your reports to arrive, so put that time to good use. The minute you send off your credit report requests, either start working on the strategies in Chapter 4 to Vanquish Your Remaining Debt or start working on laying a new foundation for your financial security by checking out Section II, Before New Credit, Break Old Habits and Beliefs to uncover how and why you got to where you are, break the debt cycle, set and achieve realistic goals, and take credit-savvy actions to buy what you want without getting back in debt.

Once you have your reports in hand, move on to Chapter 2 so you can review and correct your reports.

Chapter 2

Review and Correct Your Credit Reports

Update Your Credit Reports

Once you have your credit reports, it's time to straighten out any errors and update incorrect information. Get a pad of paper, start with one report and work your way all the way through, writing down every error you see in each portion of the report. I'll walk you through what errors to look for. Do the same for each report.

Look for Obvious Credit Report Errors First

The two most obvious errors are incorrect personal information and out-of-date information. Here's what to look for:

Incorrect personal information.

First, verify your name, address, Social Security number, and employment information. Second, confirm all listed accounts actually belong to you. If you have a common name or are a Jr., Sr., II, etc., or if you've unknowingly been a victim of identity theft, your credit report might contain information that belongs to someone else. Check the last four digits of the account numbers on the credit report against the actual account numbers on your credit cards, loan papers and your bankruptcy discharge papers. Third, look for addresses or places of employment you don't recognize. These could be clues that your information may be mixed up with someone else's or that you may have been a victim of identity theft.

Out-of-date information.

Other errors include old information that hasn't been removed from your credit report. For the most part, negative, correctly reported information that is more than seven years old must automatically be removed. Here are the exceptions:

- Chapter 7 bankruptcies remain for ten years.
- Chapter 13 bankruptcies stay on for seven years from the date you complete your repayment plan.
- Tax liens, paid lawsuits, and judgments remain for seven years from the date you paid them off.
- Unpaid lawsuits or judgments will stay listed on your credit report for seven years from the date they were entered or the time allowed by law for collecting the judgment, whichever is longer. This period varies from state to state, but it can be as long as 20 years.

Update Discharged Accounts

Once you've written down all obvious errors, look at your credit report with a more critical eye to see what other information is being reported in error. Start with accounts that were included in your bankruptcy.

Compare the discharged debts from your bankruptcy paperwork to the debts listed on your credit report. As you locate each item on your bankruptcy papers, confirm that debt is listed as "discharged under bankruptcy protection" or "reorganized under Chapter 13 bankruptcy." If a debt on your credit report is listed any other way, write that down. If any creditors are listed with active debt that wasn't discharged under your bankruptcy, add that account to your list.

Update Collection Accounts

A collection agency for a debt is generally listed *separately* from the creditor it serves. This makes it look like you have two debts when you have only one. If the debt was discharged under your bankruptcy, only the original creditor should be listed on your credit report. Write down any collection agencies that still appear on your credit report.

Unpaid Lawsuits/Judgments Hanging Around?

Contact your state attorney general's office and ask what the *statute of limitations* is for unpaid lawsuits or judgments. These will stay on your credit report until the time allowed by your state's statute of limitations or seven years, whichever is longer. Each state has its own requirements as to when that clock starts ticking, so ask for those specifics too so you know *exactly* when these unpaid lawsuits or judgments should fall off your credit report. If they still appear on your reports more than a month after that date, write to the credit bureaus and request they be removed.

Update Closed Accounts

Check for any closed accounts that are listed as open. Confirm accounts that *you* closed are listed that way and not as having been closed by a creditor.

Accounts Not Included in Your Bankruptcy

Your credit reports may also show *incorrect* information about any remaining debts—including debts you didn't list in your bankruptcy and debts that couldn't be discharged under your bankruptcy. Common places where you may find errors include defaulted student loans, back taxes, and missed mortgage payments when your Chapter 13 repayment plan ended. Anytime you have existing debts that have a bad payment history, pay close attention to them. You can bet future creditors will!

Start by confirming that *each* piece of information on these accounts is accurate. If a creditor shows you were 60 days late with several payments while your checks or receipts prove you were only 30 days late, write that information down as being incorrect, so you can report it to the credit bureau. There's a big difference between being 60 days late and being 30 days late.

Check All Your Credit Reports

Be sure to read every word on the reports from all four credit bureaus and highlight *all* incorrect information from each report. You never know which company a creditor will use to check your credit—and the last thing you want is for the negative information you cleared up on one report to show up unexpectedly on another credit bureau's report.

Even if you find incorrect information in a credit report regarding a debt for which you have a bad payment history, make sure that information is reported correctly so your credit history will be as accurate as possible.

Submit All Credit Report Errors

Once you have your notes on the four reports, you're almost ready to submit them to the respective credit bureaus. Your next step is to start a file for each credit bureau. This is where you'll keep a copy of all the letters and forms you send. And remember to always send your letters via *certified mail, return receipt requested*, so you can prove the date you sent your request. Put those little green cards in the files too.

Once your files are created, make multiple copies of your bankruptcy paperwork. You'll need four copies each of your listed debts (Schedules D, E, and F) *and* your notice of discharge (Order of Discharge).

For example, my car loan had been listed and discharged under my bankruptcy, but my Equifax credit report showed I still had an outstanding car loan, and the creditor had slapped me with a lien. Sending them my bankruptcy paperwork quickly removed the outdated information. What seemed like a big problem had an easy solution.

Now, you're ready to submit your corrections. You could submit them electronically using each credit bureau's online form, but I still recommend mailing your corrections, so you have evidence of your submissions and their responses.

Credit bureaus now provide *request for reinvestigation* or *dispute* forms that are easy to use to update your credit report. Simply print, fill out, and mail each bureau's form to update your credit report. Search *each* credit bureau's site for "dispute request form," "dispute credit report," or "dispute resolution" to find each bureau's official mail-in form *and* a list of supporting documents to include with your request. Fill out each form, listing which information is wrong on their specific credit report and stating what the correct information should be.

The credit bureaus specifically designed these forms to include all the information you must provide about your accounts. Of course, I still encourage you to include a nice, short note—even a handwritten one—along with your form. A pleasant letter often makes for speedier results.

What to Expect After Submitting Your Corrected Credit Information

Once the credit bureau receives your dispute form, they will contact your creditor to be sure that the information they have reported about your account is correct. If the creditor cannot verify the incorrect information, by law, the credit bureau must drop it from your report.

If you dispute an error and the credit bureau responds saying your creditor claims the incorrect information is correct, call or write to your creditor directly and request a letter stating that the account is current (or the correct status). Once you receive this letter, make copies and use a new dispute form to send a copy of the letter to each credit bureau that is reporting the wrong information about your account.

You can expect to hear from the credit bureau within 30 days. If a month passes and you still haven't heard anything, write another letter requesting an update on your investigation. Again, send the letter via certified mail, return receipt requested, and keep a copy for your files.

Only send supporting documents (such as receipts or canceled checks) *if* a creditor responds by saying the information is correct. Any creditor who can't back up their claims must remove *all* the bad information—regardless of whether you *ever* paid late. Without proof, your creditor must upgrade your account to show you weren't delinquent. As a result, you could wind up with positive credit information on your credit report. If they still say you were 60 days late, for example, and your records show you were only 30 days, then supply your supporting documents. Lenders view a 30-day late payment in a much better light than a payment that was 60 days late.

Continue to monitor your credit reports regularly to ensure payments on all your accounts are properly recorded. When I applied for a car loan after bankruptcy, the banker was ready to turn down my loan request based on the information in my credit report. Before my bankruptcy, I had defaulted on my student loan, and my account had been at least 120 days past due for some time. After declaring bankruptcy, I worked out a payment schedule with the student loan issuer. But a glitch in the lender's computer system showed my account becoming increasingly more delinquent every month, which was also reflected on my credit report, despite my on-time payments. Once the lender fixed the problem, they sent me a letter verifying that everything was fine and my account was current. But the creditor hadn't notified the credit bureau that they'd fixed the error. When I finally requested my credit report, I saw what my creditors had been seeing: a really bad post-bankruptcy debt—even though I had been diligently making payments on this debt after my bankruptcy. I sent a letter to the credit bureau disputing the creditor's payment history.

The credit bureau investigated and responded with a letter saying the creditor had confirmed the late payment information was correct. I sent them a copy of the letter from the student loan lender, and the credit bureau quickly updated my credit report to show my student loan account was indeed current and had been since my bankruptcy.

If discharged debts are still listed as delinquent, under collection, or charged off, your creditors may *not* have notified the credit bureaus that their debt was included in your bankruptcy; and sometimes this information just falls through the cracks. Updating and removing incorrect delinquencies is easy.

Hit a Snag Correcting Your Credit Reports?

If a credit bureau refuses to remove incorrect or out-of-date information from your credit report, submit a complaint to the Consumer Financial Protection Bureau (CFPB) (consumerfinance .gov/complaint). In your complaint, include the name, address and phone number of the credit bureau. Explain your problem, the dates you contacted the credit bureau, and with whom you spoke. Include a copy of any documents pertaining to your dispute. Send one packet to the CFPB and a second packet—including your letter to the CFPB and a copy of your documentation—to the credit bureau with a newly completed dispute form. Your packet, with the credit bureau copied on your letter to the CFPB, will prompt someone at the credit bureau to take action to resolve the issue.

Write a Credit History Statement

Bankruptcy is often caused by factors such as job loss, illness, divorce, even a lack of money management skills, that may now be under control. The Fair Credit Reporting Act allows you to add a statement to your credit report explaining any outside factors that led to your declaring bankruptcy. Or your statement could briefly outline correct information you've submitted that hasn't been updated. This statement becomes a permanent part of your credit report until you change it.

Use your statement to summarize the nature of your past problem and, if possible, show creditors how you are better able to handle credit now. If the credit bureau limits your statement to fewer than 100 words, the bureau must help you prepare a summary. Call and ask the credit bureau for help writing your statement. A representative can help you frame your credit history in the best light.

Although adding a statement about why you declared bankruptcy and what has changed to prevent it from happening again doesn't improve your credit score, it does show creditors that you have taken action to improve how you handle money, credit, and debt.

Chapter 3

Dealing with Post Bankruptcy Fallout

Bankruptcy and Your Job

In most instances, your employer is unlikely to learn you've declared bankruptcy—unless you need a security clearance, or your employer runs a credit check. What's more, your employer will probably *support* your decision because, once you file for bankruptcy, you'll be more emotionally present at work.

What your credit report says is usually only important if your job requires handling large amounts of money or you're going to be in a sensitive position. People with huge amounts of debt are considered more susceptible to blackmail, bribery, or theft, so your bankruptcy actually makes you *less* susceptible. A bankruptcy will not disqualify you at most companies. However, having several credit problems, lots of late payments, or canceled credit cards *could* disqualify you, which is why employers look a bit more favorably on a bankruptcy than on active but poor credit accounts. Bankruptcy followed by new credit problems, however, is a red flag.

By law, no employer can fire you or discriminate against you *solely* because you filed bankruptcy. Even for a government job, you can't be turned down *simply* because you went bankrupt. Discrimination against *any* employee for bankruptcy is expressly prohibited by law. If you believe you've been discriminated against or fired because of your bankruptcy, contact a debtors' rights or employment attorney immediately.

Before you start interviewing for a new job, review and confirm the information on your credit reports. Potential employers often check both your references *and* your credit report. To an employer, a good credit report indicates you can plan and are responsible. Put yourself in the employer's shoes. An employer's biggest concern is *Will this person represent my company well and not take advantage of me or mismanage my company's money?*

Employers sometimes use credit reports as a tiebreaker when they like two candidates. If you think a job offer may come down to you and one other person, be up front about your bankruptcy. The employer will appreciate your honesty and will take that into consideration when looking at your credit report. Be specific and briefly outline what led to your bankruptcy and steps you've taken to become and stay financially solvent. By law, no employer can pull your credit report unless you've signed a release giving them permission. So, you will know if an employer plans to review your credit report.

You can't control how future employers might view your credit rating. So, concentrate on what you *can* control: putting your bankruptcy and your past credit problems behind you. Future employers will be grateful to see you've dealt with these problems, because now your mind will be focused on doing your job and not on fending off bill collectors!

Credit Repair Companies

It's easy to see why many people wind up using credit repair companies. Some companies guarantee in writing that they'll get negative information off your credit report or you don't have to pay them. Don't believe it! It's true they will get information removed temporarily, because disputed items are removed from your credit report while they're under review. At that point, they take your money. Then the negative information reappears a month or two later.

Although some credit repair companies are reputable (see sidebar), many are not. Avoid any company that:

1. Asks for a large up-front fee of several hundred dollars. Legitimate companies charge a very small amount for their services, and they don't ask for their money until you are completely sat-

---

Legitimate Credit Repair Assistance

You may, after learning how to clean up your credit reports, decide you still want assistance (the same way I prefer having someone else change my oil). Legitimate credit repair companies and credit counselors do exist. They can help you write letters to your creditors to update negative information and remove or modify incorrect information on your credit reports. But you should be the one who reads, signs, and mails those letters.

If you do want to have someone else help you, make sure the company is legit. Check with the Better Business Bureau (bbb.org) where the company is headquartered. Then call your state attorney general's office to find out if the credit repair company is licensed to do business in your state. Finally, check the nonprofit Ripoff Report (ripoffreport.com) for negative reviews of the company. If the company isn't licensed to do business in your state or has a long record of complaints about it, keep your money in your pocket.

isfied that your credit reports have been corrected, based on correspondence you receive directly from the credit bureaus.

2. Says they can remove true but negative information from your credit report. The methods these companies use can get negative information taken off your credit reports only until the creditor confirms that the negative information is correct. It will again be on your credit report, and you'll be out hundreds of dollars.

3. Assures you they can remove a bankruptcy from your credit report. Unless the bankruptcy was discharged over 10 years ago (seven years for Chapter 13), there is no *ethical* way to remove your bankruptcy. There is a fraudulent way, which involves requesting your bankruptcy file from the courthouse archives, then questioning the bankruptcy on your credit report once the court file is missing. I don't recommend it.

Some bankruptcy recovery experts advocate hiring a lawyer to remove the bankruptcy from your credit report through legal loopholes. But these tactics don't help you change the underlying foundation that led you to bankruptcy in the first place. Don't invest your time, energy, and resources fixing the bankruptcy so it disappears from your credit report. Instead, invest your time and money to understand what drives your actions (or inactions) around money, change your beliefs about financial issues, and create healthier financial habits (see Section II).

The simple truth: no one can remove *true but negative* information from your credit report *for good*. Correct information, good and bad, stays on your record for at least seven years. The only *legitimate* way to remove a bankruptcy listing from your credit report is if someone else's bankruptcy is showing up on your report due to identity theft or because you cosigned a loan for someone who listed that debt in *their* bankruptcy.

To build a strong financial future, it's important that you sign your own paychecks, as the saying goes; *you* need to know how every part of your finances work, including how to correct and update information on your credit reports. I learned this lesson early on. Before my father let me drive the family car, I had to demonstrate that I could inflate and change a tire, check and change my air filter, check and top off all fluids, and change my oil. He wanted me to know how to take care of my car so I would be empowered to check and fix these common problems. I still do all of these myself (except oil changes).

You are the best person to improve or update any existing negative information on your credit reports so that they reflect you in the best light. Doing this yourself empowers you. Don't pay someone else to do it for you. If you were taken in by a credit repair scam, don't beat yourself up. Chalk up the money spent as the fee for an important lesson and move on. Get copies of your current credit reports and use the information above to update the reports yourself.

Credit Repair Company Scam You?

If you crossed paths with a less than honorable credit repair company, report the company (anonymously if you wish) to the Fraud Division at the Federal Trade Commission (FTC). Once the FTC builds a history of consumer complaints against a credit repair company, it can take action to close the company. The FTC prefers that you file your complaint online, which is very user-friendly (reportfraud.ftc.gov). The system can't take attachments, but you can paste information from documents into the Comments field of the report. Keep your documents handy in case law enforcement needs to see them. If you can't report online, you can call 877-382-4357 to report the fraud.

When a Creditor Tries to Collect a Discharged Debt

Pay attention to all phone calls or letters from creditors after your bankruptcy. Computer-generated calls and letters may go out accidentally from creditors stating that they are reaching out to collect on debts discharged under your bankruptcy or trying to repossess merchandise after they gave up any security interest in it. You can clear up the misunderstanding with a single phone call.

Any attempt to collect on a discharged debt or to repossess merchandise more than 60 days after your discharge date—if the creditor didn't previously contact you to reaffirm the debt—violates the Bankruptcy Abuse Prevention and Consumer Protection Act. If a creditor attempts to collect a discharged debt, send the following letter via certified mail, return receipt requested.

If the creditor persists and attempts to collect on the discharged debt after the date they signed for your letter, submit a complaint to the Consumer Financial Protection Bureau (consumerfinance.gov/complaint).

Do You Pay Income Tax on Discharged Debt?

Unlike debts that are *settled*, where any amount forgiven by a creditor that is more than $600 is considered taxable income, no income tax is due on *discharged* debts. If a creditor or a mortgage lender sends you a 1099-C, Cancellation of Debt, for a debt you discharged under your bankruptcy, your creditor has made an honest mistake. The 1099-C is used for debts that have been settled or forgiven.

Do not ignore any 1099 notice, or you will wind up with a great big IRS headache. To avoid an IRS problem, attach the following four items to your tax return showing the debt was discharged and should not be counted as forgiven income: (1) a copy of the 1099-C, (2) a statement that the debt was discharged under bankruptcy, (3) a copy of your Notice of Commencement of Case, and (4) a copy of your Order of Discharge.

[Date]
[Creditor's Name]
[Address]
[City, State, Zip]

Re: [Your Social Security number and account number]

Dear Sir/Madam:

On [date], I received a [letter or phone call] from you attempting to collect on the above-referenced debt.

On [date of discharge], this account was discharged under bankruptcy, Case No. [bankruptcy case number]. I trust that you will update your records to show that this debt has been discharged under bankruptcy and is no longer an outstanding debt. I also trust you will notify all credit bureaus that this debt was discharged under bankruptcy.

Enclosed are a copy of my:
• final discharge papers
• bankruptcy schedule listing your debt

As you know, any attempt to collect on a discharged debt is in violation of both the Fair Debt Collection Practices Act and the Bankruptcy Abuse Prevention and Consumer Protection Act.

Any further contact from you regarding the collection of this debt will be brought to the attention of the bankruptcy court as evidence of your violation, and I will exercise my right to sue and recover damages of $1,000 or more for each incident, as is my right. I thank you in advance for your help in clearing up this matter, and I trust that you will not attempt to collect this debt again.

Sincerely,

[Your Name]

Chapter 4

Vanquish Remaining Debt

It's time to set up a four-pronged financial strategy to expand the breathing room your bankruptcy has created. This includes catching up on any essentials, creating a savings plan, reviewing any reaffirmed debts, and paying off debts not included in your bankruptcy.

You may be tempted to start buying whatever you've denied yourself or throwing every dollar you have at your remaining debt. Please don't do either. This is *not* the time to start spending all the money you now have available. The part of you that wants to celebrate being out from under your debts by either spending money or scrimping and saving to pay off all remaining debt right now is the same part of you—your ego—that created the financial environment that led to your bankruptcy.

Catch Up on Essentials

Now's the time to review all your basic expenses. These include costs for your housing, vehicle, insurance, and health care—anything essential that you put off doing because you were trying to keep your creditors happy. Start gathering specific information on what your costs will be to take care of these items—any medical appointments you skipped, procedures you put off, or prescriptions you haven't filled, as well as any needed car or home repairs. If you canceled or reduced your auto, health, life, or homeowners' or renters' insurance, reinstate those now. You'll find tips on shopping for insurance in a credit-savvy way in Chapter 14.

Create Your Savings Plan

It's tempting to dismiss simple savings strategies. You already know how to save money, right? But do you know how to save money *right*? Does your savings balance grow every month, or do you save, spend your savings, then save again every month, like a gerbil on a treadmill? We're going to break this cycle, starting today. No more saving hundreds of dollars a month and then tapping your savings to pay your monthly bills.

Look at the amount you were paying monthly on your now-discharged debts during the three months before you filed for bankruptcy—not how much the creditors *wanted*, but how much you *actually paid* on all debts each month. Don't worry if that amount is zero; just write it down.

Set aside up to half of whatever amount you were paying your creditors before your bankruptcy; you will use this to pay any remaining debt. Take the other half and deposit it in a savings account. For instance, if you were paying creditors $1,000 a month, then you're going to set aside $500 to pay toward any remaining debts and put the other $500 a month into savings. If you weren't paying your creditors anything, gather up all the cash you can find around your home and deposit half of *that* amount into a savings account. This is an essential step.

If you don't already have a savings account, open one. If you already have a checking account at a bank or credit union, open your savings account there. If you're tempted to tap your savings account, eliminate any online access or open the account at a bank or credit union where you don't currently bank. I'm a big fan of using credit unions for savings accounts as they are often more helpful when it's time to secure a car loan (Chapter 10) or mortgage (Chapter 12). You won't ever miss money you start setting aside now, because it was already being used to pay your now-discharged debts.

Every time you receive *any* money, put at least 10 percent of that amount into your savings account. It's okay to start smaller, but I strongly suggest depositing at least $25 monthly. For now, no matter what, *do not* touch this money. Let it grow.

The savings you build now will help you achieve your post-bankruptcy financial goals. They can protect you when emergency expenses pop up while you're paying down any remaining debt, and they will make it possible for you to buy what you want without paying interest.

Reaffirmed Debts

I want to talk about reaffirmed debt next since portions of this information are time sensitive, depending on when your bankruptcy was discharged. If you didn't reaffirm any debts, feel free to skip this section.

Let's look at any reaffirmed debts you have. The sooner you do this the better, especially if you are newly bankruptcy. You have until the date the court issues your discharge *or* sixty days from the date you file your reaffirmation agreement, whichever is later. You have until that date to change your mind about reaffirming and instead add them as an amendment to your bankruptcy, so they'll be discharged. I want you to make sure *all* reaffirmed debts give you a true fresh start.

A few options are available if you reaffirmed any debt and money is still tight after your bankruptcy discharge. If you are within this sixty-day window, ask yourself two questions about each reaffirmed debt:

1. What's the worst that could happen if I *discharged* this debt?
2. What's the worst that could happen if I *missed* any future payments?

Both answers probably include *losing* the item. But missing payments on a reaffirmation agreement will impact your bankruptcy recovery more. It will increase your financial stress *and* create a new black mark on your credit report. Take the fresh start while it is available to you.

If you are still able to, canceling your reaffirmation agreement and surrendering the item is probably your best option. One family discovered their budget was still upside down after bankruptcy, with more money going out than coming in. Looking at the numbers, they realized their budget would even out if they surrendered one reaffirmed car.

To Reaffirm or Not to Reaffirm

If you're worried money could be tight after bankruptcy, you might be better off *not* reaffirming any debts other than your mortgage and possibly a car loan. You can rebuild your credit history better with a fresh start. Why tread water paying off a debt that could have been discharged under your bankruptcy?

Fear is the reason we continue paying debts that could have been discharged. Sometimes that fear shows up as guilt or shame. We're worried we will have to do without, of what might happen in an emergency, our inability to get future credit, or what others might say if something is repossessed by a creditor. Don't let your fears put your future financial freedom *and* your credit score at risk.

When you choose to keep an item that is secured by a debt, you and your creditor *must* enter into a signed agreement known as a *Reaffirmation Agreement*, where you agree to be responsible for the debt and the creditor agrees you can keep the item covered under the agreement as long as you continue paying off the debt.

A reaffirmation agreement turns a dischargeable debt into a *new*, post-bankruptcy debt. You give up your right to discharge the debt under your bankruptcy, and if you're late paying, the creditor can sue you—*and* repossess the reaffirmed item—putting a huge negative stain on your credit report *and* leaving you without the item.

Likewise, keeping a debt *without* a reaffirmation agreement doesn't necessarily give you a head start on rebuilding your credit. Future creditors are much more interested in a positive one- to two-year payment history after your bankruptcy than your payment history before your bankruptcy.

People often agonize over whether they should continue paying debts for computer equipment, tools, couches, engagement rings, appliances, and cars. You may have faced hard decisions for similar items. If your computer equipment or tools are necessary for work, your car is vital to your transportation, your washer, dryer, or other large appliance is necessary for your life—and you have no access to replacements—these items are worth reaffirming. An emotional attachment to an engagement ring may also lead you to reaffirm.

I never recommend reaffirming credit card debt that is secured by an item, as I'll explain in a moment.

On your credit report, reaffirmed debt should show as *reaffirmed*, not as *discharged* under your bankruptcy. Your payment history on any reaffirmed debt may provide a post-bankruptcy credit reference—*if* you stay current with your payments.

Reaffirmation Pros and Cons

You will almost always be better off discharging every debt you can in bankruptcy. As you rebuild your finances, you will soon have enough cash to replace the items you released. It's easy to confuse our self-worth with our *stuff*. We get emotionally attached to items that mark rites of passage. You may be attached to your car, for example, if it's the first new car you've owned. Those feelings are perfectly natural. *And* you have to decide if paying for these items is your best financial move right now. My rule of thumb is that reaffirming a debt is a good idea *only* if the debt meets these two criteria:

1. The item is a necessity for daily living such as a vehicle or *necessary* household appliance (washer, dryer, refrigerator, water heater, air conditioner, or furnace). A big-screen TV, not so much. Depending on how much you owe on your washer or dryer and how close you are to a laundromat or another place where you can do your laundry (like a friend or family member's house), you may decide *not* to reaffirm.

2. The creditor is willing to reaffirm for no more than the *current* value of the item, which may be considerably less than the balance owed, *and* is willing to create more favorable loan terms by lowering the interest rate.

Rethink why you're keeping or reaffirming any debt and ask yourself: *Is keeping this truly in my best interest?* Yes, creditors *could* come and take your big-screen television or pull up the carpet; they most likely *will* repossess the car if you decide not to reaffirm a car loan. That can be embarrassing and inconvenient—but not nearly as painful and long-lasting as having a repossession or a late payment on your credit report a year or more *after* your bankruptcy discharge. Better to take the hardest steps now, before your bankruptcy is discharged or before the period to rescind the reaffirmation agreement ends.

Redeem or Reaffirm?

When a creditor shows up at your creditors' hearing or puts a claim on the merchandise secured by your debt, they'll usually ask you to (1) reaffirm the debt or (2) surrender the merchandise. You have a *third* option, which is to pay the *value* of the merchandise (usually less than the amount of the debt). This is called *redeeming*. If you have available cash, redeeming is almost always a better choice than reaffirming a secured debt.

At the creditors' hearing, stick to your guns and calmly tell the creditor that they can either receive the *value* of the item or take the merchandise back. Chances are the creditor will back down and offer you a lower balance on the debt to get repaid *something*. At that point, you can decide to either keep the item and pay the creditor the amount they're requesting or surrender the item to them. Let me share an example of a woman who was making payments on a television from Sears. At her creditor's hearing, a Sears representative showed up and said, "Reaffirm or we'll repossess the TV." She said, "Okay, repossess it." That wasn't what Sears wanted to hear. "No, you don't understand," the representative said. "You need to reaffirm or we'll repossess." The woman said, "Well, it's worth $150 to me—take it or leave it." Sears took the $150, and she kept her television.

When you reaffirm a debt, you forfeit your right to discharge the debt in your bankruptcy. Meaning, you can be sued for non-payment if you later default on that debt. And if the item is ever damaged or destroyed, you *still* owe the debt. Think long and hard before you agree to reaffirm any debt where you are behind on payments, or the item is worth less than what you owe. Why play catch-up when you're trying to give yourself some financial breathing room? Make your bankruptcy a true fresh start so you pay only for your current expenses, while adding to your savings.

The Right Time to Reaffirm?

If you haven't filed your bankruptcy yet and you decide to reaffirm debts for nonessential items, don't reaffirm the debt when you file your initial bankruptcy paperwork. Instead, see if the creditor shows up or the debt gets discharged under bankruptcy.

In most states, unless your creditor shows up at your creditors' hearing to have you surrender the item or submits a written reaffirmation agreement that is signed by the creditor and your lawyer (or signed by you and approved by the judge before your discharge date), the debt will be discharged and the merchandise is yours.

You can resume your regular payments, and if you stay current on them, the creditor cannot repossess the item. You also won't owe any past-due amount that's built up. Basically, you'll be renting the car or other item from the creditor. Your loan will show up as discharged under your bankruptcy. Making regular payments without a reaffirmation agreement gives you time to find a replacement item which you can buy for cash. Once you have replaced the item, return the other item to your creditor. (You'll find guidance on buying a car with cash after bankruptcy in Chapter 10.)

Many people believe medical bills and past-due utility bills must be reaffirmed or your service will be cut off. This is not true. These debts can be discharged. When you include past-due medical bills in your bankruptcy, your health care provider *may* require you to pay your portion of future charges up front, in full. Any amount paid by your insurance will then be refunded to you by your doctor's office.

For utilities, any outstanding debt you list in your bankruptcy can be discharged, giving you a clean slate. Once you file your bankruptcy, the utility company can't collect on past-due amounts, but you must start making payments on new charges. Your utility company *may* require a security deposit (often the average of two month's bills) to ensure the company gets paid in the future.

Should You Reaffirm a Credit Card?

I believe it rarely pays to reaffirm a credit card. With some department store cards, some purchases may be secured by a *security interest clause* in the credit application's small print. It's a form of collateral. For example, they agree to finance your oven purchase or the new carpet that they install. You agree that until the debt is paid in full, your oven or carpet is collateral, which they can seize to pay off the debt. Because your collateral often loses value due to wear and tear, you may wind up owing more than the value of the collateral. Use the two criteria mentioned earlier to determine whether it's worthwhile to you to continue to pay these debts after bankruptcy.

Reaffirming credit card debt also can be expensive because only a portion of your payment pays down the balance. The rest goes toward interest, which accrues monthly. A frustrated man came to me after having reaffirmed a department store credit card that had a balance close to $500. He wanted the credit card to maintain a positive credit reference on his credit report. He hadn't charged anything new, his interest rate was 21 percent, and he was making the minimum $14 monthly payment.

Every month, roughly $8.50 of his $14 payment went to pay off accumulated interest, and $5.50 went toward paying off the $500 balance. We did the math together. At the rate he was paying, it would cost him $1,274 and nearly eight years to pay off a $500 credit card debt he could have discharged under his bankruptcy. After reviewing his budget, I recommended he increase his monthly payment to $22.50 so his actual debt (before interest) would be reduced by $14.50 each month. Even if he never increased his monthly payment, the debt would cost him $810 and would be paid off in three years.

This example is just one reason I firmly believe you are better off discharging all credit cards, even if they have a low balance. Creditors subtly encourage you to keep a low-balance card. What they may or may not tell you is that they're likely to immediately freeze your access to credit until you've paid off the card. And what they *won't* tell you is that once you've paid off that card, odds are they will immediately cancel the card.

Credit card marketing efforts aim to convince us that we *need* to have a credit card—at least one for emergencies, right? They've probably convinced you so thoroughly that I'll bet you can come up with mounds of examples of when you would have been lost without a credit card. Creditors use guilt tactics to convince you that the only way you can have what you want is to finance it. Somehow, they never seem to mention that you can easily buy whatever you want with cash, once you've broken the debt cycle.

After decades of helping people rebuild after bankruptcy, I still believe a *good secured* credit card will serve you better than an unsecured card. In Chapter 9 I'll talk more about rebuilding with a suitable credit card.

If you still think you need to keep a credit card, *only* reaffirm debt on a card with less than a $500 balance. Before signing a reaffirmation agreement with the creditor, make sure it clearly says your account will remain *active* and will be listed on your credit reports as an *active account*. (They will still likely freeze the account so you can't charge anything new.) If the agreement says you'll be *eligible to apply* for credit after the debt is paid off, do not reaffirm the debt; once you pay off the debt, the creditor likely will cancel the card.

Look through all the debts you reaffirmed and write each one down; then explore your options. See if you can cancel your reaffirmation agreement and return the item or accelerate repayment. In a moment, I'll share an effortless way to speed up your repayment with my DebtBuster™ strategy. You could save yourself hundreds of dollars in interest—and countless hours of lost sleep.

If you're paying on a Chapter 13 bankruptcy plan and have fallen behind on your payments or on a debt that wasn't included in the bankruptcy, ask your bankruptcy attorney about your options for modifying your bankruptcy.

How to Undo Reaffirmed Debts

If you decide to cancel your reaffirmation agreement and are eligible to do so, here are some guidelines. Depending on the item, and your tolerance for the unknown, you can cancel your reaffirmation agreement and wait to see if the creditor decides to reclaim the item. While this strategy may work with less expensive items, the creditor holding your car loan will most likely repossess your vehicle.

To surrender an item within the allowed time, call your bankruptcy attorney or the trustee or clerk for the bankruptcy court where you had your creditors' hearing. Tell them you want to surrender an item you previously reaffirmed under your bankruptcy, because you've realized you really can't afford to keep that debt. You will need to submit a revised *Intention to Reaffirm*, which will cost you about $20.

Once you submit your revised paperwork to the court, call your creditor and arrange a time to have the item picked up. Get a signed and dated receipt when you turn over the item you're surrendering. Read all paperwork carefully and do not sign *any* agreement that would make you responsible for any future debt on this item. If you're unsure about the process, reach out to your bankruptcy attorney for assistance.

The Bottom Line

No matter what decisions you made about reaffirming any debts, don't beat yourself up. You made the best decision for you *at the time*. If you did reaffirm, take steps to make sure your reaffirmation is helping you rebuild your credit. Check your credit reports to see how the reaffirmed account is being reported. It should show as being current if you've made all your payments on time since your bankruptcy.

Now, let's move forward and concentrate on eliminating any other debts that were not dischargeable under your Chapter 7 or not included in your Chapter 13 repayment plan.

Debts That Are *Not* Discharged

Debts that aren't discharged under bankruptcy fall into five categories. Here they are, in order of importance for rebuilding after bankruptcy:

1. **Secured debts reaffirmed with a creditor.** Your mortgage, car loan, or other debts you agreed to pay outside of bankruptcy, as mentioned earlier.

2. **Student loans.** Student loans are nondischargeable unless their repayment would cause an undue hardship. Listing your student loans on your bankruptcy schedule of creditors does *not* mean they will be discharged. Also, if you declared Chapter 13, you must continue paying any balances on your student loans that remain *after* your Chapter 13 repayment period ends. I'll talk more about student loan repayments in a minute.

3. **Alimony, child support, or back taxes.** If you declared Chapter 13 bankruptcy, you may also still owe alimony, child support, or back taxes. If you still owe back taxes, a good tax attorney can communicate with the IRS or state taxing authority to work out the best tax-relief strategy for you. Avoid offers for tax relief help that come in the mail. Ask your bankruptcy attorney for a referral to a tax attorney with a great reputation. You truly get what you pay for when it comes to dealing with the IRS and other tax authorities. A good tax attorney is worth the money.

4. **Income taxes not discharged under your Chapter 7 bankruptcy.** Outstanding income taxes can generally be discharged under bankruptcy if the *taxes* were at least three years old *and* your *tax returns* were filed at least two years before your bankruptcy. Otherwise, you'll have to repay those taxes. Again, it's best to talk to a tax attorney about getting these debts paid.
5. **Unlisted debts.** If you overlooked a debt that would have been discharged under bankruptcy, let your attorney or the court know immediately. You might still be able to add it to your bankruptcy, or the debt could have been discharged by default, even if it wasn't on your list of creditors.

Repaying Student Loans

Your student loans probably were *not* discharged under your bankruptcy. If you stopped making payments before you declared Chapter 7 or when your Chapter 13 student loan repayments ended *and* you still owe money, your student loans will be listed as delinquent on your credit reports until you work out a repayment schedule.

Remember: listing student loans on your bankruptcy schedule does *not* make them dischargeable. If you declared Chapter 7 and you owe student loan debt, contact your student loan servicer *now* to confirm whether your loans were discharged. The sooner you start paying student loan debt again, the quicker your credit reports will show new positive information.

GETTING STARTED

The Federal Student Aid website (studentaid.gov) has been streamlined and is *very* user-friendly. Start here to explore your student loan repayment options. Scroll to the bottom of the home page and click Contact Us. Then select the I'm in Repayment box and you'll find six different contact centers you can call, chat with, or email for help. Each center includes specifics about what they can do for you.

If you haven't made a loan payment in more than 360 days or your wages or tax refunds are being garnished, contact the Default Resolution Group (800-621-3115 or online by filling out their secure email form).

If your student loans are more current, start with *Your student loan servicer*, to log in to your student loan account. If you don't remember what company services your student loan or don't have an online account, reach out to the Federal Student Aid Information Center (FSAIC), by phone (800-433-3243), live chat during business hours, or email via their secure form. The FSAIC can help you find your loan servicer even if the Education Department doesn't own the loan.

When you talk to your student loan servicer, get as much information from them as you can about your repayment options. Each option has specific requirements. Don't agree to do anything right now. Tell the representative you need 30 days to figure out your finances and that you will get back to them to set up a plan for repaying your student loans. You'll need this time to set up your spending plan and your DebtBuster strategy so you know how much income you have available after covering your basic expenses. You want to arrange an affordable repayment plan so you can make future payments on time.

FEDERAL STUDENT LOAN OPTIONS

You have a variety of repayment options for getting back on track with your federal student loan payments, such as loan forgiveness, deferment, forbearance, rehabilitation, and loan repayment plans including loan consolidation, income-driven repayment (IDR), and direct loan repayment (standard, graduated, or extended). Learn more about each option's requirements and limitations by visiting the Forms Library at studentaid.gov/forms-library.

If you're seeking student loan forgiveness studentaid.gov is the place to get updates on loan forgiveness options. The standard forgiveness programs are still in place, but newer programs may no longer be offered.

The Loan Simulator tool (studentaid.gov/loan-simulator) is a handy tool to estimate your monthly student loan payments and compare repayment plans. Answer the simulator's guided questions with actual or hypothetical information and the system will display your options. You can even suggest an affordable monthly payment for your loans and the simulator will show you what plans are possible based on that amount. Your immediate goal is to find the option with the lowest payments, spread out over the longest time. You may eventually increase your monthly payment to pay off your loan faster by using the strategies described in the DebtBuster section. To pay down the principal on your student loan, you must specify that the extra payment is to be applied to the *principal balance*, otherwise your extra funds will be used to pre-pay your next monthly payment.

CONSOLIDATE FEDERAL STUDENT LOANS

Have more federal student loans than fingers on a hand? You may be able to consolidate them, at no cost, into one Direct Consolidation Loan. Consolidation loans use a weighted-average fixed interest rate, based on each loan's current balance and interest rate. This doesn't change the *amount* of interest you pay on your loan amounts, but it can lower your monthly payment. And you would have only one monthly payment for all loans you consolidate together.

Visit studentaid.gov/loan-consolidation to learn more about consolidation loans and fill out and submit an application. A student loan consolidator will then do the calculations and send you an estimate of what your payments would be under the consolidation plan.

PRIVATE STUDENT LOANS

Setting up payment arrangements with a private student loan service company (like Sallie Mae) can be more challenging. Your options are usually to make interest-only payments through a reduced payment plan or a forbearance plan. You might be able to reduce your monthly payment by asking for a loan modification with a lower interest rate or extended time to pay your loan, but private lenders don't usually advertise this option. At Sallie Mae, you can call the Office of the Customer Advocate (855-342-2014) or complete the online contact form (salliemae.com/about/leadership/advocate). Write on the form that you are seeking a loan modification after bankruptcy.

Erase Your Student Loans by Buying a Home?

Some state housing authorities offer special programs for first-time homebuyers who have student loans. They arrange financing that pays off your student loans, often as a forgivable deferred loan. If you keep the home as your personal residence for a set number of years, your student debt is forgiven. I will cover this more in Chapter 12 (State and Territory Housing Authorities).

DebtBuster Your Remaining Debt

Your next goal: setting up a system to pay off your remaining debt. My rule is that a debt-repayment system must help you rebuild your credit *without* leaving you cash strapped. Don't apply extra cash haphazardly toward your remaining debt. And don't postpone funding your savings account. Neither will help you get out of debt or build lasting wealth.

Instead, set up a savings account and then create a DebtBuster plan to eliminate your remaining debt quicker, while paying less interest, and building a positive payment history. Copy the enclosed DebtBuster sheet or download it from rebuildafterbankruptcy.com.

Create a DebtBuster Spreadsheet

You can easily set up your DebtBuster on the computer using Quicken, Excel, or another spreadsheet program. List each debt in order from the lowest balance to the highest balance, with their interest rate. This way you *always* know which debt gets the extra money each month. Once you pay off a debt, delete it.

SETTING UP YOUR DEBTBUSTER WORKSHEET

With the DebtBuster, tracking your debt payments *and* your progress is easy. List each creditor, one by one, in Column A.

Your *reaffirmed* debts get top billing on your DebtBuster. You are already obligated to pay these amounts under your reaffirmation agreements. Miss a payment and you risk adding negative information to your credit reports.

Second, list any *student loans.* Third is any outstanding *alimony, child support, or back taxes* (other than income taxes) you owe. Fourth is any *income tax debt.* If you haven't yet set up any income tax payment plans with the IRS or your state, you won't have specific minimum payments or interest and penalty information. Don't worry about that right now. What's important is that your DebtBuster includes every outstanding debt you owe. You can fill in the details later.

Finally, list any *other debts* you have. These could be bounced checks or other debt you forgot to include in your bankruptcy. You may also want to list debts you owe to family, friends, or local businesses. Although these debts will likely be discharged through your bankruptcy, you may have personal reasons for wanting to pay these people back.

Once all debts are listed on your DebtBuster, fill in the columns for each debt. Put the outstanding balance in Column B, and the interest rate percentage and total amount of interest per

DebtBuster Worksheet

	A	B	C	D	E	F	G
	Debt Owed To:	Balance Remaining	Interest Rate	Annual Interest Amount	Monthly Interest Amount	Minimum Payment	Minimum Payment Plus Interest
1.	ABC Credit Card	$1,200.00	20%	$240/yr	$20	$30	$50
2.							
3.							
4.							
5.							
6.							
7.							
8.							
9.							
TOTAL DEBTS:							

Put the DebtBuster Strategy to Work for You! List all your outstanding debts, balances, and the interest rates they charge under Columns A, B, C and D. In Column E write down the current amount of your monthly finance charge and in Column F write down your current minimum payment. Add Columns E and F together and enter this amount in Column G.

For example, say your balance on your first debt is $1,200. If you're paying 20% interest on your $1,200 balance, you're paying about $200 in interest annually, which equals approximately $20 as a monthly finance charge. Let's assume your creditor requires a $30 monthly minimum payment. Start by paying the minimum monthly payments (Column F) for all these debts.

If you have extra funds, pay the amount in Column G, for the bill with the lowest balance. Never change your minimum monthly payment or the monthly finance charge – creditors will reduce you monthly minimum to keep you paying interest longer. Stick to the plan!

year in Columns C and D. The current monthly finance charge from that creditor's most recent statement goes in Column E. Put your minimum monthly payment amount in Column F. Finally, add Columns E and F together and put that amount in Column G.

For example, say your balance on your first debt is $1,200. If you're paying 20% interest on your $1,200 balance, you're paying about $200 in interest annually, which equals approximately $20 as a monthly finance charge. Let's assume your creditor requires a $30 monthly minimum payment. Start by paying the minimum monthly payment (Column F) for each of these debts.

If you have extra funds, pay the amount in Column G, for the bill with the lowest balance. There's a reason I want you to put the current minimum monthly payment and current monthly finance charge on your DebtBuster. As your balance decreases, credit card companies reduce your required minimum monthly payments, so you'll pay more interest over time. Don't veer from your strategy. This system creates a steady and effortless way to dissolve your remaining debt.

Once you've added all your remaining debts, write the total for Column F on the last line of the DebtBuster. This is the amount you'll want to pay toward your debts each month, no matter what.

Which Debt to Pay First?

It's hard to say which question is more eternal. The "which came first the chicken or the egg" or "which debt first: the smallest balance or the highest interest?"

My recommendation? Use the strategy that suits you best. Psychologically, though, paying extra on the debt with the smallest *balance* first is more satisfying, as you can pay off those debts quicker and cross that debt off your list. The amount you were paying on that debt can be added to your next smallest debt, speeding up the repayment process.

Whenever you receive extra money, put at least half of that amount into savings. Once you have at least six months of expenses saved, pick the debt with the lowest balance and start paying the amount in Column G for that debt. I've included solid strategies for building savings and freeing up hidden money in your budget in Chapter 14 and Chapter 19.

PUT THE DEBTBUSTER TO WORK

Once you've built a savings reserve and are ready to tackle paying off your first debt with the smallest balance, pay the minimum payment on each debt *except* the one with the lowest balance. Let's say the smallest balance is $200 and your minimum monthly payment is $14. Pay $14 plus any extra amount you can that month. If you can pay at least $50 monthly, you'll have that debt paid off in a few months. If you have several smaller debts with nearly the same balance, pay the debt with the highest interest rate first.

Once you pay off a debt, put half of that debt's monthly payment amount into savings to continue growing your cash cushion. Add the other half of that amount to the payment for your next lowest balance. Let's say you've been paying $70 monthly on a student loan debt and you just paid it off. Now, $35 goes into savings each month and the remaining $35 gets added to the payment for your next lowest balance. This waterfall effect helps you pay off other bills even quicker. Within a year, you'll be well on your way to being debt-free *and* will have built savings.

Resist the temptation to spend extra income on new expenses or pay extra money toward your remaining debts. If you need a spending fix, go ahead and reward yourself once you have paid off one debt. Take half or all that monthly payment and treat yourself. Then go right back to the 50/50 debt payment/saving plan for the next debt you're looking to pay off. After a few splurges, you may discover you would rather put that money toward paying off the next debt so you can reward yourself with something *big* once you are debt free. You can even brainstorm free ways to treat yourself and stick that extra money in savings for something truly special—like an all-expenses *prepaid* vacation.

If you're behind on any essential expenses—utilities, car payment, insurance—this is debt. Add these bills to your DebtBuster and pay the minimum payments for these bills. Then put every extra penny you can toward catching up on those bills, while still slowly building your savings. (I've included tips on dealing with past-due utility and other bills in Chapter 17.)

The DebtBuster is meant to be flexible. When you need to make a purchase, skip the alluring *buy now, pay later* and other financing offers thrown your way. Use your newly built savings to pay cash for what you desire. That's why you have savings.

Use the DebtBuster for six months to a year. During that time, postpone nonessential purchases and not only will you find yourself in great shape financially—with savings *and* reduced or eliminated debt—but you'll also have adopted new, healthier financial habits . . . for life.

Reverse-Engineer Your Purchases

You can even use the DebtBuster strategy in reverse to plan future purchases. List items on the sheet that you want to buy, with the item's *cost* as the balance due. Each month, pay into your savings a portion of that purchase price, as if you were paying off a debt. When your DebtBuster shows you have enough cash, buy the item. Adopt this strategy for your purchases and you will *never* pay another penny in interest.

Should You Repay Discharged Debts?

You may be tempted to make good on discharged debts—a natural reaction, but *not* necessarily the *best* action. Creditors wrote off your account as a business loss. Trying to post a payment to a closed account at a large company creates a paper nightmare for them and does nothing to help you rebuild financially. Paying back loans from family and friends and repaying local companies that generously provided credit to you is easier. Once you've paid off debts not included in your bankruptcy, add any debts you want to pay to your DebtBuster. Don't broadcast your plan; just quietly implement it.

If you still want to pay back larger creditors, paying it *forward* may be your best option. Donate money to a local organization that teaches financial literacy to youth. I like Colorado's Young Americans Center (yacenter.org) founded by cable TV pioneer Bill Daniels. They create hands-on programs to help kids develop financial skills and relevant business knowledge and offer live, in-person events plus youth-appropriate access to credit to teach healthy habits. Daniels started the organization when he discovered young entrepreneurs faced challenges getting loans to fund their business ideas.

Or simply spread the word about good financial literacy content for youth, like Hands on Banking (youth.handsonbanking.org). This is the most outstanding financial literacy program I've seen. Completely free, their entertaining education video courses are designed for elementary school, middle school, and high school students. Even adults will find them helpful!

SECTION II

BEFORE NEW CREDIT, SHED OLD HABITS AND BELIEFS

Chapter 5

Lay a Foundation for Financial Success

Let's recap. Your credit reports are updated, your strategy to repay existing debts is activated, and you're ready to start rebuilding your credit score. Congratulate yourself on your progress. We can be our worst enemy after bankruptcy—or our best friend. Credit serves one useful purpose: to increase your credit score. And that *can* be done without taking on any new debt. Success in this area begins with identifying and changing the money habits, beliefs, and financial patterns that created your bankruptcy.

Many people tell me they had "great credit" before their bankruptcy. By this, they mean they paid all their bills on time each month—even if it meant living paycheck to paycheck—until something happened. Paying our bills on time *doesn't* mean we have great credit. It simply means we can pay our bills. Being *overextended* doesn't mean we have so much debt that we struggle to pay our monthly bills or live paycheck to paycheck. *Overextended* (oddly enough) actually means we carry a balance on our revolving credit (credit cards, lines of credit). In other words, we are borrowing money to pay for things *over time* that we would be better off buying with cash.

I don't say these things to be mean. I've talked with people who declared bankruptcy, got new credit, and were able to pay their monthly bills. They bought a home (or several!) and then suddenly they lost their job or their hours were cut, someone got sick, their marital status changed, they lent money to someone which left them cash-strapped, or they counted on income from a tenant who wound up moving or from a client or employer who didn't pay. Or the world turned into a sci-fi B movie and everything shut down. Bottom line, *something happened* to disrupt their carefully constructed financial recovery plan. Despite what may have happened *out there*, there is one hard truth we must face if we're going to do things differently this time.

Recognizing our role in getting to this point financially is the quickest way to start succeeding financially. Admitting that my bankruptcy was fully a result of my choices was *hard*. It was far easier to point to creditors who extended credit to an unemployed college student, creditors who wouldn't work with me when I fell behind on payments, or my lack of income as a throwaway teen. I came to think of credit pushers as drug dealers. They provided a harmful substance that made me feel good for a while. Until it didn't—until it wasn't enough . . . and then it was too much.

Drug dealers give free samples to newly clean addicts because they know an addict will always come back for another fix—which will then cost them a great deal more. Creditors do the same thing. They offer a high chance of approval, great teaser rate, or "zero interest and no hidden fees" because they're betting your debt will make them more money in the long run.

Do you ever wonder why so many people sincerely believe they *must* have a credit card for emergencies? Even more people believe that buying a car requires a car loan. And almost *everyone* believes that buying a house means having a mortgage. Buying a car or home *without debt* is considered completely impossible and unrealistic.

Most books for bankrupt consumers focus on how to quickly get credit after bankruptcy, how to get creditors to work with you after bankruptcy, and how to get the lowest monthly payments at the best interest rates, given that you've gone bankrupt. These books get you salivating at new credit offers—and lead you back into debt again right after your bankruptcy.

What you need today is a fresh start—not fresh debt. And your fresh start begins by taking a step back and examining *why* you wound up bankrupt in the first place—*before* you consider applying for new debt. (See how I used the *real* word for credit there?) This is a two-step deep dive. First, you uncover the practices, behaviors, and actions that led to your bankruptcy. Second, you start changing your thoughts and beliefs around money so you can honor your commitment to becoming and remaining debt-free.

Figure Out the Why

To understand why you wound up in bankruptcy and why your financial recovery isn't going as well as you hoped, answer the following three questions:

1. Where are you starting from financially?
2. What factors truly contributed to your bankruptcy?
3. What drove you to make the choices you made?

Where Are You Starting from Financially?

Remember the house I talked about in the Introduction? When you lay the foundation for a house, where you start depends on the ground beneath you. Is it smoothly graded or full of rocks? What possible issues lurk beneath the surface (like the underground spring that ran through the neighbor's site) which at any moment could wash away all financial progress? Are you thinking of using an existing makeshift structure as the foundation for your financial house, or would you be better off rebuilding from scratch?

Where you start will depend on your financial situation at *two* points in time: just before your bankruptcy and right now. Sit with each of the following questions and answer them honestly and factually, including as much detail as you can about what was going on in your life at the time—without blaming yourself or anyone else:

1. When was the last time you were able to pay all your bills on time every month?
2. When did you stop paying your unsecured creditors?
3. Which secured debts were you behind on or constantly struggling to pay?
4. When, after you could no longer pay your debts, did you begin to struggle each month to pay your daily expenses?
5. What debts, secured or unsecured, did you keep after your bankruptcy?
6. What *new* debt do you have since your bankruptcy was discharged?
7. Where do you struggle to keep up with your expenses or find yourself unable to create what you want in your life?
8. What's usually going on in your life when you can save money, *and* when you find yourself using your savings to pay your monthly bills instead of moving forward a cherished goal?
9. What fear was behind the financial decisions you did or did not make?

Take a break and let these questions and your answers settle around you.

What Factors Contributed to Your Bankruptcy?

In addition to the role you played in your bankruptcy, outside factors may also have contributed. Your next task is to identify these outside factors so you can create new patterns to prepare for the unexpected.

Circle all items in the following list that contributed to your bankruptcy, and add any others not listed below:

- Job loss, reduced hours, or less overtime pay
- Unexpected medical expenses or a chronic medical condition
- Family breakup due to death, divorce, incarceration, or violence
- Depleted or lack of emergency savings
- Harassing creditors unwilling to work with you
- Late payments that led to penalties, fees, and higher interest rates
- Natural disasters such as fire, flood, tornado, or hurricane
- Insufficient or lack of insurance
- Excessive spending
- Gambling, substance abuse
- Emotional spending
- Identity theft
- Loans to friends or family who never paid you back
- Lack of financial knowledge

Put an asterisk (*) next to any item you selected whose impact might have been prevented or minimized if you had only known specific financial information at the time. Remember: no judgment here—just information gathering.

What Drove You to Make the Choices You Made?

We all make choices with our finances. Rather than judge our past (or current) financial choices, simply recognize them and acknowledge where you are willing to make different choices today.

We always make the best choices we can *at the moment we make them*. We make choices because we don't see any other options. We make choices by not acting when our action *could* make a difference. We make choices out of fear.

For instance, when a work situation changes, we're confident we'll find new work in a few weeks—a month or two tops. So, we live on savings and credit cards and don't think about cutting expenses. Then weeks turn into months—and sometimes years. Meanwhile, we *chose* to keep the extra car, keep the kids in private schools, or pay for multiple extracurricular activities. We keep the big house rather than move to something smaller or back in with our folks. We choose 80 percent insurance coverage for the lower monthly premium rather than pay a higher monthly amount for full coverage. We choose not to scale back our holiday spending and continue dining out while our income is reduced. We choose not to pay attention to how much is coming in and going out of our accounts.

We choose not to *talk* about money—and sometimes not to even *think* about money. We don't want to talk about the credit cards we (or a spouse) use for binge shopping, because we don't want to deal with potential emotional (or physical) outbursts when we bring up money issues. We don't educate ourselves on the possible pitfalls of keeping the mortgage in the divorce while letting our spouse be responsible for the joint credit card debt—and then end up with both the mortgage and the credit card debt when our spouse promptly declares bankruptcy. (Divorce attorneys, unfortunately, don't always know bankruptcy law.)

We have hundreds of reasons for the choices we made in our relationship with money. And they all seemed like a good idea at the time. But these choices add up until we've dug a financial hole so deep that bankruptcy is the only way out. And now that's in the past.

There is *no* upside to blaming yourself (or anyone else) for winding up in bankruptcy court. Simply *recognize* and *honor* the choices you made at the time you made them. You may find this phrase helpful: *It seemed like a good idea at the time.* Repeat after me: It *seemed* like a good idea at the time. It seemed like a good idea at the time—for whatever reason you had—or you certainly wouldn't have made that choice.

We tend to look at catastrophic events as *unexpected*—something we can't plan for. But that belief is false. We *can* plan to protect ourselves from unexpected events: lost jobs, illnesses, a family member's death or disability, divorce, fire, hurricanes, a disabled car, or even identity theft. Planning won't eliminate the impact of these events, but it does blunt the financial damage.

Let's face it. Not all of us learned how to save money. Not all of us learned to ask the *right* questions to make informed financial decisions. Our ingrained money habits and beliefs start young, *and* they can be easily changed if we choose to change them.

As a child, I was an awesome saver. I had a whale bank instead of a piggy bank, and pretty much my entire allowance, money I received for babysitting, and financial gifts went into Whaley. Occasionally, I'd shake out all my money to bask in my abundance. One day, in addition to my bills and coins, a piece of paper in my dad's familiar handwriting fell out. The paper simply said, "IOU $50".

My dad knew I was a saver, and when the cash flow from his construction business was slow, he started tapping my savings to buy our groceries and gas. Unconsciously, this taught me not to save—because someone would just come along and take it from me. That fear contributed to my bankruptcy when I was twenty-one.

I learned some new financial strategies as I rebuilt after bankruptcy, but I still hadn't learned how to ask the right questions. Less than a year after purchasing my first home, I was laid off. I took on some side gigs, but every month I dipped into my emergency savings to pay the mortgage. Depleted, I finally called the mortgage company, explained my financial situation and was transferred to the workout division, where they used HUD's assignment program to modify my loan for me. I didn't *know* I should reach out to my mortgage company to see what my options were *before* I spent all my savings. I could have beaten myself up for not knowing and for spending my savings, leaving myself cash-strapped. Or

I could acknowledge that spending my savings *seemed* like a good idea at the time.

If I had known about HUD's assignment program, I would have entered it shortly after I was laid off to reduce my monthly mortgage payment, which would have enabled me to support myself with savings until my income increased again. I made a different choice—one that seemed like a good idea based on my knowledge at the time.

Knowledge Is Power

Knowledge truly is power. Not having any or all the information we need to make informed decisions leaves us on edge, uncertain. The unknown is just a space in our brain where we keep ourselves in the dark. It's time to move yourself out of the darkness and into a space where you'll have more financial self-confidence and financial freedom to get clear about the way money works in your life, so you can make the best financial choices.

To do that, make a list of whatever you want to know financially. We don't know what we don't know—and new information often leads to more questions. So, keep your list handy and write down all the new questions that come up as your knowledge grows. I created *Bounce Back from Bankruptcy* because people had questions about what to do next, as I did. So, I set out to answer those questions. Not sure what you even want to ask? Use these as starter questions:

- What do I need to look for in a good credit card?
- How do I learn what the fine print in a contract really means?
- How do credit builder programs *really* work?

You may be more than ready to take control of your finances, or a part of you may still wish someone else would handle it. You may even prefer *not* to know anything about money matters. But the more you know, the more you can easily create a secure financial future for yourself. While you may be tempted to farm out your credit report disputes and updates, following through on those steps *yourself* gives *you* knowledge. And that knowledge empowers you.

As you gain new financial knowledge, your beliefs about money and the way you handle your money will begin to change. This is how you create a healthy relationship with money.

Heal Your Relationship with Money

Healing your relationship with money isn't a one-and-done. The process is like peeling an onion, layer by layer. Every now and again, revisit this information and push yourself to uncover the next layer of obstacles where you sabotage your financial security—knowingly or unknowingly. The more often you explore what you believe about money, the easier you can build a positive net worth after bankruptcy, where you *own* more than you owe.

Despite our best intentions, few of us have truly healthy relationships with money. The first time I heard Travis Tritt's ballad "Best of Intentions," I visualized him committing to his spouse, fulfilling that commitment throughout the years—occasionally falling short as we all do—and assuring his spouse that, even when he fell short, his intentions were pure.

Then I saw the music video.

Travis plays a man who is in and out of jail, expressing remorse for all the times he let his wife down. He had the best of intentions, but he never took action to avoid situations that would land him in jail. He never committed himself to change.

What's that got to do with improving your relationship with money?

How often do you let the distractions in your life keep you from doing what you set out to do? We always seem to be searching for legitimate excuses for why we're not making the financial changes we say we want to make. We had good intentions, right? The drawback is that good intentions always remain *intentions*. Something we *meant* to do but didn't. *Intending* to do something isn't the same as *doing* it. You know that saying about the road to hell being paved with good intentions, right?

In Chapter 7, I will walk you through how you can consciously commit to turning an intention into a *goal*—and then accomplish that goal. For now, let's figure out what your intentions are. What *exactly* do you want to change? Circle any items on this list that align with what you want to do, and feel free to add others!

- Stop living paycheck to paycheck.
- Stop feeling that I don't have *enough*.
- Stop feeling that I can't afford what I want to do, be, or experience (for myself or my loved ones).
- Stop feeling indebted to others.
- Stop arguing with my family about how we spend money.
- Start feeling more comfortable about giving and receiving money.
- Start creating real savings, investments and wealth.

Commit to Change

After bankruptcy we may intend to avoid debt, never carry a credit card balance, and *definitely* do things differently this time. But we don't commit to eliminating situations that add to our debt. Firmly convinced our bankruptcy was due to circumstances beyond our control, we ignore how *our* attitudes and actions around money contributed to our bankruptcy.

Right after a bankruptcy discharge, new credit is tempting. We wonder whether bankruptcy truly *is* a 10-year mistake. We worry we've ruined our credit forever. The holiday season approaches, and we're tempted to spend money before we have it, turn to one of the widely marketed quick lending options and find ourselves making the same old money mistakes.

Rationalizing when we spend more money than we truly want to spend is a quick way to get caught in the debt cycle. By looking within, we can learn more about whatever stops us from fulfilling our intention to handle our money in a healthier way. It usually comes back to fear. We're afraid that:

- other people will think we're cheap, poor or stingy;
- someone will buy us something more expensive than what we bought them;
- our children will think poorly of us if we don't buy them what they want;
- our children will be shunned by their peers if we cut back on what we give them;
- we will never have the life we truly desire; able to afford to have children, a nice car, a home of our own, start our own business or travel more.

We use our fears to sabotage our intentions. We point to the obstacles that fear tosses up and declare "I would have, but . . ." or "I was going to, but. . . ." When you catch yourself in this mental game of Twister, make these two commitments to yourself:

- I am committed to healing my relationship with money.
- I am committed to removing all obstacles I've created to avoid honoring my commitment to heal.

The goal is to acknowledge our obstacles and then look beyond them to identify the *fear* that causes us to create them in the first place. Let's use your bankruptcy as an example, starting with just the facts.

You went bankrupt.

While honoring your commitment to pay off a particular debt, you may have encountered an obstacle:

- Creditors wouldn't work with you to negotiate reasonable monthly payments.
- Your home was about to be foreclosed on.
- Clients or employers were slow to pay you.
- Your paperwork was destroyed in a natural disaster.
- You were physically or emotionally overwhelmed by the stress of your finances.
- Unexpressed anger, resentment, or envy sabotaged your efforts.
- You couldn't bear to look at how much you owed.

Our *debt* may have been discharged, but the obstacles—the reasons our debt happened—either still exist or have the potential to show up again. Unless we make inner changes. Unexpressed feelings can make us angry or righteously indignant. Fear of rejection or fear of the unknown can immobilize us. Commit every day to identify and eliminate one small obstacle you've created to achieving financial security. Turn your good intentions into firm commitments and step out in faith, leaving fear behind.

In addition to making the two commitments noted above, which are from my workbook *Heal Your Relationship with Money*, the following commitments are equally important:

- Develop my financial knowledge and financial independence.
- Become radically honest about my finances.
- Fully empower others to be financially independent.
- Accept that I am *solely* responsible for and the source of my current financial situation.
- Learn to enjoy my money.

To become radically honest with yourself, ask: *Is my goal to be truly financially free, building a positive net worth, or is my goal to get back into debt as quickly as possible by getting new credit?* Don't delude yourself into believing that you're getting credit "in case of an emergency," taking on a car loan because it's the only way you can afford a *reliable* car, or trying to improve your credit score so you can get credit at low interest rates like everyone else. The fact is most people who get a new credit card after bankruptcy carry a balance from month to month within a year of their discharge date. I was one of them!

Chapter 6

10 Steps to Break the Debt Cycle—For Good

After bankruptcy, many people believe their bankruptcy was *entirely* out of their control and due to outside circumstances. If we hold this truth, we risk going bankrupt again. As Maya Angelou said, "I did then what I *knew* how to do. Now that I know better, I *do* better." Taking a small step to become aware of our role in our situation helps us do better.

For decades, I've taught my *Break the Debt Cycle—For Good* workshop, which has helped countless people create a new approach to money and credit. If you follow the 10 steps below, from the workshop, you can transform your financial situation, creating financial security and solvency.

Step 1. Become Willing to Stop Adding Any New Debt

Interrupting the debt cycle starts with a willingness to do better, to do something different. We must move from debt management to debt repayment and then to credit leverage. Become aware of hidden debt traps that are designed to lure you back into debt, and implement strategies that the credit-savvy use regularly (as shared in Chapter 8). Your goal is to be able to harness the freedom of a credit card without the burden of new debt.

Step 2. Free Yourself from Indebtedness of the Mind

What makes you want to take on debt? Where does having extra money make you nervous, and why? When we identify the root cause of our debt cycle and our money patterns and beliefs—the resentments that keep us indebted to others emotionally, psychologically, *and* financially—we can transform everything. Download for free my *Heal Your Relationship with Money* workbook (rebuildafterbankruptcy.com). The workbook offers 28 questions to help you identify the core beliefs that have created your attitudes about money, debt, and prosperity. Recognizing your patterns, financial prejudices and misperceptions, and attitudes about lack has incredible transformative power.

Step 3. Gain Clarity about What You Have

You have the power to decide what changes you want to make to free up the financial energy that's currently trapped in your life. Simplify your life by releasing things that no longer serve you (including relationships and clutter). Get comfortable making short-term changes to create long-term results. Our egos love telling us we're losing something. The truth is, you're *gaining* your financial freedom—without it having to come from somewhere outside of you. Clarity helps us release our attachment to what *is* so we make room for what we truly desire. Replace your desire to stay vague about money issues with clarity and learn how to effectively review and make money moves that give you control over your financial world.

Step 4. Slow Your Debt Repayment

Take a few minutes to review the DebtBuster repayment plan you've created for yourself and notice where you're wanting to move faster. Revise your plan so it's slow and steady—to ensure it's sustainable. Reorganize your repayment plan so every piece of it works best for *you*. Stop hating your remaining debt (and your past debt) and start embracing your debt as a valuable tool for boosting your self-worth and self-confidence.

Madly trying to get debt-free and using credit as a tool for wealth-building, without transforming your beliefs and creating financial balance, is the surest road back to bankruptcy court. Teach yourself how to view debt as simply a *thing*. Not a thing that has power over you, but a thing that simply exists. Create a repayment plan and a plan forward that gives you the best emotional, psychological, and financial benefits. Slow and steady really does win the race. You've already started creating your financial security net with the actions you've taken so far to bounce back from your bankruptcy. Keep up the good work!

Step 5. Become a Better Steward of What You Have

Practicing the fine art of financial avoidance and procrastination contributes in subtle ways to your financial struggles. You have the power and ability to create what you desire. It all starts with baby steps. Begin to recognize and honor your financial choices. When you learn to respond differently to new financial situations as they occur, pat yourself on the back for each positive step, no matter how small. Breaking the debt cycle is an exercise in freedom. It's a chance to creatively find even more ways to transform the debt cycle—within yourself, your family, and your community. Remember the old *I Spy* game? Use a similar strategy to spot the ways in which you self-sabotage your prosperity. Then decide if you're willing to replace those behaviors with truly empowering actions and thoughts.

Step 6. Cultivate Patience

As you begin experiencing the benefits of less stress and greater control over financial events in your life, you may find yourself chomping at the bit to make changes, rock the boat, and speed things up. This is the biggest form of self-sabotage. Recognize it and look for ways in which you're comparing yourself to others. Identify ways to tap into your inborn sense of enjoyment. Slow your roll. Remember that the repayment plan and credit restoration steps you're setting up for yourself work if you're willing to stay on the steady, slow path. Work on fine tuning and managing your cash flow, and building forward momentum, as you create a solid savings base and repay your remaining debt.

Step 7. Value Yourself More

In my book *The Art of Tithing* I talk about how giving and receiving are the same thing. Our struggles with both often contribute to our debt cycle. As you overcome financial struggles by using and becoming comfortable with the concrete strategies you're discovering, you'll begin to understand the true value of non-monetary things, including your time, energy, and wisdom. When a financial situation pops up that requires you to use your savings, or you want something you can't purchase because you don't have *enough*, you'll come face-to-face with your feelings. Rather than acting on impulse, you can explore and act on financial options that expend less of your time, energy, and money. You'll stop self-sabotaging yourself and begin to explore and remove your self-imposed obstacles to receiving. You'll move from feeling entitled to being empowered.

Step 8. Harness the Power in Knowledge

Fear of the unknown often disempowers us. The psychology of belief demonstrates that when we encounter information that contradicts our long-held beliefs, *cognitive dissonance* occurs. Our brain simply can't wrap itself around a life without debt that is vibrant and effortless and financially satisfying. So we subconsciously rebel against the changes designed to take us in that direction.

It's not unlike the man who read my book, then decided the process was too slow, so he focused his efforts on getting credit after bankruptcy as quickly as possible—touting the fact that he and his wife had access to all sorts of credit eight months after his bankruptcy, building up huge external trappings of wealth. He taught others how to do the same and then wound up drowning in debt and going bankrupt again. This is not what I want for you. Instead of learning how to game the system, explore your rebellious streak around the process. Focus on gaining knowledge that increases your financial self-confidence and self-esteem.

The difference between paying cash or financing with debt is the difference between freedom and slavery—between living in the present and living in the past. An acquaintance who knew the power of cash wanted to buy a new pickup truck. He walked into the dealership with a check, told the dealer what he was looking for, and said the amount of the check would start with the number 2. He didn't care if the total came to $29,999.99—that was the most he was going to pay for the truck he wanted. And that's exactly what his new truck cost him. Know what you want and harness that knowledge so you can willingly walk away from credit and increase your spending power—or at the very least be comfortable in the knowledge that you're making the most informed decision about credit. Review all your current financial decisions and adjust any that aren't serving your best needs.

Step 9. Focus on What You Truly Want

Move away from the belief that you want or need *more money* to have what you want. What you really want is to know how to get what you want with the money that you have. We'll explore this in Chapter 7, GoalGetting, which will help you create and move toward your goals in a balanced way.

Step 10. Measure Progress, Not Perfection

Challenges are going to come up during the process of breaking this cycle of boom and bust as you bounce back from bankruptcy. Emotionally, psychologically, and spiritually, you're going to face obstacles. You'll get to see exactly where you sabotage yourself. You'll have the opportunity to support your dreams, and you'll begin to relax and enjoy creating a life where debt no longer rules your world and financial peace is your new reality.

Bottom line, money is *energy*. Nothing less, nothing more. Money has no power to control our actions—our *thoughts* control our actions. Start with a financial worry that is weighing on your mind. Maybe you're concerned about meeting this month's mortgage or rent payment. Your goal is to come up with enough money to pay for your housing. Whatever your financial concern, move yourself through the above 10 steps. Work toward progress, not perfection. Don't beat yourself up if you can't do everything at once. Take it one step at a time and keep moving forward, harnessing the power of your financial thoughts using a technique I call GoalGetting. Consider this *your* fresh-start financial literacy program.

What Do You Think You Lack?

Money isn't the only place where we feel lack in our lives. We may feel we lack knowledge, time, energy, or motivation, for example. I've been sober for 40 years, and in the beginning I found it challenging to write. My first year of sobriety, without a cigarette and a gin and tonic within easy reach, I would sit at my typewriter drawing a blank. I couldn't put two words together, much less two sentences. My sponsor suggested I set a timer for 10 minutes and write, then call her back. I reset that timer and made that phone call every 10 minutes for hours. Then suddenly, I would discover I had completely missed the timer going off and had written for an hour.

Forty years later, I still set a 15-minute timer when I write. I often find myself hitting *repeat* again and again as my fingers fly across the keyboard. Other times, I use the next 15 minutes to move my body, do other tasks, then return to my desk when the timer goes off again. Use this timer method to create more of whatever you think you lack.

Chapter 7

GoalGetting

The Power of GoalGetting

Our financial knowledge and habits are heavily rooted in how we were raised. My parents never talked about money—but they often *argued* about it. For years, I thought money was something taboo, so I never set any financial goals other than to *make it through the day*.

Many of us *set* goals, but few *achieve* them. Why? Because we seldom break our goals into manageable steps. One small step you take today toward achieving one goal determines whether you achieve—or get—your goal. Columnist George Will observed that "Europeans shop for what they *want*. Americans shop to *discover* what they want." No wonder we Americans spend so much. We're trying to discover *what* we want.

Today, we start with what we want and work backward. Sit somewhere quiet and ponder what you really want. What are your true desires? List things you really want to be, do, or experience. Here are a few of my past goals: paying a $500 dental bill, plane tickets to see my sister, gardening supplies to start seeds indoors, enjoying three weeks in Paris. All were goals I achieved by focusing on what I really wanted. What do you *really* want? Write it all down. It could be as simple as new socks or as wild as an interstellar trip to Mars.

As the first step in the GoalGetting strategy, record your top 10 goals below. Don't worry about filling in the second column yet.

My GoalGetting Strategy, Dated _____

My Top 10 Goals	3 Small Actions I'll Take
1.	1. 2. 3.
2.	1. 2. 3.
3.	1. 2. 3.
4.	1. 2. 3.
5.	1. 2. 3.
6.	1. 2. 3.
7.	1. 2. 3.
8.	1. 2. 3.
9.	1. 2. 3.
10.	1. 2. 3.

Next, pick the goal you want to work on first, then list a small action in the second column that you're willing to take today toward getting that goal. Don't go all gung ho committing to and taking so many actions that you burn yourself out. Start with one tiny action a day that you're willing to take toward a specific goal. Whether you're trying to achieve a short-term goal this month or a long-term goal years from now, you *get* your goal one step at a time.

Here's how goal-getting works for a financial goal. Let's say you want to take your family on a vacation to Disney World®. Fill in the blanks below regarding your goal:

1. The goal you want to achieve. *My goal is:* _____
   _____

2. The date by which you want to complete your goal. When do you want this to happen? Do you want to take your family to Disney World six months from now? Set a doable deadline and be willing to be flexible. *My goal date is:* _____.

3. How much money is needed to make this goal a reality? This is where you start your small tasks. You want to get clear on exactly what achieving your goal will cost financially. Not guesses. Real, factual numbers. The numbers may change as you move toward your goal. In fact, you may find your goal is less expensive—and more doable—once you know the true cost. Do your research. What *will* it cost to go to Disney World for one week? How much will airfare be for the time of year you'll be traveling? What's a rental car cost compared to driving yourself, or the cost of renting a car from home *and* driving yourself compared to flying? What are your housing options? Hotel, home swap, campground? On-site lodging or off-site? What are the different ticket prices to the parks you want to

visit? What would the cost of food and souvenirs be? Based on your research, let's say you determine your costs will be:

Vacation Expense	Cost
Nonstop airfare for four people	$800
3-day theme park passes	$1,300
Turo car rental for 7 days	$300
Housing at a resort with a full kitchen	$1,400
Food/souvenirs	$700
Unexpected expenses	$500
TOTAL:	$5,000

Armed with your research, you can calculate what you require financially. *The amount needed to make my goal a reality is: $_____.*

4. What's your starting point financially? To reach a goal, you have to know where you stand financially *now*. What amount can you set aside *today* toward this goal? Don't be discouraged if the answer *appears* to be zero. Gather your pocket change, add it up, and put it in a jar or box with the goal written on it: Disney Trip. Then write down your starting point for this goal. *I have this much set aside for my goal: $_____.*

5. How much do you still need to make your goal a reality? Look at your answer to Question 3 and subtract the amount from Question 4. If your trip costs $5,000 and you have $32.17 in spare change, you need $4,967.83. Divided by six months, that's $828 a month, or $27.60 per day, that you'll need to save to make your goal a reality. No judgment. Just information. Information is power. *I need to set aside this much: $_____.*

6. How frequently (daily, weekly, monthly, other) will you contribute to your vacation fund? If you want to contribute something every time you get paid, and you have regular paydays, total how many paydays you have between now and when you want to achieve this goal. Divide the amount in Question 5 by this number to see how much you need to contribute each payday to realize your goal. *I need to set aside this much each day/week/ month/paycheck: $*_____.

If the answer to Question 6 doesn't seem doable financially right now, review the various parts of your plan and brainstorm other options. For example, you could:

1. Postpone your trip for an extra year. That way, you have 18 months (or 78 weeks) to save $4,967.83, at a rate of $276 per month. More reasonable? That's just $9.20 a day.

2. Pare your trip expenses to reduce the total amount needed. If your family likes camping, you can pack your essential camping gear and rent a campsite at Disney's Fort Wilderness for about $80/night. If you don't want to bring a tent, you can rent a tent for $40/night. Or stop at Walmart on your way to the campsite and pick up a decent roomy tent for around $80. Staying at any Disney resort property usually includes free transportation to and from Disney parks, and various package deals can reduce the cost of your theme park tickets and even eliminate the need for a rental car if they offer an airport shuttle.

3. Share expenses with another family and stay off-site at a complex that offers free shuttle service to a Disney property.

4. Stay near the ocean, visit Disney for only one or two days, then visit other sites like Cape Canaveral.

Anything is possible when you're taking a single action each day toward your goals. Once you've successfully taken one action toward your goal each day for a few months, gradually increase your pace to two actions a day. Make a single phone call, research a single piece of information. Every day, ask yourself, "What one thing can I do toward one of my goals today?" Then do that one thing.

If you do more than one thing that day, great! But be careful of burning out. One way to discipline yourself to the slow and steady approach is to force yourself to do *only* one thing a day toward a single goal for 21 days. By then, you might be going bonkers about not making faster progress, but you'll create a habit of taking action daily and will see how each action brings you closer to your goals.

Engage Your Whole Family in GoalGetting

Having a group goal is the easiest way to get the whole family involved in GoalGetting. Make a game out of seeing where you can save money toward a family goal everyone is excited about, like season tickets to the WNBA, horseback riding at the Grand Canyon, watching a space shuttle launch in person, or building a backyard pool. Work together to figure out the cost and to free up the money in your everyday expenses or generate extra money to set aside for your goal.

You don't have to wait to save for your goal when you still have debts to repay. Simply allocate a percentage of the money you're currently saving to go toward your goal. That way, you'll make progress toward both eliminating your remaining debt *and* making your goal a reality.

Teach your whole family how to think critically and involve them in decision-making about how they want to spend money. Don't criticize or dismiss anyone who has a desire to spend money on something. Instead, use it as an opportunity to help them see the power of making choices based on intention rather than impulse—of choosing to save for a bigger goal in the future instead of spending money on something that gives short-term pleasure.

Decades ago, while visiting with friends in Illinois, their 10-year-old daughter wanted McDonald's for dinner. It was payday, and her dad, as usual, had cashed his weekly paycheck on his way home. He asked her to sit with him at the kitchen table, then handed her all the cash, saying, "Let's see what we've got here." He had her make piles as he called out expenses—this much for a portion of the upcoming mortgage, this much toward each utility, then amounts toward the car payment, gas, insurance, groceries, and so on. When he finished going through the list of expenses, she counted out the remaining $30. Then he asked her a question: "Would you like to spend this $30 on McDonald's tonight or put it in the envelope for our Florida trip?" She said, *"Florida,"* then hugged him and left the room—a beautiful way to teach money management *and* demonstrate the power our choices have to create our future.

You'll be amazed at how quickly you, your spouse, and kids will decide you all want to achieve the family goal, or a personal goal, more than spending money on convenience or impulse buys—especially if you sit down together and say, "Let's see . . . we can have these extra premium channels on cable, or we can switch to the lower-cost version with commercials and put $15 each month into our vacation fund." Ten $15 decisions generate $150 in savings! Add pictures of your goal to your savings container so you can visualize yourselves enjoying the goal.

Involve family members, even the smallest children, in choosing the actions they want to take to move the family goal forward and feed the dream. Turning off the lights when they leave a room, for example, can free up money that would have gone toward the electric bill. One family's daughter proposed she could clip coupons for everything the family bought; her mother gave her 10 percent of the grocery savings to put toward her own goals.

Make progress toward reaching at least one goal today. It doesn't matter how tiny that progress might be. One step forward daily will get you to your goal.

Review and update your goal sheet daily, and pick another action you'll take tomorrow to move your goal forward. Encourage all family members to do the same, whether they're working toward the group goal or their individual goals. Sharing ideas and achievements can lead to some lively conversations and bonding time.

Chapter 8

Make Credit-Savvy Moves

Being credit-savvy is *easy* . . . really! A few simple changes in your thoughts, attitudes, and actions will help you make only the best credit decisions moving forward. If this information were taught in school, few people would *ever* carry a balance on any account, except to keep their money working *for them*. Anyone can extend credit to you, but not all credit is in your best interest. Arm yourself with this knowledge and follow the guidance in this chapter to change how credit and debt work in your life.

Too often, we use credit to extend our income to get what we want *now*, which leads me to a hard truth: If your goal is to get credit again as quickly as possible, you will likely go bankrupt again. Creditors count on your desire for credit after bankruptcy outweighing your desire to bounce back after your bankruptcy, to become financially solvent.

Simply put, credit is debt. Our primal brains have been programmed to think credit *good*, debt *bad*. But credit can be a heavy anchor if you get caught in the cycle of having *monthly* debt, where you use future income to pay for current expenses. At that point, credit *is* debt—different words for the same thing.

So, before we talk about new ways to get credit and move to the next level of rebuilding after bankruptcy, let's look at how you can become a credit-savvy consumer, firmly focused on your goals, becoming financially secure and solvent, so credit never again becomes the burden of debt.

You may be thinking *this time will be different*. When I talk with people who are deep in debt a few years after their bankruptcy, I can easily trace their financial problems back to the moment when their credit became their debt, using simple detective work. In reviewing their credit account statements, I look for the first month they didn't pay the balance in full. I ask them what was going on in their world at that moment. They tell me of an occurrence that caused them to buy something they didn't have the money for at the time—usually something essential. Tickets to visit a family member, a new household appliance, and car repairs typically top the list. They increased their monthly payment and paid off the debt in a few months, which included the regular expenses they charged on that account as well as the interest that had accrued. The cycle repeated following another unexpected occurrence. Then two emergencies happened close together, and they racked up more debt which became impossible to pay off in a few months. The sizable monthly payment couldn't keep up with their ballooning debt until that whole amount was just enough to cover their new minimum payment.

If this has happened to you, Section IV can help you get out from under the crushing debt. But if you are just now bouncing back from your bankruptcy, you can break that cycle right now. It takes very little time to become a credit-savvy consumer, and the knowledge you gain could save you hundreds, even thousands, of dollars.

Let's say you need an expensive car repair. Your ready cash is tied up or needed for other upcoming expenses. The dealer offers you the opportunity to use their financing. It seems like your only option; you can make monthly payments, and there's *no interest if paid in full in six months*.

Sounds great—except that interest on the *entire* amount financed starts *accruing* when you buy the item. No matter how much you pay during that six months, if you still owe even a *penny* when the offer expires, you must pay *all* accrued interest. The benefit: you have extra time to pay off the debt. The drawback: your purchase will cost you approximately 30 percent more if you don't pay the balance in full in six months *and* you will continue to pay that 30 percent interest rate on the balance every month until it's paid in full.

Such offers make good financial sense in only two scenarios: (1) You have the cash set aside in savings and you're simply using the credit line as a way to avoid taking your money out of savings right now, or (2) you have no other way to get the funds and need to use this financing to get your car repaired.

If you're using your savings, pay the monthly minimum until the month *before* your no-interest period ends, then pay the balance in full. If you're using the credit line to truly replace money you don't currently have, divide the bill by 5 so that you will pay the bill in full *before* those six months are up, to completely avoid any interest charges.

Let's say the bill is $2,000. Divided by 5, you need to come up with $400 each month, or $100 a week, to pay the entire bill before the interest-free period ends. Use the strategies in Chapter 14 and Chapter 19 to free up every possible penny to cover the $400 monthly payment—pay more when you can.

The Fine Print Says the Quiet Part Aloud

When it comes to getting you to buy something, the enticing marketing copy is *always* in big type. The stuff they don't want you to know? The stuff that will cost you money? It's all in the *fine* print. My spouse laughs at me for doing it, but I *always* read the fine print—as annoying and time-consuming as it is. The fine print of all contracts and financing or credit applications contains the true hidden costs, increased fees you might incur, and changes in company policies that may cost you more.

When my teenage son opened a checking account that came with a debit card, he intentionally kept his balance low to resist the temptation to spend and had us transfer funds from his savings when he wanted to level up. He hadn't read the fine print in the account agreement, which outlined he could have four monthly free transfers and would pay $15 for each additional transfer. He was giving the bank $30 a month to access his own money. Realizing it, he adjusted to weekly transfers to avoid these fees.

Creditors, banks, utilities—basically any company you give money to—send notices and statements alerting you to changes in their terms. Creditors *must* give you advance notice of financial changes and give you a chance to close your account or change the way you do business with them. The changes go into effect if you don't object. That's why it might seem as though creditors *suddenly* raise your interest rate without warning. They give us warnings, but we generally don't read them.

Listen to Your Buyer's Remorse

Ever have second thoughts about a large purchase right after you sign the financing agreement and hand over your deposit? This *buyer's remorse* can be your best friend. You may be able to change your mind, undo the contract, and get your money back. The details will be in the fine print. Laws vary by state, but in general you have three to five business days from the day you sign the contract to cancel it and get your deposit back.

Expect the Unexpected

We all know that eventually we may need to have a car repaired, an appliance replaced or a cavity filled. We're surprised by these expenses because we *pretend* they won't ever happen. Instead, what if you began setting aside funds to cover these expenses (or a portion of them) before the expense becomes an emergency? Of all the credit-savvy guidance I can offer, this one action can be the hardest to follow—not only for a potential emergency purchase, but also for unexpected enjoyment (a vacation, a gift).

As a credit-savvy consumer, you need to remember that creditors *want* you to add new debt to your current expenses. Little dollar signs light up in their eyes when you reach for credit as the solution. Instead, when you're tempted to buy something on credit for enjoyment or you want to set aside funds for those unexpected automotive repairs, appliance replacements, or medical expenses, crunch the numbers so you know *exactly* what your purchase will cost. Start with small $250 savings goals for the emergency repairs. And build those savings slowly. Look for ways to generate a little extra money each

---

The Truth About Once-in-a-Lifetime Deals

I laugh at sales pitches that claim you'll never get this low price again. It's a *one-time offer* and you must act fast to buy now or miss out forever. Growing up in a family that owned a small business, I learned an important lesson about sales pitches. The truth is, if a company really wants your business, you can *always* buy what you want at the super sale price. When dealing with small or local companies, that great low price will either still be offered after the advertised deadline, or you can buy the item somewhere else. Larger businesses will find a way to offer the same sale price again in a few months, because they know the low price draws customers. A good deal is a good deal—but it's never actually a once-in-a-lifetime deal.

month and set aside something to achieve your goal. Look for sales, compare prices and take advantage of coupons. If the unexpected happens, use those savings, finance whatever you need to finance, and don't charge anything else until your balance is paid off.

Layaway:
Best Alternative to Buy Now, Pay Later

Credit-savvy consumers know that sometimes the best way to use credit is through a layaway or prepayment plan. Instead of the credit card approach of buy now, pay later, with layaway, you *set aside the item now, pay as you go, and take possession when it's paid for.* Small businesses often will agree to such a plan if you ask. You put down a deposit—usually 10 to 30 percent—and then make weekly or intermittent payments toward your purchase, which stays at the store until it's fully paid for. When you make your final payment, the store lets you have your merchandise—and you've paid no interest.

Beware of *eLayaway* programs offered by stores like Sears and Kmart. They're actually buy now, pay later programs. Others like Walmart are up front about offering buy now, pay later options. Two well-known chains that still offer true layaway programs are Burlington and Jostens (the high school ring company).

Don't Charge Consumables

Decades ago, I was a weekly guest on a financial radio show. The host asked me to talk about college students and debt. I asked my intern, who was a few years out of college, what she charged on her credit card in college that she wished she hadn't. She was okay with charging her books and travel expenses to get home for the holidays. But she regretted having charged beer runs, late-night pizzas, and spur-of-the-moment expenses for things with no lasting value. My advice: don't use your credit card for anything that won't exist next month.

The True Cost of Three Easy Payments

I love advertisements that hawk *three easy payments of $9.95* without ever telling you the cost if you were to buy the item outright. Not only that, but only the fine print tells you about the usual *convenience fee* you'll be charged for the privilege of paying in installments, which total $29.85, with an extra dollar or so tacked on to each installment as a convenience fee. That means you'll pay $32.85 for the item. The purchase price if you were to pay for it in full? $25.95. The company makes an extra 25 percent if they can convince you to make those three easy payments.

Burlington (burlington.com) offers a 30-day layaway. Your deposit must be $10 or 20 percent (whichever is more), and you'll pay a $5 service fee. If you don't complete your layaway payments within the 30 days, they'll charge a $10 or 10 percent cancellation fee (whichever is less), and any payments you made are transferred into store credits that you can use later.

Jostens (jostens.com) offers a 12-payment layaway plan for high school rings. Your payments must be made every 14 days for roughly 22 weeks. There's no service fee, but your ring must cost at least $425 ($501 if you're in Ohio). You will be charged a $100 cancellation fee if you miss a payment—and they'll refund all your money directly to you.

SECTION III

CREDIT AFTER BANKRUPTCY DONE RIGHT

Chapter 9

When You Are Desperate for Credit

I once saw a sign that said *save 100% when you don't buy anything*. Sometimes, though, you must spend money. And after bankruptcy, you want to spend money in ways that help you rebuild your credit. There are excellent ways to do that, and some ways you will definitely want to avoid—all of which we cover in this chapter.

You may be worried that you'll never get credit again. You may be glad to be rid of credit card debt for now. You may even swear you'll *never* touch another credit card for as long as you live. No matter how you feel about credit cards, they can offer a quick way to rebuild your credit history so you can qualify for lower interest rates on insurance, car loans, and mortgages. That's our goal, after all: to have every dollar you spend be a dollar that saves you money.

I challenge you to think about *credit* the way I do: credit is *debt*. Wanting credit is simply the desire to have and use more money than we have available right now. Rather than make our money work smarter for us, *credit* creates a situation where we are using money we haven't yet received. Creditors *let* us use tomorrow's money today, and they make it sound as though they're doing us a favor—when they're really setting us up for financial failure. That's especially true with short-term lenders and so-called credit-building programs.

Short-Term Lenders

Pay attention to what the financial advertisements you see on television and in other media *aren't* telling you—like the DriveTime app that lets you pick the down payment and monthly payment amounts for your next car but never mentions anything about the car's total price. The companies that offer buy now, pay later options, cash advances or payday advances try to sell you on buying now and paying later with no *hidden* fees. Few of these companies help you rebuild your credit, but these all can and will hurt your credit.

The Klarna credit card, issued by WebBank, is a popular option. It's advertised as a fee-free and interest-free option that's superior to high-cost credit cards. You can purchase pretty much everything in installments, even your burrito dinner (if it's over $35), thanks to their partnership with DoorDash. After paying 25 percent up front, you pay a quarter of the purchase price every two weeks for the next six weeks, interest-free. Miss a payment, though, and they'll charge you interest ranging from 28.99 to 35.99 percent. FICO is now including buy now, pay later data in their credit score calculations. In 2024, 25% of all buy now, pay later users had at least one late payment. And nearly half of all users would likely experience a lower credit score. That negative information is the last thing you want as you're trying to build positive credit after your bankruptcy.

Like Klarna, most cash advance and payday advance companies are financial technology companies that *partner* with banks. These short-term lending programs are designed to get you to pay fees that exceed any interest you'd pay on a credit card. To use these companies' programs, you must open an account with their bank, set up a monthly direct deposit (designed to collect your paycheck) into that account, and then get loans from them. Their marketing is outstanding, magnifying the discontent that comes with having to wait to get paid for your work on your *payday* and asserting that *you* should be able to decide when you get paid. To me, they're no different than payday lenders in what they do to you financially. You might not be paying 700 percent interest as you would with a payday lender, but they'll still cost you between 100 and 575 percent in interest. Think about that . . . are you willing to pay almost six times the original purchase price just to have the thing you want right away?

Credit-Building Programs

Don't get me started on self-proclaimed credit builder programs. My favorite bad actors *lend* you money, put that loan into a savings account, and then you repay the loan—in full—over time. Let me repeat that: They *lend* you $1,000, but you never have access to the $1,000 from the loan. Instead, they put the loan proceeds into a savings account (which may or may not earn interest). All of this happens on paper. You make payments on the loan (which may or may not include paying interest). Once you've paid half the loan amount, they often then graciously give you access to that $500, usually through a secured credit card, which you can use to charge things and then must make monthly payments on. If you don't pay the balance on the secured account in full, you pay interest on the remaining amount. Miss one payment on the original loan *or* the secured credit card balance and you create black marks on your credit reports after bankruptcy.

When it comes to credit-building opportunities, the industry offers endless versions with various terms and conditions. One credit builder simply gives you access to two of the most horrid secured and prepaid cards on the market, issued by First Progress Bank and First Latitude Bank, respectively.

Credit-Building Program Red Flags

Credit-building programs are heavily advertised for a reason: they make the *company* scads of money. Before you jump at one of these offers, check it out thoroughly, read every word of the fine print, and pay attention to these warning signs.

1. The bank affiliated with the program gets horrible ratings. All genuine *bank* credit cards are backed by an FDIC-insured issuing bank or a NCUA-insured credit union that reports your payments to the major credit bureaus and protects your deposit on a secured card. Most credit-builder and cash app programs are *financial tech companies* that have connected themselves with a bank. In addition, many company names *sound* like familiar bank names but they aren't. They count on you accepting, without verifying, that the named company is truly a bank. If you're talking with a financial tech company or if the bank uses another bank to issue their credit card, ask for the *full* name of the issuing bank. Without an issuing bank that is a member of the FDIC, it's not a real credit card.

   Most financial tech companies—like Klarna, Chime, Credit Builder Card, and others—are connected to substandard banks. First, verify the issuing bank's name using the FDIC's BankFind Suite (banks.data.fdic.gov/bankfind-suite/bankfind). Then check the Better Business Bureau (bbb.org) to see the bank's *reviews* and *complaint* history. If the bank isn't legit or has many negative reviews and complaints, take a pass. Do the same for any credit union. It should be federally insured by the National Credit Union Administration (NCUA), which offers to credit unions the same protection the FDIC offers to banks. Visit mycreditunion.gov to search for a credit union by name. They recommend using a single search word like "digital" rather than the whole company's name. Check the credit union's Better Business Bureau listing as well.

2. The interest rate is listed vaguely as *based on your personal situation or based on your zip code*. They won't tell you the rate you will be charged until you plop down money to apply. Authentic credit cards disclose their rates up front, and good credit cards don't charge an application fee. Don't give any company money for a credit card until they tell you their interest rate in writing.

3. The company declares that as a program member you're eligible for a *collateralized* credit card, even if you have bad credit. Collateralized simply means *secured*—and what they're offering is usually *not* a good secured card.

4. The company lures you with a credit line of *up to* $1,000. Be alert to those two magic words: *up to*. The credit line you'll qualify for will likely be much lower—often $350 or less. Their recommended secured card will generally charge you an application fee and an annual fee, and sometimes will provide *no* grace period—meaning you'll pay interest on every single transaction from the moment you make a purchase.

Create Your Own Credit Builder

The biggest issue I have with credit-builder programs is that they are designed to rebuild your credit by getting you into debt. These programs play on our desires and fears. Instead, save your money and put it into a secure savings account with one of the companies that truly builds your credit. They'll issue you a credit card with a credit limit equal to your savings and will report your payments to the major credit bureaus every month—simple, straightforward, and with minimal risk to you. If you fall behind on your monthly payments, you close the account, pay off any outstanding balance with your savings account, and you're good.

Prepaid Credit Cards

I don't recommend *any* prepaid credit cards. A prepaid card does nothing to rebuild your credit rating. Most issuing companies don't report your payments to the credit bureaus, and prepaid cards can't be used for some transactions, like renting a car, unless your name is embossed on the front. Prepaid credit cards are basically fancy debit cards that *cost* you money. Unlike your friendly bank debit card, a prepaid credit card often charges fees to do simple things like adding money to your account (known as *reloading*) or checking your balance. Many also charge a monthly fee.

Debit Cards

Most debit cards give you the convenience of a credit card while helping you develop (and maintain) the discipline of spending only the cash you have, because the money is drawn out of your checking or savings account.

When you receive your debit card, it will usually have a Visa® or Mastercard® logo (some have Discover®) and look exactly like a regular credit card except for tiny type that says *Debit Card*. You can use your debit card anywhere Mastercard or Visa is accepted (including at the Olympics, as I can personally attest!).

Is a Debit Card Right for You?

Your debit card not only looks like a credit card, but it acts like one too. You can use it to order goods and services in person, online, or via phone instead of carrying wads of cash. You can purchase airline tickets and reserve a hotel room without having to prepay. But most rental car companies won't accept a debit card to reserve a car. (There are ways around that, as you'll see in Chapter 11.)

The main way credit cards and debit cards differ is in how you pay for your purchases. Unlike the line of credit you have with a credit card, you must have the money in your account at the time of purchase when using a debit card.

With a credit card, a merchant checks to see whether you have enough credit available on your card to buy what you want to buy. Then they charge that purchase amount to your credit card account. At the end of your billing cycle, they send you a statement showing everything you bought during that period and the total amount you owe. This is your *bill*. You then either pay your bill in full to return your debt to zero, or you pay a portion of your statement balance and carry the remainder to the next month. At that point, the credit card company charges you interest (known as a *finance charge*) on that remainder, and both the remaining balance and the interest charge are added to next month's statement.

With a debit card, a merchant checks to see whether you have enough money available in your checking account to buy what you want to buy. The money is then subtracted from your checking account, either immediately or within three business days, as if you paid using a check. Your card's limit is your *current available* checking account balance.

Here's the catch: The amount your bank *says* you have and the amount you *really* have available in your account may differ. You may have written checks that haven't yet cleared your account, or withdrawals or purchases that are still pending and haven't posted to your account. Fortunately, modern technology (and consumer protection laws) lets your bank put a partial or full *hold* on amounts a merchant is attempting to collect from your account. This allows the business to verify or authorize payment from you after confirming the amount available but before removing the funds from your account. While the process isn't flawless, it can protect you from getting hit with fees *every* time you spend more money than you may have in your account.

Ready to Get a Debit Card?

If you decide you want a debit card, make sure to ask your bank the following questions:

Does the bank protect me against fraudulent charges? Most banks offer the same protection for stolen or fraudulent use of your debit card as they do for credit cards. Ask your banker what your liability would be if your card is stolen or used fraudulently, and make sure you're comfortable with the answer before requesting a debit card. Many banks (and credit card companies) offer free *fraud alert* options, where you'll receive a call, text, or email if a charge looks suspicious. If you respond that you did not authorize the transaction, the fraud team will disable your card and restrict your account. You'll still need to follow up with your bank on the fraudulent charges by filling out their paperwork, changing your account password, and possibly getting a new debit card.

Does the bank protect me if I have a dispute with a merchant? A good debit card will give you the same *chargeback* right that credit cards offer, by disputing any merchandise problem for you.

If the card you're considering passes these two tests, then it's time to select from the different available debit card options. Find out answers to these questions:

How much will the bank charge for me to get cash from another bank's ATM using my debit card? It's standard practice for another bank chain to charge you a convenience fee (up to $5 per transaction) for using their ATM. But *your* bank may also charge you when you use that other bank's ATM. To avoid these fees, only withdraw cash from your own bank's ATMs. You might instead want to bank at a credit union that belongs to the CO-OP Connected Credit Unions network (I'll talk about "Credit Union

---

Turned Down for a Debit Card?

Generally, no credit check is needed to get a debit card. However, if you bounced more than two checks in the past year, you may need permission from your bank to have a debit card. A *savings sweep* can help you avoid bouncing checks in the future or having insufficient funds in your checking account when you make a purchase. This is especially helpful if you're not clear on when automatic recurring purchases are withdrawn from your account. A savings sweep automatically moves money from your savings to your checking account to cover incoming expenses that exceed your current available balance. Check with your bank to see if they offer this benefit and what fees they charge when using the savings sweep.

Secured Cards That Make the Grade" in a moment), which has more than 30,000 surcharge-free ATMs throughout the country.

What are my daily limits for purchases and cash withdrawals with my debit card? This is very important, especially if you want to use your card for large purchases. Years ago, my Land Rover was in the repair shop. When I went to pay the $1,200 bill, the purchase was declined, even though I had ample funds in the account. Turns out the bill exceeded the daily purchase limit on my card. Fortunately, I called my bank just before closing time and they raised my daily limit for that day, so I wasn't stranded. Most banks also limit the amount you can withdraw each day at an ATM, which is usually $400–$1,000.

When you open your account, you can specify what daily limit you want to set for transactions and withdrawals. You can also go into the bank and have them change the limits for you. Sometimes you can check and change your limits online. Some banks offer in-branch ATM machines that allow larger withdrawals, and you can always withdraw larger sums at the teller window.

When will deposits be credited to my account, and when will charges be subtracted? Money generally goes out of our accounts faster than it gets deposited. Every time you make a deposit, ask specifically when your money will be available and whether any hold is being put on your deposit. Most banks make a small amount of a check available immediately, but not the entire check amount. Make sure you know *exactly* how long every deposit will take to clear so you don't spend money that's not yet available. Otherwise, the dreaded overdraft police will send out their notices to the check reporting services if a delay creates a negative balance in your account. When possible, cash large checks at the bank the check is drawn from. Then deposit the cash into your account at your bank.

Whenever you use your debit card, get a receipt (paper or electronic), then check all receipts against your bank statements or online bank ledger. Subtract any transaction fees directly from your checkbook on the day you use your debit card to help you avoid overdrawing your account.

The Downside to Debit Cards

Debit cards are a great way to avoid running up debt, but a debit card will *not* help you rebuild your credit. In fact, although it can help you avoid negative references on your credit report, it can also hurt your credit if you overdraw your bank account, which can happen easily with a debit card. Overdrafts show up on your check reporting services reports, which banks review when you apply for a car loan or mortgage.

A credit card that reports to the major credit bureaus is usually needed to rebuild your credit to the point where creditors will offer you a mortgage or a car loan. Avoid using credit-builder programs, as discussed earlier. I recommend getting a debit card *and* one good secured credit card.

It's easy to make transactions or write checks from your checking account without remembering to track them. Popular cash apps like Apple Pay, Venmo, and Zelle make it easy to move money around. If you're not tracking those expenses carefully, you can easily bounce a check or find yourself overdrawn.

How Much Credit is Enough

The only point of having a credit card is to improve your creditworthiness, which lowers your insurance rates and the interest rate you'll pay on a mortgage or car loan. You only need enough credit to give you access to funds in an emergency—funds that you'll have built up in savings but may not have on hand or accessible in the moment you need them.

Beware of *preapproved offers* for credit that appear in your mailbox. These days *preapproved* simply means you passed their first screening test, which is usually that you are breathing and have an address. If you read the fine print of these preapproved offers, you'll typically see that they *do* check your credit report before you qualify. Every application you submit puts an inquiry on your credit report, which tips off future creditors that you're desperate to get more credit. Opt out of these offers using the strategies in Chapter 13.

You may be surprised at how little credit you truly need to put new, positive credit information on your credit report. Carrying a monthly balance on your credit card does not help your credit score—but it can *hurt* it! Calculate how much you know you could pay off within two months if you found yourself in debt. Be conservative in your estimate. Your goal here is to figure out the lowest credit limit you should apply for so that the card's balance can be paid in full within a few months. This protects you from getting in debt again just as you're starting to get back on your feet.

As for how many cards you should have, I urge you to get only *one* credit card for personal use. If you have a business, get a second card to use only for business expenses. One low-limit card will do wonders to help you rebuild your credit history without risk. Over time, as you pay your bill *in full* each month, the creditor will raise your credit limit. You've demonstrated you are a good credit risk, and now they want to entice you with more credit so you'll also become a *profitable* customer—paying them monthly interest.

I will always remember a conversation I had with a credit card executive. He was laughing at a newscaster who referred to the rising number of late-paying consumers as "deadbeats." The executive explained that in their industry, a *deadbeat* is the customer they never earn any interest from because they pay their bill in full each month.

Regardless of how high your creditor raises your credit limit, continue charging only what you can afford to pay off in full each month with money you already have in savings, not money you're earning this month. One effortless way to raise your credit score is to never charge more than 30 percent of your total credit limit and pay your previous statement balance in full each month. If your credit limit is $1,000, for example, always charge less than $300 each billing cycle. This shows *future* creditors you're able to handle credit responsibly and that you don't view credit as an extension of your income. Despite common lore, carrying a balance on your credit card and paying interest *does not* increase your credit score.

Bottom line: You do *not* need a big credit line to buy what you want. Consistently take the small steps discussed next and you will soon be able to have whatever you want, when you want to buy it— without debt.

Never look at what the *monthly* payments are for anything when you're buying something on credit. If the salesperson asks how much you want to spend each *month*, respond with your bottom-dollar offer for the *total* cost if you were paying with cash. This way you learn to plan for purchases you want to make, allowing you to have what you want, when you want, without adding any new revolving debt.

Steps for Debt-Free Credit Card Spending

Controlling your credit card spending and building a positive credit history is easy, regardless of your past spending habits. Just follow these steps:

1. Get a secured credit card with no more than a $500 limit. You can't fall into enormous debt with a $500 credit limit. Start with a $200 to $500 limit and charge no more than 30% of that limit ($60–$150 a month) to improve your credit score.

2. Use your credit card to charge small recurring expenses that require a card on file—those monthly expenses that are almost always the same amount so you can easily track your spending: subscriptions, dental insurance, internet, things like that.

3. Whatever amount you charge, put that amount in your savings account the day you make the purchase. Then use the money in your savings account to pay the bill in full each month.

4. Never charge anything that's on sale if you're carrying a balance. Your purchase will cost you much more than the discount if you're paying interest on it.

5. Only charge what you can pay in full when the bill arrives. For larger essential purchases, only charge what you can pay off in a few months. If a bill arrives with a higher balance than you can pay in full, do yourself an enormous favor. Stop all auto payments, stick your credit card in a plastic bag filled with water, and put it in the freezer. Don't use your card for anything until your bill is paid in full.

6. Add your credit card statement due date to your calendar to more easily keep on track with your payments.

7. Always pay the statement balance in full.

8. If you are allowed to make payments more often than once a month and you want to get in the habit of only spending money you *already* have, check your credit card balance online daily—not how much *credit* is still available but the amount you currently *owe* for this billing cycle. Then pay what you can on that amount today.

9. If your credit card company limits the number of payments each month, pay weekly if possible (ask how many payments you can make each month). This creates a habit of buying only what you can pay for *today*. Too often we buy what we know we can pay off at the end of the month or on payday with money we've just received. By paying for your purchases weekly, you avoid that debt cycle *and* you rebuild your credit. Achieving this level of financial freedom can be done in a few years if you train yourself to avoid the credit traps lenders use to lure you into debt.

10. Set up autopay for the minimum payment. Your credit card's only purpose is to create a positive credit report reference. You never want a late payment for several reasons. First, creditors are allowed to raise your interest rate, and being late by even one day can be extremely expensive. Second, being late adds a black mark to your credit report, which tells creditors you are still a bad credit risk. Third, autopay eliminates the risk of missing a payment because you've misplaced the bill or overlooked the email notification that your statement is ready. It happens more than you know. People in areas hit by floods, fires, hurricanes, or an illness know all too well how easy it is to miss a payment and the unfortunate results of doing so.

11. Prepay your credit card bill if possible. When you need access to more credit on your secured card, you don't have to make additional deposits to your savings account. Instead, some secured credit cards let you *prepay* your credit card bill. Your credit line will still be the same, but you will have a negative balance. Say you have a secured credit card with a $200 credit line and you need to charge $450 worth of travel expenses this month. If you have a zero balance and prepay $250, you temporarily increase your credit line to $450. You're not actually increasing your *credit* limit; you are increasing your purchasing power. Every holiday season, or before a vacation, I used to send in an extra few hundred dollars so the money I spent was already credited to my charge card.

Following the above strategies will increase your credit score and help you stay out of debt. Now that you know how to make your credit card work for you, let's look at some different card options, starting with one you might already have.

Using a Zero Balance Credit Card That Wasn't Discharged

Because you don't have to list credit cards with a zero balance on your bankruptcy schedule, you could use this credit card account to rebuild your credit. *But*, as noted earlier, chances are good that the creditor will close even fully paid accounts when they discover your bankruptcy. In a Chapter 13 repayment plan, your trustee's approval would be needed to reopen the account, and you would pay all new charges on that credit card *outside* your repayment plan.

How do these creditors find out about your bankruptcy? Credit bureaus give creditors a monthly list of Social Security numbers for bankruptcy filers. Your creditors then compare their cardholders' Social Security numbers against bankruptcies listed on Equifax's Bankruptcy Navigator Index®, Experian's Bankruptcy PLUSsm, and TransUnion's CreditVision®. When creditors discover a recent bankruptcy filing, they often cancel accounts without warning, to protect themselves against losses. Nothing's quite as embarrassing as taking your bestie to lunch or attempting to buy something with your zero-balance credit card that you didn't include in your bankruptcy, only to discover that the creditor has canceled your card.

Sometimes creditors accidentally list these zero-balance open accounts on your credit report as *discharged under bankruptcy* even when they were not included in your bankruptcy. If this happens, you may be able to convince the creditor to reopen your account.

Call the creditor's customer service department and get the phone number for the corporate office. You can sometimes find this number on the bottom of a creditor's website or on their Contact page. Call and ask for the name of and mailing address for the director of consumer affairs. Send this person a brief good-faith letter that includes a proposal to minimize their risk if they keep your account open. You can use the sample letter on the next page.

Send the letter via certified mail, return receipt requested.

[Date]
[Director's Name]
Director of Consumer Affairs
[Address]
[City, State, Zip Code]

Re: [Your account number]

Dear [Director's Name]:

I have been a customer of yours since [date you opened the account with them], with my account in good standing.

While I was forced to declare bankruptcy on [date of bankruptcy discharge], I kept your account out of my bankruptcy because I valued my relationship with your company.

[Add a paragraph here stating the status of your account with them, such as "my account was closed by your representatives on such-and-such date" or "my account is listed on my credit report as having been discharged under bankruptcy, but that is not correct."]

Since I have been a customer of yours for [number of years], I would really like to keep this account active and am writing to ask that you reopen this account.

I understand you may be reluctant to continue an account for a customer with a recent bankruptcy on their credit report. I believe you can minimize your risk if you limit my credit line to [$500 or half your existing credit limit, whichever is greater].

I appreciate your taking a chance on a longtime customer who is working to rebuild [his/her] credit, and I trust you will reinstate my account within the next 30 days.

Sincerely,
[Your Name]

Choosing a New Credit Card after Bankruptcy

Credit cards come in all flavors, including secured, unsecured, and prepaid cards. Some charge high annual fees, some charge interest varying from moderate to outrageous, and some allow no grace period on purchases while others give you 21–30 days from the date your bill is issued to pay your balance without accruing interest. If you elect to receive your statements in the mail, the clock starts ticking on the day the statement is *mailed*—so your grace period will appear shorter.

When looking for the best credit card after their bankruptcy, most people focus on finding a card with a low interest rate, a low or no annual fee, and the highest credit limit they can get with the lowest security deposit. Some of these factors are important, but not the *most* important. The best credit card will depend on what you want out of it. No matter what factors are most important to you, when rebuilding your credit, any credit card you get (secured or unsecured) must meet certain criteria, which I'll talk about in a minute.

Beware of online *best of* lists for secured and unsecured credit cards that are good for people with bad credit. For starters, the methodology they use is flawed and often doesn't pay attention to what's truly important for rebuilding your credit. In addition, these lists generally contain credit cards that pay websites and companies affiliate fees for their recommendation, which means the *website owner* makes money every time someone clicks the link or applies for that card. I'd be okay with that if their recommendations were the best cards for you, but they're usually not.

Despite the wide variety of cards out there, a secured card will be your best option after bankruptcy for the reasons I'll explain. But not all secured cards are created equal.

Find Your Best Credit Card

The marketing geniuses at credit card companies have worked hard to convince you that having a secured credit card in your wallet is about as desirable as having a skunk in your house. Creditors work hard to convince you that the security deposit ties up your money. When you're bombarded with offers for *unsecured* credit cards, my advice to get a *secured* credit card may seem silly. But the truth is, a secured card provides you with a safety net against building up debt and also minimizes the fees and interest the creditor can collect from you.

A *good* secured credit card looks and acts like a regular Mastercard, Visa, or Discover card. The only difference? You deposit money as *collateral* for your credit line rather than having the company extend credit. Companies minimize their risk of default, and you rebuild your credit score. The money is yours. It's often deposited in a savings account (and in some cases earns interest). You enjoy all the benefits of a regular credit card, including establishing a positive credit history.

As long as you handle your credit responsibly—paying what you owe on time every month and using less than 30% of your credit line—your credit score will rise quickly. Within a few years you may find you have sparkling credit. Your creditor will review your account and often eventually offers to convert your secured card to an *unsecured* credit card, returning your deposit plus any earned interest.

Another benefit: if rising debt on a secured card threatens to sink your newfound financial solvency, you can close your account with one phone call and a follow-up letter, then pay down the balance until your security deposit will cover any remaining balance, and once again you will be debt-free. Financially, a good secured credit card offers you a better deal than any unsecured or prepaid card or any cash advance, cash app, or payday loan option you'll encounter after bankruptcy. Use the following checklist to find the best card for *you*.

SECURED CREDIT CARD CHECKLIST

Most banks and credit unions have a few general requirements for all secured credit applicants. Once upon a time, credit union membership was limited to people who met very narrow criteria. Fortunately, many credit unions now offer memberships to anyone who belongs to a nonprofit organization that is a member of that credit union. Whether you choose a bank or a credit union, getting a secured credit card usually requires that you:

- be at least 18 years old,
- have a phone, and
- reside in the United States.

As long as your debts have been discharged and you have no outstanding liens, your bankruptcy won't count against you. If you haven't already cleaned up your credit reports, take those steps in Chapter 2 *before* applying for a credit card or any other loan.

To reestablish your credit with a secured credit card, make sure you analyze all credit offers you receive. You want to apply for only one card. Don't apply for several cards at once. Too many new inquiries on your credit report raise a red flag with creditors—and can *lower* your credit score. The following nine questions will help you easily identify the *one* credit card that best suits you.

Banks and credit unions merge, credit offers change, or you may have found this book in 2030 or beyond. Even if the cards I recommend here are no longer available or their terms change, I want you to have all the information you need to pick a *good* secured credit card. Winnow the cards to ones that offer the best chances of increasing your credit score while minimizing the amount it costs you to do so.

One by one, run the cards you're considering through these questions. The minute you get a no, cut the card from your list and move on to the next one (with the exception noted in Question 1).

The conditions in the first two questions won't jump out at you on all applications or marketing materials, because they may not be addressed. Even if the credit card issuer currently meets these criteria, policies change. Because banks aren't *required* to disclose this information, get the answer in writing. I've included all the essential details I analyze with credit card offers so you can figure out which offers are good for you. Review the credit application, visit the company's website, read their terms and conditions and disclosures carefully, and email, chat with, or call the creditor and ask these questions:

1. For how long does my bankruptcy have to be discharged before I can apply for your secured credit card? Some cards let you apply right away while others require you wait until your bankruptcy discharge is several years old. Don't dismiss the card right away if you will have to wait to apply for it. Instead, get answers to all the other questions so you can decide for yourself whether this card is worth the wait. Some companies don't offer their secured credit card to anyone with a bankruptcy on their credit report.

2. Do you report my payment history on this card every month to at least the three major credit bureaus? Future auto loan or mortgage lenders won't see your good credit habits unless your payments are regularly reported to Equifax, Experian, and TransUnion (and hopefully Innovis). When you're ready to take out a car loan or a mortgage, you want your good payment history to shine through. A secured credit card issued by a credit union that may or may not report your credit history is the one exception *if* you'll be financing your car and home through that credit union. They will see your good payment

history from your credit card account, whether or not they report your payments to the credit bureaus.

3. Do you report my credit card without mentioning it's a secured card? Only you and your creditor should know your credit card is secured by your savings. When a bank lists a credit card as secured on your credit report, other creditors immediately know the card is not really issued to provide *credit*—it's secured by your collateral (your security deposit). This won't help you build a positive credit history, so make sure the secured card you select is *not* listed as secured on your credit reports. Again, if you think you'll apply for future credit through the same credit union you're seeking a card from, it matters less how they report your secured credit card.

4. At what point will my secured card switch to an unsecured card? The best issuers of secured cards want you to succeed. Some start reviewing your account after seven months, while others wait a full year. If they find you've made timely payments on their account and on all other accounts reported on your credit report and you're using your credit wisely, the best companies will convert your account to unsecured and return your security deposit. Some issuers (like Merrick Bank) never convert you to an unsecured card.

5. What is your grace period for purchases, between when my billing period ends and my payment is due? This tells you how much time you have to pay your bill once you receive it. The best cards offer grace periods of at least 21 days. To make my recommended list, the creditor has to offer a minimum 21-day grace period. If your credit card has a grace period for purchases *and* you pay off your entire balance each month by the due date, you won't pay interest on your purchases. I don't recommend using your credit card for cash advances, as most cards have no grace period for these amounts and

you'll be paying interest from the moment you withdraw your money.

6. What interest rate do you charge, and what causes that to change? All cards I recommend calculate your interest rate based on the U.S. Prime Rate *plus* a set percentage. Currently the prime rate is 7.50%. Your interest rate falls when the prime rate is lowered and rises when it is increased. Some secured card issuers *increase* your interest rate (either temporarily or permanently) if you make a *single* late payment. On a positive note, some credit card issuers *reduce* your interest rate if you put your account on autopay or if you request electronic instead of printed statements.

7. What fees do you charge? All creditors I recommend charge either no annual fee or an annual fee under $30; others charge an outrageously higher annual fee or a monthly fee for your card. Some charge for late payments while others give you a pass for one late payment but charge for any others. Some charge if you go over your credit limit. Some charge if you take out a cash advance, transfer a balance from another card, or use your card in other countries. And some don't. Knowing what these fees are helps you budget for or avoid them.

8. How much will my credit line be, and can my credit limit increase over time? Your security deposit is the amount of credit you can access for most secured credit cards. Capital One offers a $200 credit line but allows your initial security deposit to be $49, $100, or $200 depending on your credit score when you apply. Most creditors let you make additional deposits into your secured savings account to increase your credit line. Others randomly increase your credit line as you demonstrate you are a good credit risk. Only use additional credit if you can pay off the entire amount you charge within two months. And avoid any cards with a credit line that is *less than* your security deposit.

9. Do you pay interest on my security deposit? It's not a deal-breaker if they don't. It's a treat to find a bank that pays interest on your secured savings account all the time. Credit unions that offer secured credit cards always pay interest (or, as they call it, *dividends*) on your secured savings. Secured credit card issuing banks usually only advertise that they pay interest on your security deposit when interest rates are rising, as they know it may sway you to choose them. When you're earning money on your savings, don't just focus on the highest-yield savings account. Instead, subtract what you'll be *paid* in interest from what you'll be *charged* in interest if you carry a balance, to get your *net* interest rate. Don't automatically *assume* a higher yield on your deposit equals a higher *net* interest rate. Always do the math.

Once you've found the best card for you using the above criteria, either call the toll-free number to request an application or download an application from the company's website. While it's tempting to quickly apply online, take your time. You want to see *all* the fine print, which is usually found in a document called *Terms and Disclosures* or *Fee Disclosures*. Read every word of the document. If you're unsure about what anything means, ask questions. And get the answers in writing. Fill in all blanks on the application. Blank areas will delay processing or disqualify you completely. If you have a co-applicant, his or her information must also be complete. Remember to sign the application—sometimes signatures are required in several places.

Most banks let you deposit your security money using an automatic draw from your checking or savings account, or using a personal check, cashier's check, or money order. Personal checks can take a few weeks to clear. If you want your credit card sooner, use the automatic transfer option or send a cashier's check or money order.

SECURED CARDS THAT MAKE THE GRADE

Here are the *only* secured credit cards from banks and credit unions that *currently* meet my stringent requirements.

Having grown up in small towns, I'm a big fan of community banks, so I'll start there. The Independent Community Banks of America provides credit card services to community banks through their subsidiary, TCM Bank. This is TCM Bank's *sole* purpose. You can *only* apply for this card through a community bank. Find a community bank near you at directory.icba.org. Not all community banks offer secured credit cards, but those that do often offer the secured Visa listed below, which is specifically designed to help you build and rebuild your credit. Should your monthly payment ever be more than 30 days late, TCM Bank will automatically close your credit card account, use your security deposit to pay your outstanding balance, and return any remaining security deposit. Visit the credit card section on your bank's website to see if they offer this card:

TCM Bank Secured Platinum Visa (available only through your community bank). No application fee is required, your payment history is reported to the major credit bureaus, and the card is *not* reported as secured. Your security deposit can be between $300 and $5,000, and your deposited amount will be your credit limit. Their annual fee is $29, and they provide your FICO credit score for free to help you track your progress. After 13 months, they'll review your account information and convert you to an unsecured credit card if you've made all payments on time, kept your spending within your limit, have no delinquencies on other accounts, and have a 660 or higher credit score.

You can manage your card online at mycardstatement.com or through the MyCard Mobile app. TCM Bank uses your average daily balance to calculate your interest at the end of each billing cycle. The annual percentage rate (APR) for this card is currently 25.49 percent (prime + 17.99%).

Other solid secured card options are listed below.

Bank of America BankAmericard® Secured Mastercard (bankofamerica.com). This card has no annual fee and a 25-day grace period. Your secured deposit can be from $200 to $5,000. They don't report your card as secured and offer account text alerts to remind you when your payment is due or when autopayments are made. Periodically, they will review your account and decide whether you qualify to have your security deposit returned. The interest rate is currently 25.24 percent (prime + 17.74%). Their customer service is 100 percent based in the United States. While Bank of America offers other secured cards—notably reward cards—I recommend avoiding them. Although they offer 1 to 3 percent cash back on your purchases, their interest rate is 3 percent higher (28.24%). Carry a balance and you negate any cashback benefit. Because most purchases earn only 1 percent cash back, you'll be paying *them* an extra 2 percent for no reason.

CapitalOne Platinum Secured (capitalone.com). This is CapitalOne's credit rebuilding card. You get a minimum $200 credit limit, and your maximum limit can climb to either $500 or $1,000 based on your creditworthiness. The better your credit, the smaller your required security deposit. Depending on your creditworthiness, your security deposit will be $200, $99, or $49. The drawback with this card is that you may wind up with a larger credit limit than you can pay off with your security deposit if you get behind. For a starting credit limit above $200, send them a larger security deposit and *that* amount will be your initial credit line. Their interest rate is 29.74 percent (prime + 22.24%). There is no annual fee, and the card has a 25-day grace period. The only penalty fee they charge is a $40 late-payment fee.

To help you rebuild your credit, they won't issue you this card unless your monthly income is *at least* $425 higher than whatever amount you pay in rent or for your mortgage. Your bankruptcy must have been discharged before you can apply. If a Capital One account was included in your bankruptcy, it must have been charged off for more than 12 months by the time you apply.

Discover it® Secured Credit Card (discover.com). Discover used to be the runt of credit card issuers, but today their cards are accepted in almost as many places as Visa and Mastercard. Discover goes the extra mile to get your business. While the 27.24 percent interest rate (prime + 19.74%) is a bit steeper than that of other secured cards, this is a *cashback* rewards card. During the first year you have the card, Discover matches your cashback amount dollar for dollar. Pay off your balance in full each month and they'll be paying *you* to use their card.

Your security deposit can be $200 to $2,500, in increments of $100. This initial deposit will be your *minimum* credit limit. Discover determines your *maximum* limit based on your income and ability to pay. They review your account after seven months. If you've made all payments for all Discover accounts on time for six months and kept all other credit accounts current, you will likely get your security deposit back after that first review. Should your finances get tight and you decide to close your account and pay your full balance, your deposit will be returned within 90 days. Like Bank of America, Discover has a 100 percent U.S.-based customer service division.

U.S. Bank® Secured Visa Card (usbank.com). Many people rave about the secured *reward* cards offered by U.S. Bank, but I'm a bigger fan of *this* card. At 28.24 percent (prime + 20.74%), this card's interest rate is lower than those for the reward cards. Reward cards in general have higher interest rates and many entice you to spend more simply to get the rewards. The U.S. Bank rewards card doesn't offer any other special perk beyond the rewards. The security deposit for all U.S. Bank secured cards is $300 to $5,000, made in $100 increments. They'll review your account after 12 months and graduate you to a traditional card if you qualify, returning your security deposit in the process. If you don't qualify, they'll continue to review your account and convert you once you do. There's no annual fee, and late-payment penalty fees can be up to $41.

Vectra Bank Visa Launch Secured Card (vectrabank.com). Vectra's Launch Secured Card keeps getting better and better. Its interest rate of 16.49 percent (prime + 8.99%) is substantially lower than rates for other secured cards, *and* it pays interest on your security deposit. The annual fee is $25, and the grace period is 25 days.

CREDIT UNION SECURED CARDS THAT MAKE THE GRADE

My favorite credit unions that offer good secured credit cards are next. Confirm the credit union you're joining is NCUA-insured and is a member of the CO-OP Financial Services network (co-opcreditunions.org). Visit their Locator page and click the Does My CU Participate tab. Being a member of a CO-OP credit union gives you access to over 30,000 ATMs, as noted earlier, as well as 5,000+ branches of other credit unions, where you can do business as if it were your home branch. You can withdraw, deposit, and conduct all other transactions at these locations. And your purchases using these cards are protected.

Digital Federal Credit Union—DCU (dcu.org). My first corporate job was at Digital Equipment Corporation, which organized DCU in 1979, so I have a fondness for this nonprofit credit union, and *anyone* who qualifies can join this credit union. You're *automatically* eligible if you belong to one of a handful of local or national associations (with annual memberships ranging from $10 to $120) that are DCU members. You can join the association of your choice when you apply for membership in the credit union. Check DCU's Membership Eligibility page (dcu.org/membership/member-eligibility.html) to find links to these associations. It's a great way to support a local nonprofit organization *and* get access to one of the best secured credit cards available. You can apply for the secured credit card at the same time you submit your membership application, as long as your opening account deposit equals or exceeds your secured savings deposit. You will be a DCU member for life, even if you never renew your association membership.

The DCU Platinum Secured Visa interest rate of 15.75 percent (prime + 8.25%) is even lower than Vectra's, and it can never go above 18 percent. There are no fees for cash advances, balance transfers, foreign transactions or if you go over your credit limit. You will pay $35 any time your payment is late. If your account ever becomes more than 60 days past due, your interest rate will jump to 18 percent. The card offers a 25-day grace period.

You can complete and submit your membership application online. Your membership automatically gives you a free primary savings account, which can be opened with a mere $5 deposit. The first $1,000 you deposit into a primary savings account earns up to 5.5 percent interest. You then need to open a secured savings account and use those secured funds to apply for your DCU Secured Visa. The only way to increase your credit line is to deposit more money in that secured deposit account.

GTE Financial (gtefinancial.org). You can become a GTE member if you join their nonprofit financial educational club, CUSavers ($10 lifetime membership fee). Their application is only available online. Be sure to check the box that you want to join their CUSavers organization. Their financial education center includes financial counseling and financial literacy workshops. GTE offers both secured and unsecured versions of their Go Forward Mastercard. Your chances of approval will depend on your *current* credit history. The amount you deposit in your secured savings account will be your credit line ($1,000-$30,000). The secured card carries a fixed interest rate of 17.99 percent. With the unsecured version, your rate varies depending on your creditworthiness and can be as low as 13.24 percent. There is no annual fee or application fee. The grace period is 21 days.

If a payment is returned for any reason, you'll pay $25. Late payments will cost you $30 for the first one and $41 for additional ones. Once you've made six consecutive on-time payments, they'll reset your late fee to $30. While the secured card is reported as secured on your credit report, after six months of positive payment history you can apply for the unsecured version and stand a good chance of being approved.

SECURED CARDS I'M LESS WILD ABOUT

Some secured cards you should *definitely* avoid, but others I'm just leery of for specific reasons. I'm including them here as they meet my stringent requirements, but they also have a few quirks.

Citibank Citi® Secured Mastercard (citi.com). Your bankruptcy must be discharged for at least two years before you can apply for this card, which means you have to wait two years to start building a credit history from a revolving credit source. This card charges no annual fee, and the grace period is 23 days. Your security deposit can be $200 to $2,500, which will be your credit limit. Within 18 months, they will refund your security deposit. Their interest rate is 26.74 percent (prime + 18.99%), *but* if a payment is late a single day (or your payment is returned for insufficient funds), they can automatically raise your interest rate up to 29.99 percent (the maximum rate allowed by law). And that penalty interest rate may apply indefinitely. Plus, they charge you a late fee and returned payment fee of up to $41. One plus: they let you pick whether you want your payment due date to be at the beginning, middle, or end of the month—a nice touch to help you balance your monthly expenses.

Merrick Bank® Classic Secured Mastercard (merrickbank.com). Merrick offers a teasingly low 22.70 percent interest rate (prime +

15.2%) and has a 25-day grace period. They give you a $200 credit line for a $200 security deposit (maximum deposit: $3,000). They immediately charge you a $36 annual fee, reducing your credit line to $164; after that, they charge you $3 a month. While they review your account every few months and increase your credit limit, they don't *ever* convert your account to unsecured. The only way you get your deposit back is if you pay your account in full and close it.

Chapter 10

Buy a Car after Bankruptcy

After bankruptcy, you'll be considered a subprime borrower for a car loan, due to your reduced credit score. Currently, 6.6 percent of those subprime auto loan borrowers are behind in their payments by 60 days or more—compared to a mere 0.4 percent of borrowers with higher credit scores—which means that many folks who declared bankruptcy and then got a car loan quickly afterward now have new negative information on their credit reports. To help you avoid becoming one of them, I've included my smartest advice on ways you can buy a car after bankruptcy.

Need a Car Now?

Need a car before your credit report is completely cleaned up, or while making payments on your Chapter 13 bankruptcy? Focus on buying your car in a way that creates a true fresh start.

First, if you don't use a vehicle often, look for solutions that require little to no financial commitment:

- Carpool or borrow a car.
- Use a car share service, public transportation, or a transport company like Super Shuttle, when available.
- Walk or ride a bike or scooter if able.

Steer clear of expensive ride shares like Lyft and Uber whenever possible.

Second, if a car *is* a necessary part of your daily life, your best bet is to pay cash for your next car. When I say buy a car for cash, I'm not talking about doling out tens of thousands of dollars. I'm talking about shopping around for a reasonably priced, reliable, previously loved car. The last thing you want is to spend thousands of dollars in interest, pay higher car insurance rates, *and* risk a late car payment when you're rebuilding.

Your first car after bankruptcy might not be the best-looking one on the block. But if it gets you from point A to point B every day, without you having to make payments each month, you're at a big financial advantage over anyone else who pays (monthly) for the privilege of parking his dream car in the driveway. You soon *will* be able to pay cash for the car you truly desire, *if* you're willing to make a few changes in the way you approach buying a car *now*—a goal the other guy may never achieve.

The quickest way to *truly own*—not finance—your dream car, is to focus on a car that will provide good, reliable transportation. Too often we buy cars based on *outer* appearances. We want the sunroof, the power windows, the Bluetooth hookup, the Bose stereo, and the alloy wheels. We approach car shopping like dating.

Buying a Car While in Chapter 13

Still making payments under your Chapter 13 bankruptcy? If so, you will need your trustee's permission before buying a car. Chances are good the trustee will work with you to fit the car into your budget—especially if you save up the cash to buy a *used* car. Start small. You should be able to buy a decent 10- to 15-year-old car for $2,500 to $7,500. Be sure to have any car inspected by a trusted mechanic before you buy it.

Attracted to what's on the outside, we sometimes overlook major *internal* flaws that otherwise would be dealbreakers.

Don't get distracted by the bells and whistles. You don't want a used car that looks good on the surface but needs thousands of dollars for unexpected repairs. Focus on what the owner tells you about the *mechanical* parts of the car. Does the car have a new battery, tires, brakes, muffler, timing belt, transmission, alternator, distributor, carburetor, or radiator, for example? When were these items replaced or repaired, and can the owner provide receipts for the work done or direct you to the mechanic or dealership that did the work? Have all recall issues been fixed? I'm a big fan of car sellers who have all the maintenance receipts and mechanical records for their vehicle; it's a sign the car may be less likely to need expensive repairs. An owner who regularly maintains their car and takes care of problems early is a find.

Now, *where* to look for this amazing vehicle?

1. Ask everyone you know. Put the word out about what you're looking for in a car. Because my car loan was listed on my bankruptcy and my car had been sold at auction, it was impossible for me to get a decent car loan right away. I let everyone know what was important to me in a car. I wanted an automatic, reliable car to make long-haul drives from Maryland to visit family in Florida and Illinois—preferably something with a good-sized cargo area. A friend's boss had a 6-year-old Honda Civic hatchback that had been in two minor fender benders. She lived in the District of Columbia, had bought a BMW, and didn't have room to park two cars; she needed the car sold *fast*. A bit crinkled in the back and very reliable, the hatchback was mine for $200.

I drove that car for five years and put a total of $1,000 into it for a new clutch, muffler, and brakes. For five years I had no car payment. Instead, I used my "car payment" money to pay off debts not included in my bankruptcy. Grand total, I spent $1,200 on my car over five years, plus what I paid for regular maintenance. I sold the car to a college student for $500 (150% more than what I paid). My *total* cost came to $700—or $140 a year.

More recently, when my son turned seventeen, we asked friends to spread the word that we were looking for a car for him. A friend of a friend shared that her mom was selling her car because her vision had gotten to a point where she didn't feel comfortable driving. Within a few weeks, he was the owner of a well-maintained 2012 Ford Focus. He paid $2,500 in cash—money he'd saved while working at two jobs.

2. Look for private local sales. Search for private-party ads that say *ugly but reliable, well-maintained,* or *hail-damaged.* Shop the classifieds, Craigslist, Facebook Marketplace, Nextdoor, and local bulletin boards at coffeehouses, houses of worship, grocery stores, and bookstores.

You're looking for a car that's mechanically sound but may have some minor damage. If you like the way the car drives, review the maintenance records to see what service has been done on the car and when repairs and recalls were done. If the records are incomplete, ask a trusted mechanic where you get your vehicle serviced or repaired to inspect the car and give you an idea of what price they would pay if *they* were buying the car.

I'll go into more detail about finding the best car for your needs and your finances in a minute, but first, figure out what you truly want in a car.

What's Important to You in a Car

When I started looking for my next car after the Honda Civic, I wanted a used Toyota Camry. I listed the features I wanted the car to have, the feelings I thought having the car would give me, and why I wanted *that* car, in particular. When I examined *why* I wanted the Camry, I discovered that, subconsciously, I wanted others to see how successful I was. That sent me back to the drawing board for a deep dive into what I *really* wanted and needed.

I listed the specifics of what I needed in a car and why, plus features I considered optional. My specific criteria: a well-maintained, four-door sedan with cruise control, tilt steering wheel, AM-FM cassette stereo, and power windows. Of course, I'd have loved the car to have a leather interior, sunroof, power locks, and a CD player. But I stuck with the basics so others would know what type of car I wanted.

A four-door car so passengers could easily get in and out. Cruise control so my leg wouldn't fall asleep while I was driving long distances. A tilt steering wheel to easily get in and out from behind the steering wheel without adjusting my seat. A cassette player to listen to my favorite books on tape and motivational tapes. And finally, I wanted power windows so I wouldn't wear out my arm at toll plazas.

What criteria are important to you and why? List them on a piece of paper and put the list somewhere you can see it throughout the day (your bathroom mirror is a great location). Tell everyone you know what you're looking for in a car, so they'll keep you in mind when they come across cars that meet your criteria.

Focus on the essence of what you want and work from there. Don't limit yourself by stating the specific make and model you desire. The car I had in mind was a Toyota Camry. I wound up buying a car I had never heard of—a Chrysler Cirrus—which was made on the same assembly line as the Toyota Camry but cost $13,000 less. I put 300,000 miles on that car before I swapped it for a Range Rover—bought with cash.

Insure Your Insurance

When you're ready to insure your car, take out comprehensive/collision insurance—at the very least until your car loan is paid off and you have enough savings to repair or replace your car. This way, if your car gets totaled or stolen, you're not stuck paying a car loan on a car that is a pile of junkyard tin or gone for good.

Keep the deductible as high as you can afford and your insurance premiums will be cheaper. I started out with a $100 deductible. Once I had saved $250, I raised the deductible to $250, then $500, and so on until I had $1,000 in savings and my deductible was $1,000. I still have a $1,000 deductible. Create a separate savings account specifically for your insurance deductible so you have the money on hand if needed.

Check the Value of What You Want

Once you know what you want in a car, I recommend you pretend you're from Missouri (the "Show Me" state) unless you already are. First, visit iseecars.com, click their Research tab, then select Studies and Guides, where you'll find research on the most reliable cars for the money. This website offers free reliability ratings for all makes and models, classified by model generation (a version of a vehicle before major changes were made in its style or mechanics).

After you narrow your options, visit rerev.com. Scroll down to the footer and, under Car Insights, click Years to Avoid. Here you'll find more details on the best and worst makes and models—including information on likely issues and estimated costs if your car needs those repairs.

Having done your homework, you're ready to buy your car. Iseecars.com has the best search engine for selecting all the things you want in a car (although a cassette player is unfortunately no longer available). More importantly, these deep-dive car geeks have crunched the numbers so that you can see the price of different options. Who knew that a brown or white 2006 Toyota Tacoma would save you $800 on your purchase price or that a blue one would cost you an extra $450? Scroll to the bottom of the website page to see all the ways to save money by selecting different features.

Buy a Car Without Debt

Once you've bought your reliable car, paid off any undischarged debts, and built savings to put toward your down payment, you're ready to go out and get a 5- to 10-year-old car. It's surprising how many reliable cars in this age range can be found for under $10,000. Take your time deciding what car you want and be flexible. My former spouse and I shared a car for an entire year, rising early to arrange car schedules, which was not an easy feat as we lived 30 minutes from everything. The right car will appear while you're saving the money to pay for it.

Keep Financial Goals in Mind When Financing

For the record, I am not *anti*-car loan. I'm pro-*building financial independence*. Having a teenage son, I view cars like boys view sneakers. High-end sneakers can run hundreds of dollars, and teens rush to snap them up. Yet there once was an uber rich teen who wore $99 sneakers—specifically, 574 Core New Balance sneakers—and he still does. What did young Barron Trump know that other teens often don't? He knew high-end sneakers lose their value the minute you wear them. And he also knew what he *wanted*: comfortable, stylish sneakers at the best price possible. Whether it's shoes or cars, why pay more when you can get the same or better quality for less?

Before you jump at the opportunity many financing apps offer to *set your own terms* for your down payment and monthly payment, let's first get clear on your financial goals around your car purchase. You want to pick a vehicle that's priced to fit into your financial goals over the next three to eight years. The average car loan term is six years, although some dealers offer to spread your payments over eight years, which is *not* as good as it sounds. Before you start pricing cars, ask yourself these questions, and be as honest as you can:

1. How much do I want to pay in total? Most people look at the *selling price* but forget to add in the interest paid on the loan and all the dealer fees, which increase your total debt significantly.

2. How much will registration cost me? Many states charge registration fees based on the assessed value of the car, regardless of its condition. In general, the more your car is worth, the more your (often annual) registration fees will likely be.

3. How much insurance do I want to pay on this car? The more expensive or fancy the car and the lower your credit score, the higher your insurance costs.

Tips for Financing with a Credit Union

Many credit unions now offer *indirect lending*, which is a form of dealer financing. Unless you must go *in person* to the credit union to apply for your loan, chances are you're being offered an indirect loan. With these loans, you wind up paying an origination or dealer fee. This is a fancy fee the dealership gets simply to *process your loan*. Translated, this means that they're getting paid for filling out your loan paperwork.

When in doubt, call your credit union and ask, "Is the origination or dealer fee paid by me or the credit union?" If they don't know or tell you that you pay the dealer fee, go to the credit union branch, do your paperwork there, and pocket this amount.

4. How much is the car I want to buy *actually* worth given the miles it's been driven and the car's condition? I'm a big fan of vincheck.info for gauging the value of a vehicle. You can look up just the make and model or enter the unique vehicle identification number (VIN) to see more details about a specific vehicle. The site provides the average, above-average, and below-average prices for each particular vehicle—plus extensive vehicle information—completely free.

5. How much of a down payment can I make on a vehicle? The larger your down payment, the lower your car loan amount— which means *less* of your money gets paid as interest over the life of the loan. Before you decide on a down payment amount, be sure you've set aside savings for potential repairs.

6. What interest rate is offered, based on my credit score? The higher the rate, the more you'll pay over the life of the loan. The *average* interest rate if you have a 600 credit score is 9 percent; it's 8.4 percent if your credit score is 700. The highest car loan interest rates are 24.5 percent. Do not let any subprime lender convince you to pay more than 12 percent if your credit score is at least 475.

7. What is the total I'll pay for this vehicle over the life of the loan? Add your registration fee, insurance costs, maintenance and repair set-aside funds, and down payment to the bottom line of your costs and write down that total amount.

8. What will my monthly car expenses be? Include your car payment, monthly insurance, fuel, and so on. Where else would you want to spend some of this monthly amount?

9. What will I have to give up or postpone if I buy this car? Look at the total cost of the car over the life of the loan. What other long-term goals will need to be delayed if you spend this amount on your vehicle?

Where to Find the Best Car Loan

Once you know what's on your credit reports and have updated them to frame your bankruptcy in the best light possible, search for the best loans from these lenders:

1. A credit union where you're a member. Credit unions offer members excellent interest rates on car loans, as long as your bankruptcy is at least a year old and your payment record after bankruptcy is clean. If you have the credit union's secured credit card in addition to having your checking and savings accounts at the credit union, your interest rate will be even better.

2. A lending network search company, like LendingTree. Their interest rates will be higher, but your chances for approval will be better than what's offered through dealer financing.

3. Your banker. Most banks no longer offer auto loans for private-party sales. They only finance sales from big-brand dealerships in their specific network. Even so, you could get up to a 2 percent lower interest rate if you have the dealer finance the vehicle through your bank.

4. The dealer's finance department. Before I talk about this option, promise me you won't do business with *bad credit, no problem* dealers. Those guys will sell you an overpriced car and stick you with a high-interest car loan. If you can qualify for a car loan at their interest rates, chances are you can get a loan with a lower interest rate on your own.

Please don't let a dealer talk you into taking higher-interest financing just because your dream car doesn't qualify for lower rates at your credit score. This is a personal, emotional manipulation that sales professionals are trained to use. Spoiler alert: it ends with you overpaying for your car.

Best Way to Buy a Car from a Dealer

Buying from a dealer will almost always be a more expensive option than buying from a private party. If you do buy your car from a dealer, keep the focus on the *purchase price* you want to pay and the *mechanics* of the car—not the bells and whistles. Steer clear of answering the question of how much you can afford to pay each month. Armed with your research from above, specify the maximum amount you're willing to pay for a particular car. Let's use $10,000 as our target price.

The dealer wants you to commit to as large a monthly payment as you can afford, in order to charge you more interest. They will constantly try to get you to commit to a *monthly* amount. Never, ever share the amount you've budgeted monthly for your car payment. Instead, calculate how much car you can afford to pay off in two years. If you can afford to spend $250 a month on a car payment, then you can afford to finance $6,000 over two years. You don't want to tell the dealer you can spend $250 a month because the dealer will want to hook you up with a $250 payment for 48 months, financing $12,000 instead of $6,000.

A good dealer will work with you to buy the car you want to buy at the price you want to pay. A good dealer will stop trying to sell you on the low monthly payment as soon as they see you are serious about spending no more than the price you've determined. Put down as much savings as you can afford toward the total price of the car. This will help you get a better deal on the interest rate, but as you'll see in a minute, the interest rate you're charged isn't as important as the fact that you're about to add another piece of good credit to your credit reports.

After you've agreed upon a car and a price, tell the dealer how much you can put down and that you want to finance the balance. If you can put down $3,000, you'll finance the remaining $7,000. But don't finance the loan over two years. Instead, ask to have a 48-

month loan. This way your required car payment is around $180 (based on a 10% interest rate). While you might be able to pay more, don't burden yourself with a locked-in higher payment. And don't let the dealer convince you that your bankruptcy *requires* you to pay a higher interest rate. If your credit score is 600 or higher, you shouldn't be paying much more than 8.5 percent interest.

Once you have signed the loan agreement with a $180 required monthly payment, pay the $250 you've budgeted for the car payment each month instead. You'll have the $7,000 loan paid off in 33 months if you do. Or pay $300 a month and have a zero balance in just over two years. You want to make that extra monthly payment amount optional for a reason. Financial situations can change in an instant, and you don't want to find yourself saddled with a huge debt burden if something happens. If you're still building up savings (or your down payment depleted your savings), pay the true payment amount of $180 and put an extra $70 per month into a car expense fund to cover future maintenance and repair costs, to minimize your stress around paying for these inevitable costs.

Wait as Long as Possible to Finance

Your credit score determines the interest rate you pay, which determines your monthly payment amount. If you can, wait for at least two years after you start rebuilding your credit before you get a car loan. A solid two years of on-time payments to your secured credit card account can result in much lower interest rates—and a lower car payment.

Should You Get a Co-Signer?

You may find you need to finance a car before lenders are ready to lend you money or before your credit score is high enough for you to qualify for the lowest interest rate possible. While I advocate for paying cash for a car you can afford before taking on new debt after your bankruptcy is discharged, circumstances may require you to get a vehicle that you must finance. Depending on your credit score, financing on your own could be extremely expensive. In this case, a co-signer can come in handy.

The ideal co-signer has good credit and is willing to vouch for you and take over payments if you're unable to pay. The benefit is that you'll get a much better interest rate. The drawback is that if you don't make good on your payments, your co-signer could end up owning the car, and your default or late payments will affect *their* credit.

One way to reduce a co-signer's risk is to sign a contract that says two things: that you are personally liable for paying them if you ever default on the loan *and* that within two years you will apply for a loan in your name only or the car becomes their property. During those two years, you can improve your credit enough to get a car loan in your name alone, without a co-signer. In some instances, a lender will even remove an existing co-signer.

To remove a co-signer, meet with the lender who holds the note on the car you currently have (or with the dealer who arranged the financing for you). Bring with you a recent copy of your credit reports showing your on-time payment history for the past twenty-four months. Also bring a notarized letter from your co-signer stating that you have been the one making the payments all these months.

If it's not possible to remove the co-signer, continue to pay the current loan until it's paid off, increase your payments to speed up the process, or ask the lender what interest rate you'd qualify for if you were to sell this car and buy a different one.

Have a High-Interest Car Loan?

You're not alone if you already bought and financed a car at a high interest rate. One man shared that his car loan not only had a high interest rate but an *outrageous* one. If you're in the same pickle, you might be able to get out from under the high interest rate, especially if you have a solid two years of on-time payments, using one of the following two options:

1. Refinance the loan at a lower interest rate. If you bought a brand-new car that's now less than 2 years old—and especially if you financed through a dealer—you may be able to refinance the loan at a lower interest rate at a local credit union or bank. Ask if they offer refinancing for recently purchased cars. Credit unions offer their members excellent interest rates on car loans, as long as your bankruptcy is at least a year old and your payment record after bankruptcy is clean.

2. Go back to the original lender. Speak to the local finance manager or write a letter to the company president. Calmly explain that without a lower interest rate you will have to sell the car. With this letter, you put the ball in the lender's court. They will often make you a counteroffer of an interest rate somewhere in the middle between your current rate and the one you're asking for. If your current interest rate is 14 percent and the going interest rate is 8 percent, ask for a 10 percent interest rate in your letter. If the lender counteroffers, decide how high you really want to go. The lender has three options:

   • Get as much interest as they think they can get from you.
   • Accept the percentage you asked for.
   • Risk getting nothing when you either sell the car and pay off that high interest loan or default on the loan.

If you're sending a letter rather than speaking with the lender in person, send the letter via certified mail, return receipt requested, and keep a copy for your files. See the sample letter on the next page:

[Date]
[President's Name]
[Name of Lender]
[Address]
[City, State, Zip Code]

RE: [Your automobile loan number]

Dear [President's Name]:

On [date you purchased your car], I obtained a car loan from your company to finance the purchase of a [type of car, year, make and model]. The interest rate I received was [percentage interest rate], which is extremely high. This interest rate is so high, in fact, that I am faced with a dilemma: Either I convince you to reduce the interest rate to a more reasonable one of [indicate the rate you'd be willing to pay] or I will be forced to sell my car.

I would like to continue my relationship with your company, but I cannot continue to pay this high interest rate. I look forward to hearing from you in the next 30 days to see whether we can lower this interest rate to [the rate you listed above].

Sincerely,
[Your Name]

Don't Lease a Car Unless You Must

Leasing deals look good at first glance, but the fine print can sink you. I strongly recommend *against* leasing unless you're a business owner and there's an *incredible* tax advantage to leasing through your company. Leasing is tempting because it lets you drive a more expensive car than you can afford to buy. If that's your main reason for leasing, I urge you to reconsider and *buy* a different car instead.

With a lease, your monthly payments may be attractive, but when the lease ends, you will have paid thousands without having bought anything. If you decide to lease, be sure you get a *closed-end* lease that gives you a choice to walk away from the car once the lease expires.

To get the best lease possible, you need to know two numbers for the make and model you're considering: the *dealer cost* and the *residual value*. The residual value depends on the length of your lease. Subtract the residual cost from the dealer cost, to see what a fair value would be for you to pay over the life of your lease. If your lease payments total more than that number, you're overpaying.

Remember to stick with a car you can afford. Once all your debts are paid off, you can turn your sights on that sportster or that off-road beast. For now, stick with an affordable car that will get you where you need to be going. You'll reach a positive net worth a whole lot faster if you rebuild your finances by creating assets. If you decide to lease even with my warning, at least you'll know you're not overpaying.

Trading In with an Upside-Down Loan

Be particularly careful about trading in a car and getting another car with a car loan if your present car is worth less than the amount of your current car loan. This is known as being "upside down" on your loan. When you are upside down, the lender will usually roll over the remaining balance you owe into your new car loan. When you add the outstanding debt from your old car to the new car loan amount, you are even *further* upside down the minute you drive off the dealer's lot. If you must trade in a car with an upside-down loan, trade down, not up. I once met a man who so badly wanted to cut his car debt that he traded his Corvette for a Chevette.

From Bankrupt to Buying with Cash

Follow these strategies and you can—within a decade—go from bankrupt to buying a new car with cash, like a woman I know. She leased an Isuzu Rodeo for three years. As her lease was ending, she wanted to trade the Rodeo for a Ford Explorer, priced at $30,000. I suggested she set up an alternative plan. She used the GoalGetting strategy (from Chapter 7) to create a 10-year goal to *own* an Explorer outright.

Her monthly lease payments on the Rodeo had been $380. The residual value—the amount to buy the Rodeo when her lease ended—was $6,000. She purchased the Rodeo and financed the $6,000 with a three-year loan, reducing her monthly payment to $180. Instead of paying $180, she continued to pay $380 monthly and paid the loan off in 18 months. For the remaining 18 months, she continued paying $380 into her *savings* account.

At the end of the three years, she owned the Rodeo outright *and* had $6,840 in savings to put toward the Explorer. She chose a 2-year-old Explorer that had all the bells and whistles she wanted. Her cost? $22,000. She put down $7,000, traded the Rodeo for $4,000, and financed the remaining $11,000 over five years, at 6 percent. Her new monthly payment: $212.

She continued paying $380 each month, paying off this new loan in 18 months, after which she kept paying $380 monthly into her savings for another 18 months. Eight and half years after she set her goal, not only did she own a 5-year-old Explorer outright, but she also had $11,400 in savings so she could buy her next car with cash—and never pay another cent in interest on a car loan. This could be you.

Chapter 11

Travel Without Credit

Many airlines, rental car agencies, and hotels offer *some* form of credit-free travel options—including gift cards—but times have changed. Fewer accept cash payment, and none accept traveler's checks. Many no longer keep cash on the premises for safety reasons. PayPal and digital wallets are becoming more popular. Debit cards are often allowed for payment but not for reservations. And some companies *require* a credit card on file.

Companies are also big on offering *buy now, pay later* options, which are—repeat after me—debt. And forget about prepaid credit cards for travel, which I've already mentioned are *huge* financial drains. Unless the prepaid card has your name embossed on it, most travel companies won't take it for reservations. I don't mean to sound like Paula Pessimist, though. I do have some solid suggestions for traveling using the payment method that works best for *you* when you're flying, booking a rental car, or selecting a hotel.

The keys to seamless travel without credit are to (1) plan in advance and (2) double-check current policies. Companies merge and change policies frequently. Make your reservations early if you want to use available cash options. And use these insider tips to maximize your ability to use cash, a debit card, or a bank transfer to pay for your travel:

- Join travel reward programs and list your debit card as your *primary* payment method. With this information on file, many airlines, hotels, and rental car agencies let you both reserve *and* pay with your debit card.

- Call the specific *location* and ask the *location manager* about their specific terms. Some have companywide policies; others may have flexibility in their cash or debit options by location— even in the same city.

- Use a travel agent to book your travel. Local travel agents still exist and will gladly book any flight, rental car, and hotel for you, and you can pay with a bank or wire transfer, cash, cash app, and sometimes a debit card. Joining AAA will get you access to top-notch travel agents. You can talk with them virtually or, if you're in one of the 14 states (or Puerto Rico) where AAA has local offices, you can make an appointment and book your trip in person. Travel agents are also helpful if you want help setting up a travel itinerary.

Fly Without a Credit Card

Today, every major airline accepts debit cards. Remember, an ATM card from your bank is different from a debit card. A debit card will have a Visa, Mastercard, or Discover logo. Even if you love to travel, think twice before signing up for an airline-specific reward *debit* card. Reward cards often come with extra fees (including an annual fee) and can cost more than they're worth to you, as mentioned in Chapter 9.

All three U.S.-based international airlines (American, Delta, and United) also accept PayPal—which draws from your bank account or PayPal balance, as you wish. And most airlines offer several convenient get-into-debt—I mean, buy now, pay later— options. But cash is also king sometimes. Some airport ticket counters, travel centers near airports, and travel agents still let you buy airline tickets with cash. And all three major U.S.-based airlines have ways you can buy your tickets using their specific modern-day layaway option:

American Airlines. American lets you buy gift cards (virtual or plastic) that you can use for purchasing flights *only*, and they never expire. Each gift card can be between $50 and $1,500. You can use up to eight gift cards per transaction, and your balance carries over until the gift card is at zero. Lots of ins and outs, but a straightforward program. To redeem your gift card, you must buy your tickets online at giftcards.aa.com, unless you want to call in your reservation for an additional fee (800-677-9555).

Delta Air Lines. Delta offers gift cards that can be used for any Delta flight worldwide or any Delta Vacations® package that includes airfare. You can select your own value for each card, ranging from $50 to $2,000. Delta gift cards never expire, and there are no service or inactivity fees charged. You can buy these gift cards at delta.com or through retailers like Albertsons, Bed Bath & Beyond, Best Buy, CVS Pharmacy, Home Depot, Kroger, Lowes, Publix, Rite Aid, Safeway, Target, Walgreens, and Walmart. When you buy through a retailer, you save on shipping charges. You can even add gift cards to your wedding registry at Honeyfund, The Knot, and Zola.

Redeeming Delta gift cards is simple. You can redeem online at delta.com/redeem or by calling 800-225-1366. For vacation packages with airfare, redeem online at delta.com/vacation, by calling 800-800-1504, or in person at Delta's Airport Customer Service. If you redeem online, you can use a maximum of five gift cards per transaction (no matter how many tickets you're buying). If you need to redeem more to complete a transaction, call 800-225-1366 and a reservation specialist will help you.

United Airlines. United's gift card option is called TravelBank. To fund your TravelBank, you must sign up for a free United MileagePlus account. You can then buy TravelBank certificates in six different amounts (from $50 to $1,000), up to $5,000 per day. Anyone else with a Mileage Plus membership can also buy certificates on your behalf. Funds added to your account will show up within seven days. The TravelBank cash stays in your account for five years from purchase, but you must either deposit or redeem some TravelBank cash every 18 months or your account can be closed and your money will be forfeited. Unlike with American or Delta, you can use United TravelBank cash for your ticket, baggage fees, and seat upgrades. You redeem TravelBank funds as if they were a travel certificate, in any usual way you book with United.

Rent a Ride without a Credit Card

There are three key moments in the life of your car rental: reservation, rental pickup, and return. No major company accepts cash as payment at *all* locations. Most car rental agencies have both corporate and individual franchise locations. If you want to pay cash or reserve a car with your debit card, call the rental location where you'll pick up your vehicle to ask about their specific policy and find out what they'll need from you. You can often find a list of franchise locations and their phone numbers on the company's general policy page, by searching for *franchise* or asking customer service for a list of franchises in the area where you will be picking up the vehicle.

In general, you'll need to meet the following requirements:

- Have a clean credit report showing your bankruptcy has been discharged (or you're current on Chapter 13 payments) and your accounts are up to date.
- Be at least twenty-five years old.
- Have been employed at your current job for at least 12 months.
- Provide a recent phone bill listed in your name, a copy of your driver's license, proof of current collision and liability insur-

ance (without it, you're required to buy their insurance), and a recent utility bill showing your current address.

- If you're using a business credit card, your name must be on the card.

Almost all rental agencies offer prepayment deals, but their cancellation policies can be stiff, though not usually as costly as nonrefundable hotel prepaid reservations (more on that in a minute).

Read the fine print about when you would need to cancel a reservation to avoid paying some or all of your prepaid amount. If you use a *pay now* option with these companies, your cancellation window may be 24 or 48 hours—you'll get a portion back if you cancel before then and nothing back if you miss the window. So, make sure you know *exactly* when the deadline is to cancel, or you risk losing your money. I recommend looking at the agency's debit card and cash options instead. To me, the discount on prepaid car rentals isn't worth the risk of losing your money if your travel plans change.

In the United States, the three main car rental corporations—Avis, Enterprise, and Hertz—all have high-end, mid-range, and economy brands. These are highlighted below, along with Turo, a peer-to-peer car share company, which I believe is the best car share option for credit-free travel.

Avis Budget Group (Brands: Avis/Budget/Payless/zipcar). Some Avis locations take debit cards for reservations if they first deem you creditworthy, meaning they will run a credit check. They use Equifax, so if you have a security freeze on your credit file, lift it before you're traveling or they won't be able to check your credit. Debit cards are not allowed if you're picking up a premium vehicle, and not in Philadelphia and certain areas of New Jersey at all. Avis will put a $100 to $300 hold on your card above and beyond the full rental price, which may not be released for two weeks. If you want to use a debit card for a pay now option at Avis, first call the

---

Tricks for Renting with a Debit Card

Most rental car agencies will take your debit card as payment when you return the vehicle, but none take debit cards for *reservations* except when you are:

- enrolled in their company's rewards program *and* list your debit card as your primary payment method;
- renting in New York or Michigan, where credit cards are *not* required for reserving or picking up a vehicle; or
- picking up at an airport location *if* you show your travel itinerary containing your round-trip departure information. Some airport locations require two valid and current forms of picture ID. It can even be your Costco card or work ID. Some companies require additional documents, so call the pickup location and confirm *exactly* what documentation they require when you pick up the vehicle. Most rental agencies include this information on their website; always double-check current requirements.

---

location and confirm they can deem you creditworthy. Whatever card you use to reserve is what you'll need to present at pickup; if your credit hasn't been vetted, you may not be able to pick up your vehicle.

Only a few Budget locations take debit cards for payment. You can use their pay now option to prepay, but a credit card is needed.

Payless puts a $250 hold on your credit card when you prepay—you cannot use a debit card.

I understand the appeal of zipcar. They let you rent by the hour or the day, but I'm not a big fan. The required membership will cost you $9/month or $90/year. You get 200 free miles a day ($0.67/mile after that), and their rental rates are higher than those of most car rental agencies. If you need a car only for a few hours once a month or so, their $12–$19/hourly rate is reasonable.

Enterprise Mobility (Brands: Enterprise/National/Alamo). A few locations take cash for payment at the *end* of your rental only.

Call the location where you're picking up your vehicle and ask about their policy.

Hertz Global Holdings (Brands: Hertz/Dollar/Thrifty/Firefly). Hands down, the Hertz group is the best rental option for credit-free travel. If you're renting from a non-airport corporate-owned Hertz location, you can often use a debit card to reserve *and* pick up your car.

Dollar often lets you reserve and pick up your car with your debit card if you make your reservation at least 24 hours in advance and have a second proper photo ID. Your rental car must be *compact through full size only* unless your debit card is in your Dollar Express rewards profile. Dollar doesn't check your credit, but you must have sufficient funds in your bank account to cover the entire rental plus $500. If you've previously rented through your Dollar Express membership, no extra hold will be placed on your card.

Thrifty waives the hold if you're an established rewards member and your debit card has a Visa logo.

Firefly is Hertz's international budget car rental agency, with branches in Mexico, the Caribbean, Australia, New Zealand, Europe, and the Middle East, as well as select U.S. locations. If you use Firefly, book through a travel agent; their website is a hot mess.

You can use your debit card for reservation and payment if it's already in your rewards profile for all Hertz brands. Hertz also allows *cash* payment at all *corporate* locations for all rentals at all four brands—if you first apply for their Cash Deposit Identification Card. You can download the Cash Deposit ID Card application at images.hertz.com/pdfs/cashdepositcard.pdf.

Read the entire application so you know what you're agreeing to when you rent. Fill out the form completely and send it via certified mail, return receipt requested to the address listed, with a check or money order enclosed for the $15 nonrefundable processing fee, which pays for a credit check. (A money order will be processed faster.) If you also travel for business, fill out the information so you're prequalified for both.

Once you're approved and are issued the Cash Deposit ID Card, you have the right to leave a cash deposit at all Hertz brand locations. The deposit will be equal to the amount of the full rental plus a deposit to cover incidentals. You agree to pay any balance in cash when you return the rental car.

Turo (turo.com). Turo lets you reserve and pay with Apple Pay and Google Pay, as well as a bank-issued debit card, including debit cards from online banks Chime and Ally. The only prepaid card they allow is Lead Bank's Revolut US (but your payment history isn't reported to the credit bureaus). You can reserve a car and select *pay later* at no extra charge. Depending on your rental length, Turo runs your payment either two days or seven days before your rental starts. In New York, you must use a credit card to *reserve* a car, but you can *pay* with any of the above.

Turo is often a third cheaper than most rental car companies. Your first 1,000 miles in a rental are free ($0.50 /mile above that), and you can get a full refund if you cancel more than 24 hours before your rental starts. If you want to pick up and return your rental to an airport (free), simply type in the airport name as your rental loca-

---

Transportation Tips for Business Travel

1. If you already know where you need to spend your days, look through a AAA travel book or a map app for hotels close enough to your business meetings so you won't need a rental car, and use the free hotel airport shuttle if available.
2. Use a car share service like Lyft or Uber for short distances.
3. Have your employer (a) arrange a car service where they can pre-pay any charges, (b) give you a company card so you avoid having to "cash qualify" with the rental company, or (c) give you a travel advance so you don't have to pay the car rental out of *your* pocket.

tion. Or the car owner will deliver the car to you at the location of your choice and pick it up again for a small fee. You can rent pretty much any car, anywhere, and you select the vehicle's make, model, and year. Vehicles are individually owned, so check recent reviews for the listed vehicle to make sure it's in top form. Additional drivers who have a Turo account can be added at no charge.

Our family uses Turo often, and it comes in handy in curious ways. One time, while staying in a small town with no ride-share or taxi service, I discovered that I'd left my headlights on and drained my battery. AAA had already jumped it once, but it didn't stick. I realized that if I needed a new battery, the closest auto parts store was nearly three miles away. I'd have to walk there and back, carrying a car battery the whole way. Or if something else was wrong, my car might need to be at the mechanic for a day or so. I quickly checked Turo for options and found a Subaru Ascent to rent for $48 a day, less than a mile from my location. I could pick it up there, or for $5 they would deliver it to me.

Hotels and Other Housing

Almost all hotels accept debit cards for reservations and at check-in. They will place a hold on your card for your entire stay plus an extra amount for incidental expenses. Hotels now offer online prepayment options, where you can use a debit card to reserve and pay your bill in advance, locking in a slightly lower price. These are generally *nonrefundable*, so I'm not a fan unless you have no other option. Plans can change quickly, and you'd be out your money. Many hotel chains also accept buy now, pay later virtual payment, which—like lipstick on a pig—is just a way to dress up *debt*, so I discourage using those.

Like car rental agencies, many hotel chains have merged and now are owned by a handful of corporations but still operate independently. To find out about a particular chain's policy, call the specific hotel location and ask about its *credit-free* policy. Some hotels have companywide policies, others decide policies by location. Below are the policies at seven major chains that have helpful credit-free options, including my favorite, the family-owned Drury Hotels.

BWH® Hotels (800-780-7234; bestwestern.com). This includes a variety of Best Western hotel brands, WorldHotels™ and SureStay® hotels. All BWH properties are independently owned and operated and have their own credit-free payment options. Although their website says they require a credit card for all hotel reservations, you *can* use your debit card to purchase online—and your full stay may be charged when you make your reservation.

The Best Western Gift Card can be used at all BWH brands except for the WorldHotels properties. Not all *locations* accept the Best Western Gift Card, so call ahead and confirm before you purchase and get details on your location's specific policy. Some locations only let you pay lodging charges with your gift card, while others let you use it for other services. You'll find each location's contact information at the top of its individual overview page. Best Western Gift Cards do not expire and in some cases can be reloaded. If you're unable to buy the gift cards online, you can call 833-632-0867 for help.

Drury Hotels (800-378-7946; druryhotels.com). This chain of 150 properties in 27 states has always been family-owned and operated. Brands include Drury Plaza, Drury Inn & Suites, and Pear Tree Inn. Drury no longer accepts cash as payment when checking in, except at two locations in Missouri and two in Texas. At all locations, you can check in with a debit card and a hold will be placed for the entire amount of your stay, plus $50 for incidentals, with funds released within 10 days. You can also pay using mobile pay apps (Apple, Google, or Samsung).

Drury has always been ahead of the curve, offering gift *certificates* decades ago. They've now switched to gift *cards* (available as physical plastic cards or electronically). Gift cards can be used at check-in for *all* properties, to pay for your room stays and pretty much everything else, including upgrades, valet charges, pet fees, and in-house purchases, including at their Kitchen + Bar late-night restaurants. You can buy cards in any amount from $10 to $2,000 and purchase multiple cards in a single transaction. Gift card balances do not expire. To purchase gift cards, visit giftcard.druryhotels.com or call 866-892-7890 for assistance. You can also store them in your Apple or Google digital wallet.

Some Drury locations offer a credit card authorization (CCA) form, which allows your boss, friends, or family members to put your charges on *their* card. The cardholder can choose to pay just the room and taxes, all charges, or somewhere in between. The form includes various check boxes for the cardholder to choose. For these CCA reservations, Drury puts a hold on the card equal to the cost of a one-night stay with tax. Call the hotel directly to make your reservation and request the form. Ask if they want the form returned via fax or email, and get the necessary information. The form *must* be completed and returned at least 48 hours before you check in, so take care of it immediately to ensure your reservation is confirmed. When you check in, you will need to show a valid photo ID.

If you travel for business, approved direct bill accounts are also available. Check with the specific Drury location for details.

Hilton (800-445-8667; Hilton.com). Hilton's 24 brands include Waldorf Astoria, Conrad, DoubleTree, Embassy Suites, Homewood Suites, Home2Suites, Tru, Hampton Inn, and all things Hilton. Hilton has previously offered a unique type of gift card, which is an American Express-branded debit card. The program is currently paused while they work out technical difficulties.

A safer bet—and a good backup option in case your attempt to use a Hilton gift card fails—would be for a family member or friend to submit (via fax) a CCA form so the hotel can use this person's credit card for your charges. Your friend can elect to cover all charges, just room and tax, meals charged to the room, retail sales, and any recreational activity costs. They can specify a maximum amount they will be responsible for, which will be charged up front—at checkout any unused portion will be refunded to the credit card.

Hyatt (800-233-1234; hyatt.com). At a Hyatt brand property, you need a credit card to book a reservation online. Hyatt Gift Cards can be used at participating hotels in most countries in North, Central, and South America, and the Caribbean. When you redeem Hyatt Gift Cards, you earn World of Hyatt reward points. You can buy up to $10,000 worth of gift cards ($25–$2,000) daily. The cards never expire, and there are no service fees. Whoever has the card can use it, which is handy if you and your family travel frequently but not always together. They can be used to pay for room stays, dining, spa services, and other amenities.

Someone else can pay for your room with their credit card if they fill out the Hyatt CCA form (hyatt.com/help/faqs). The form's dropdown menu shows you whether the property you select accepts CCA payments and prepopulates the fax number. If the property doesn't take the form, don't worry. Call the property directly and ask for directions on how to arrange the third-party payment. Once approved, you just need to show up with an ID—and possibly present a debit card for extra charges.

Intercontinental Hotels Group—IHG (800-465-4329; ihg.com). IHG's 19 brands cover a wide variety of travel styles and include InterContinental, Kimpton, Crowne Plaza, voco, Holiday Inn, Staybridge Suites, and Candlewood Suites. Only Kimpton offers a gift card (through Buyatab, web.buyatab.com); the card is reloadable ($10–$2,000), with one reload allowed every 24 hours. The gift card never expires and has no service fees. Kimpton gift cards can only be used in the Americas and in a few other locations.

MarriottBonvoy (800-228-9290; marriott.com). Marriott's 39 brands include Renaissance, Ritz-Carlton, Westin, Sheraton, Courtyard by Marriott, Fairfield Inn, SpringHill Suites, Residence Inn, and Element. All but 10 brands accept Marriott GiftCards and eGiftCards, which you can purchase at gifts.marriott.com or at a participating hotel. Cards are sold in increments from $25 to $2,000. You can buy as many cards as you want, up to $10,000 a day. The cards never expire.

You must contact the specific location to confirm they accept gift cards. A credit or debit card is required to reserve your room, and you can then use your gift cards to pay upon arrival. Gift cards can be used for your hotel stay amenities like dining, spa services, and golf rounds. Marriott has no restrictions on the number of gift cards you can use in a single transaction.

Some hotel locations also accept CCAs where someone else can put your room charges on their credit card. They must call the hotel's front desk directly, and it can take up to a week for them to process the CCA form, so plan ahead.

When you travel on business, you can completely bypass the need for a deposit by guaranteeing your room with a corporate credit card and then paying cash for your room on arrival.

Wyndham Hotels (800-407-9832; wyndham.com). Wyndham encompasses 25 brands, including La Quinta, Wingate, Ramada, Baymont, Days Inn, Super 8, Howard Johnson, Travelodge, Micro-tel, Hawthorne Suites, Tryp, WaterWalk Extended Stay, and all things Wyndham. All Wyndham properties require you to use a credit card if you're reserving a room online. However, you can pay with your debit card when you arrive, if you prefer. Some locations let you pay for your stay with cash, but you must call them directly for details.

Many other smaller hotel brands like Four Seasons, OMNI, and Trump Hotels offer gift cards as well. Call your favorite and ask about their gift card program. Then grab your suitcase and start packing. Now you can travel anywhere you want, without worrying about needing a credit card. Bon voyage!

Chapter 12

Buy or Rent a Home after Bankruptcy

Your next big financial move may be buying a house. Imagine going from bankrupt to owning your home outright and then buying your next home for cash in seven to 10 years. Not only is it possible, but it becomes highly *probable* when you focus on putting your money to work for *you* instead of your creditors. And if you want to stay in your current home once you're mortgage free, you can use your savings to buy a smaller vacation or rental property.

Enough daydreaming about where you'll be financially in 10 years. Let's get back to purchasing your home now. Your home is the one major asset that *generally* appreciates, or gains value, over the years rather than losing value.

Once you've updated your credit reports and have been making payments for two years since your bankruptcy discharge on either a car loan or a credit card that are being reported to the major credit bureaus (double-check to make sure!), you'll likely be eligible for a decent mortgage rate. You can buy a home earlier than that, but I encourage you to be patient. Otherwise, your home may cost you more in the long run. After taking major steps to change your use of money and your attitude toward your finances, it's time to talk about homebuying.

In general, if you're repaying debts through Chapter 13 bankruptcy, your trustee won't let you buy a home until your repayment plan is complete. But there are exceptions, as I'll share later.

Find Out Your Current Credit Score

While we spent a lot of time in Chapters 1 and 2 talking about your credit *reports*, here we focus on your credit *score*. This three-digit number is created by information compiled from your credit history and widely advertised as the single most important number in your life. Your creditors would have you believe that you *are* your credit score and that you can't make a large purchase without a good one. In truth, you can buy anything you want, regardless of your credit score.

Two different credit score compilers exist, so you may hear a lender refer to your FICO score, while another may call it your VantageScore. FICO has a complicated numerical system for determining your credit risk with different versions and different formulas for calculating your score depending on whether you're seeking a mortgage, a car loan, a credit card, or insurance. As a result, you actually have 10 different possible FICO scores.

VantageScore (created by the three major credit bureaus) compiles your credit score by looking at factors they believe best determine your ability to use credit in a healthy way. With VantageScore your rental payments are often considered, while medical bills are not. For both, their credit score calculations don't consider *paid* collection accounts at all and medical bills in collection are dealt with differently than other collection accounts. Under the VantageScore system, your most recent six-month history of on-time payments counts more with a new lender than late payments on paid-off debts or even your bankruptcy—as long as you're not *maxing out* your available credit.

The following table tells you, from highest to lowest, what the credit score calculators consider most important.

A good rule of thumb is that a credit score above 700 will still be a passing grade (good credit risk) for both companies. And for a mortgage, a credit score as low as 620 can still get you a decent interest rate. Remember: the higher your credit score, the less interest you will pay.

FICO Score	VantageScore
Have you consistently paid your accounts on time?	What total amount of credit do you have available, what total amount do you owe, and what percentage of your credit are you using?
How much do you owe on your accounts?	Do you have a healthy mix of credit types, and what's your experience been with them?
How long have you had a credit history?	Have you consistently paid your accounts on time? Late mortgage payments count more.
What mix of accounts do you have— revolving, mortgage, unsecured?	How long have you had a credit history?
How many new credit accounts have you opened in the past two years?	How many new credit accounts have you opened in the past two years?

A mortgage lender will receive the credit industry's version of your credit scores from your credit reports (they can see these scores; we can't). But you can get a look at the FICO score that's available for consumers on the MyFICO website. Bypass the subscription options and order specific reports only when you need them at myfico.com/products/fico-score-credit-reports. Select either a report from one specific credit bureau for $19.95 or a report from all three for $59.95.

As I shared earlier, *knowing* about any negative credit information lurking on your credit reports helps you take steps to improve how creditors view your creditworthiness for buying a home. Follow the strategies in Chapter 2 and you'll start building a firm foundation for improving your credit score. Start taking action now so you'll be more attractive to mortgage lenders and other creditors when you're ready to buy a house.

Keep Housing Costs Affordable

When you talk to lenders about preapproval, be up front about your bankruptcy—and highlight everything you've done so far to rebuild your credit since then. Most lenders offer to preapprove you for a mortgage equal to 28 to 32 percent of your pretax income to cover principal, interest, taxes, and insurance. Many people feel like it's financially stretching to have nearly a third of their income dedicated to housing—and that doesn't even include utilities, maintenance, or repairs! May I suggest something else?

Request to be approved for a mortgage based on 20 to 25 percent of your pretax income. You would qualify for a smaller loan, paying less each month for your housing. Yes, you'd be buying a smaller house, unless you increase your down payment. It's a worthy trade-off for creating a cushion against unforeseen expenses by paying less each month for your housing. I know it can be tempting to use tricks like no-money-down, 40-year, adjustable-rate or interest-only mortgages with a balloon payment to give you the illusion of being able to afford a more expensive home. Play it safe and buy a smaller, more affordable home and build your equity quickly by paying off your mortgage as soon as you can.

Once you know how much your lender thinks you can afford, shop for houses that sell for at least $25,000 less than that amount. This will give you a cushion against becoming overextended if your finances suddenly change.

When the housing market is overpriced, don't let the higher sales prices burst your bubble or tempt you to overspend. Instead, pretend you're fishing. Be patient. Save your money, spend time getting clear about everything you want in a home, and watch for when prices begin dropping and delinquencies and foreclosure filings begin rising. This is when you'll get the most value for your money. Banks will be desperate for qualified homebuyers, and overextended homeowners will be grateful to get out of their loans.

If you're part of a two-income household, maximize your spending power. Ask your lender what loan amount you would qualify for using just the higher salary. My late colleague Pete Dickinson, editor of "The Retirement Letter," and his wife used this strategy. His wife was a librarian with a steady paycheck, and he was a writer whose income varied. They bought their first home based on his wife's income and paid it off early. Then they bought a second home in Prescott, Arizona, which they rented out until they were ready to retire. Using this strategy, you could own your home outright within 10 years. Continue putting that extra money into savings and you'll soon be able to buy your next home with cash.

Or do like the contrarian investor Richard Band did. He and his family never moved from the three-bedroom bungalow he and his wife bought when they first married. As his children became adults, he eventually added a second story, to accommodate visiting children and grandchildren.

When I bought my first home after bankruptcy, my lender told me I could qualify for up to $150,000. Armed with that information, I started shopping for houses in the $125,000 range and bought a two-bedroom, two-bath bayside bungalow for $121,000.

In general, you'll want to get a 30-year conventional loan with the lowest possible payments—and with as little money up front as possible. That's why I strongly recommend getting an FHA or VA loan, especially if you're a first-time buyer or haven't owned a home in at least three years. With these loans you make a lower down payment—3.5 percent of the home's selling price or less. The FHA is known to grant mortgages to folks with 2-year-old bankruptcies.

If you have a negative post-bankruptcy credit history, don't despair. You can still become a homeowner, but you will have to be more creative with your financing. For instance, saving more money to put down 30 percent could improve your chances of getting a mortgage.

When you find a house you like and you're ready to buy, ask the seller's broker what company currently holds the mortgage on the house, because you want to give them the opportunity to keep the mortgage. Call or write the lender and say:

I'm planning on buying the house at [this specific address]. I understand your company holds the mortgage, and I wanted to give you the opportunity to keep the mortgage. I'm looking for the best mortgage package you can offer on a 30-year fixed-rate loan.

Regardless of what lender you select, ask how many points are included in the mortgage rate package. The low interest rate you're being offered may come at the cost of paying more at closing in the form of points. With points, you basically prepay interest or "buy down" your interest rate. This reduces your monthly payments but can also drain your savings account balance. Each point on a 30-year fixed-rate mortgage costs roughly 1 percent of your total loan amount. If you borrow $250,000, each point would cost you an additional $2,500 at closing, to reduce your interest rate by 0.25 percentage point (taking your 6.25% interest rate down to 6.0%). There are much better ways to cut the amount of interest you pay over the life of your mortgage, as I'll explain in a bit.

One way to avoid surprises when buying a home is to get prequalified for a mortgage, so you can read all details of the mortgage loan package including the negotiable terms like points. For instance, some sellers are willing to split the cost of the points as well as other costly items like transfer taxes, but these details must be included in your purchase agreement. Ask your broker and the seller's mortgage holder for an estimate of closing costs so you can see how much money you'll need at the closing.

Most real estate agents—even buyer's brokers—will encourage you to fill out their contract on the spot and offer it to the seller. Don't do it. The only way to protect your interests and make sure you get the best deal possible is to read every word, write down all the questions you have, and (with your questions in hand) ask a real estate lawyer to review all the documents, point out any red flags, and answer all your questions before you sign a contract to purchase the property.

Reduce Your Closing Costs

Closing costs can be very expensive, usually 1 to 5 percent of the home's purchase price. Here are four possible ways you can reduce your closing costs. I used all these techniques when buying my first home. Instead of having to pay anything at closing, I received a check for $1,018:

1. Roll as many of your closing costs into your *mortgage* as you can. Some items *must* be paid separately at closing, but others can be rolled into your mortgage. Ask your loan officer for a list of charges that can be included in your mortgage.

2. Split closing costs with the seller whenever possible. Sellers will commonly pay half the points and transfer taxes, but only if you ask.

3. Roll closing costs into the *purchase price* when possible. If the mortgage amount you plan to take out is less than the home's appraised value, see if the seller would be willing to bump up the contracted price of the house so you can get that extra money back from the seller to pay part of your closing costs. Make sure

your contract clearly states this change, with a clause such as the following: *Seller agrees to pay an additional $5,000 to Buyer, to be used for closing costs.*

4. Have the seller pay you at closing for any needed repairs. The house I bought after my bankruptcy needed a lot of work. When I had the house inspected, I made a list of 10 needed repairs. Then I gave the seller two options: either make the repairs or pay me the cost of the repairs at the time of closing. The seller made some of the repairs and paid me for the others. The total cost of the remaining repairs was about $4,000. My closing costs were just under $3,000, which meant I had a bit over $1,000 due to me—hence, my $1,018 check at closing.

The Consumer Financial Protection Bureau has an excellent 28-page PDF booklet called *Your Home Loan Toolkit: A Step-by-Step Guide*, which I highly recommend. You can download a free copy at cfpb.gov/owning-a-home. Scroll down the right side and you'll see it listed under Downloadable Resources. It's only available electronically, so you'll need to print a copy.

Where to Get Your Down Payment

Most lenders let you borrow 80 to 90 percent of a home's value. This means you'll need a down payment that covers 10 to 20 percent of the sale price *plus* your closing costs. For an FHA mortgage, your down payment can be as little as 3.5 percent of your loan amount, and you can roll most closing costs into your loan as mentioned above.

The only money I paid to purchase my first house was my $3,000 down payment. I had intentionally saved this money in my company's 401(k) plan. By law, you can withdraw money from a 401(k) account for the down payment on your primary residence— the house you're going to live in. *Withdraw* the money instead of borrowing it, for two reasons. First, *borrowing* the money gives you access to only 50 percent of your account's value, versus 80 percent for withdrawing. Second, money you *borrow* from your 401(k) must be paid back—with interest. And if you stop working for that employer, you'll need to pay *all* the money back right away. Job insecurity and layoffs can happen anytime. Living on your savings while paying back a retirement plan loan creates extra stress you do not need.

One last important step when withdrawing money from your 401(k) plan: have your plan administrator withhold and submit to the IRS any unpaid taxes from when your money entered your tax-deferred retirement account so you won't be hit with an unexpected tax liability on April 15.

If none of these down payment options are feasible, see if you qualify for down payment assistance through your local housing authority.

Little or No Money for a Down Payment?

Every state (plus the District of Columbia and most U.S. territories) has a housing authority or housing agency. These organizations offer special programs for first-time homebuyers, emergency responders, teachers, veterans, first-generation homebuyers, and those who have gone bankrupt, among others. These funds are usually provided as down payment assistance. The housing authority may offer you a grant, forgivable loan, low-interest-rate loan, or bridge loan that helps you bridge the gap between the amount you have available for a down payment and what the lender requires.

These programs do not usually provide *direct* assistance (although a few do). Instead, they provide a list of approved lenders who will determine your eligibility for each program based on your state's criteria. The lender will explain to you the maximum loan amount, sales price limit (the most your home can cost), and the income limit (how much your annual income can be) for where you want to purchase.

Once the lender has gathered all required information from you and qualified you for a loan program, the lender works with the housing agency to help you secure your loan through the best program. Your best option might be a combination of assistance through local grants and down payment assistance programs for a specific county or municipality or other nonprofit organizations.

Most organizations provide lists of lenders, real estate professionals, and housing counselors who are certified to work with their programs. I recommend first selecting a lender who you're comfortable with and asking them for referrals to real estate agents they've worked well with, as well as homebuyer education courses they recommend that meet the homeowner education requirement for your loan issuer.

The criteria for receiving a homeowner grant or loan vary by location, but you'll need to at least meet the following minimum requirements:

- Be a first-time homebuyer *or* not have owned a home in the past three years.
- Have decent credit—usually between 620 and 680 depending on the program. They use combined credit reports to determine your credit score by picking the middle score or using the average of the three.
- Your bankruptcy should have been discharged at least a year ago, and there should be no new negative credit information in your file. Federal lending guidelines require a waiting period after bankruptcy, the length of which depends on the type of loan you want, the type of bankruptcy you filed, whether your last mortgage was discharged under bankruptcy, and your *current* credit score.

- Have an income that is at or below specific income limits (using annual income or Area Median Income). You will likely qualify for some program if your income is no more than 80 to 120 percent of the Area Median Income for a family of your size.
- Be ready to live in the home within 60 days of closing on your mortgage (the property cannot be rented out). Some programs allow you to buy multi-unit properties with up to four living units. You can then live in one unit and rent the others.
- Have a signed purchase agreement for your home before you *apply* for the mortgage.
- Have copies of your federal income tax returns from the past three years.

The Homebuyer Assistance Process

The first and second steps of the homebuyer assistance process vary; you'll first need to either take a homebuyer education class or connect with a lender. Even if you're not yet ready to buy, financial coaching from a housing counseling agency can help you increase your credit score, reduce debt, and learn effective budgeting strategies that will help you buy a home sooner than you otherwise could. Many housing stability counseling programs are free. They can help you create a specific action plan and assist with a variety of credit, budgeting, and other financial matters. NeighborWorks America (neighborworks.org) offers a directory of the nonprofit financial counseling agencies in their network.

The homebuyer assistance process follows six steps:

STEP 1. EDUCATE.

Take the state's homebuyer education course. Most assistance programs require you to complete such a course *before* you purchase your home and provide them with a copy of your course completion certificate. Even if it's not mandatory, I recommend taking the course. You will learn vital information for navigating the assistance programs and learn which ones you're eligible for, which area lenders work with the housing authority's programs, and what documents each potential lender requires. Some programs require financial counseling too.

STEP 2. ASSESS ELIGIBILITY.

After completing the course, contact a recommended lender so they can analyze your monthly income, your credit history, and your debt level. This will help them determine how large a mortgage loan you're eligible to receive. This is the assistance program's version of preapproval. Your lender will be your contact through the whole process, working to get you a qualifying mortgage and registering you for the program.

If a loan officer isn't named specifically on the housing authority's list of approved lenders, tell them you want to speak to a loan officer who has experience working with the housing authority's programs. A home is a major purchase; you and the loan officer must communicate well together, and you should fully understand your program options.

STEP 3. SEARCH.

Start scoping out homes within the program price limits and the lender's suggested price range (keeping in mind my 20%–25% guideline in the Keep Housing Costs Affordable section earlier in this chapter). This saves you time and frustration. You don't want to find your dream house only to discover you can't finance it through the program. Use a real estate agent who is already familiar with the state's programs, preferably a *buyer's broker*. The real estate commission you pay at closing is for your agent to negotiate the sales price and other items, explain the terms of the contract, and guide you through the home inspection process.

STEP 4. REVIEW.
Read every word of the contract and all additional documents, and make a list of questions. Reach out to your buyer's broker and a real estate attorney to have them review everything as well.

STEP 5. APPLY.
Once everyone agrees to the terms of the purchase and you have a signed contract with the seller, meet with your lender to fill out a mortgage application. This is when you'll get more exact numbers of how much money you will need for your down payment and your closing costs. Respond quickly to requests your lender makes for additional information. Your loan could be processed in as little as 30 days. Your lender may issue a conditional approval so you can set a closing date while you gather additional information for your lender. Again, read all the mortgage and assistance program documents, get written answers to your questions, and have both your lawyer and buyer's broker review all papers before you sign—they might be able to change some items in the contract and save you money.

STEP 6: CELEBRATE!
It's time to close on your new home. Because housing authorities go through the closing process so often, you can usually expect your closing to go very smoothly. The closing will usually take place at the title company's office (often a lawyer's office), and you will have many documents to sign. Ask for a copy of all documents in advance of the closing so you can read them through completely and get any remaining questions answered.

State and Territory Housing Authorities

In this section, I've included basic information about programs offered by each housing authority. Contact your housing authority as soon as possible to find out if you're eligible for any of the programs and to learn about each program's application process so you can begin to take steps to qualify.

Although many states have additional agencies and programs in individual regions or counties, the list below generally contains information only for the *main* housing authority and that organization's contact details. Programs sometimes run out of money for the year; sometimes funds get replenished, and other times programs expire. If a program you're interested in is no longer available, talk with your lender or the program manager to see when or if the program will be reinstated.

Alabama

Alabama Housing Finance Authority (ahfa.com; 800-325-2432). AHFA's First Step program offers below-market interest rates on 30-year fixed interest mortgages through AHFA-recommended lenders. All borrowers are eligible for Down Payment Assistance (DPA) of up to $10,000 or 4% of the sales price, whichever is lower. The DPA is issued as a 10-year secured second mortgage. An Affordable Income Subsidy Grant is available for closing costs if you use the HFA Advantage loan; grant funds depend on your income. Alabama restricts properties being used for business or commercial use, so confirm with your lender which program will be best for you. AHFA's Step Up program helps if you can afford a mortgage but need assistance with your down payment.

Alaska

Alaska Housing Finance Corporation (ahfc.us; 907-338-6100). The AHFC's website is user-friendly. If you can't find what you're looking for, scroll down to the "site map" in the footer. You must be a resident of Alaska *and* be current on any child support payments. Alaska offers a variety of specialized buyer programs, including funds for veterans (and some active-duty military). You are required to read Alaska's tax-exempt booklet—which is a fancy name for an easy-to-read 11-page PDF, with an attached affidavit where you attest that you've read every single word of the requirements for getting a program loan. Complete Alaska's free homebuyer course to receive a certificate for a $250-$350 credit toward your program fee. You can take the self-directed *Finally Home* online course, but I highly recommend taking the 6-hour *HomeChoice* class instead. Alaska's down payment assistance programs are run through governmental, nonprofit, or regional programs. You could be eligible for a grant, deferred payment, forgivable loan—or a combination of all three.

Arizona

Arizona Industrial Development Authority, Department of Housing (homeplusaz.com; 602-584-7587). To get a feel for Arizona's programs, first read through the Home Buyer Resources, and the Frequently Asked Questions pages. Ask the loan officer: Do you charge an *origination fee* for loans you process through HOME Plus? If they say yes, take a pass. In Arizona, origination fees are *allowed* but are not *required*. All fees and amounts charged are at the lender's discretion. No reason to pay more for your loan than necessary. If they say they don't charge an origination fee, get that answer in writing before moving forward. The Arizona Is Home Mortgage Assistance Program offers below market rate 30-year fixed mortgages, along with an additional 4% of the loan amount which you can use for your down payment or closing costs if you'll be buying in a rural county. Their HOME Plus program is available statewide. Arizona's down payment assistance is offered as "silent" second mortgages which are fully forgiven once you've owned your home for three to five years. Sell before then, and you'll owe only the amount remaining for the unforgiven months.

Arkansas

Arkansas Development Finance Authority (homeloans.arkansas. gov; 501-682-5900). ADFA offers two strong options for home-buyers. Both programs offer 30-year fixed-rate mortgages with no pre-payment penalties. The best way to find an approved lender is to use the orange *Find a Lender* button or enter the zip code where you're looking to buy. Some loan programs are county specific while others are statewide. Down payment assistance is in the form of a non-forgivable second mortgage with a 10-year term. You can use the funds for your down payment or closing costs as needed.

California

California Housing Finance Agency (calhfa.ca.gov; 877-922-5432). California's programs are only operated through approved lenders and every home zoned in the state as a single-family residence is eligible—including condominiums and double-wide manufac-tured homes. Some Accessory Dwelling Units, guest houses and in-law quarters may also qualify, so check with your lender. Cali-fornia offers first mortgage programs *and* down payment assistance programs. CalHFA's MyHome Assistance Program is where you'll find the state's DPA and closing cost programs. California offers an additional program if you have lost your home in a FEMA-declared disaster. School employees, fire department employees, veterans and others may be eligible for additional assistance.

Colorado

Colorado Housing Finance Authority (chfainfo.com; 800-877-2432). Colorado has a nicely laid out drop down menu that walks you through their website. Type "income limits" in the website's search bar to see the most recent income and purchase price limits. Only the First Step and HomeAccess Programs have purchase price limits. The *Help for Homeowners* tab includes interview questions to ask prospective lenders or real estate agents, plus mortgage calculators and even fillable spending plan worksheets. The Consumer Resources section includes links to other down payment programs and low-income home purchase finance options. Colorado provides resources for Black and African American homeowners looking to create generational wealth, and loans if neither you nor your parents owned a home *in your lifetime* or if you lived in foster care and have never owned a house. Colorado also offers all paperwork and its Homebuyer's Education course in both English and Spanish. Colorado offers new primary mortgages, refinances FHA loans previously issued by the program, and provides deferred or forgivable down payment grants and second mortgages for your down payment and closing costs.

Connecticut

Connecticut Housing Finance Authority (chfa.org; 860-721-9501). Most CHFA loans require you to take a Homebuyer's Education Course. All CHFA courses are offered free and cover a variety of helpful topics. I highly recommend taking them all, including their Pre-Purchase Course and optional free counseling, a Pre-Closing Course *and* Foreclosure Prevention Course. Interest rate reductions are available for mortgages if you're buying in a targeted area, and for residents of public housing, veterans, military families and their surviving spouses or civil union partners (if the service member died due to military service or from injuries sustained in military service), some state troopers and police officers, teachers, or if you or someone in your household is permanently disabled. One unique program is the Smart Rate Pilot Interest Rate Reduction Program. A mouthful that offers a mortgage interest rate reduction if you have outstanding student loan debt ($15,000 or more), in good standing—whether current or deferred—so you can become

---

Whoever's in New England. . . .

FHLBank Boston (fhlbboston.com) offers three programs through their member banks and credit unions across six New England states (Connecticut, Maine, Massachusetts, New Hampshire, Rhode Island and Vermont). FHLBB requires you to take a Homebuyer Education course from one of their approved Homebuyer Counseling Agencies if you apply for one of these programs:

1. The Equity Builder Program grant provides assistance with down payment, closing costs, up to two points, rehabilitation expenses and even homebuyer counseling costs if you're a first-time home-buyer. Search for "EB members approved" to see a list of banks and credit unions that participate.

2. The Housing Our Workforce Program provides DPA grants even if you're not a first-time homebuyer. You must contribute at least $2,000 from your own money (no gifted funds). You can receive other gifts, but the $2,000 must come from your own money. This grant is forgiven monthly or daily. Once you've occupied your home for five years it's fully forgiven. Before then, you'll need to repay any unforgiven balance over $2,500. Search for "HOW members approved" to see a list of banks and credit unions that participate.

3. The Lift Up Homeownership Program provides five-year forgivable down payment and closing cost assistance to first-generation homebuyers and people of color purchasing their first home. You must contribute a minimum of $1,000 from your own funds. You can't combine this FHLBB program with either of the other pro-grams, but you can combine it with other down payment programs outside of FHLBB. You'll find a link to participating banks and credit unions on the Lift Up program page.

a homeowner sooner. Many Connecticut cities and towns also offer down payment assistance in the form of low-interest loans or grants, so pick an experienced loan officer who knows the local programs. To qualify for the Time to Own forgivable down payment assistance program, you must have been a Connecticut resident for the past three years.

Delaware

Delaware State Housing Authority (KissYourLandlordGoodbye.com; 302-739-4263). Delaware's programs are as straightforward as their website with two nearly identical statewide programs. I recommend selecting a lender and then asking for referrals to housing counselors and realtors who are familiar with the programs offered. Create your dream team and increase your chances of success. Each program offers a straight up Smart Start first mortgage and the option to add one of two deferred down payment/closing cost loans. Their Lender tab lists a limited number of lending organizations; to see more lenders, fill out the DSHA contact form and request a complete list. If you're buying a fixer-upper, pay attention to listed lenders with the little house icon—they're the ones familiar with the FHA 203k Limited Program.

District of Columbia

Front Door (frontdoor.dc.gov). So much is going on in Washington, DC to help people buy and keep their homes—the district created this dynamic homebuyer website with contributions from fourteen different DC agencies, a handful of partner organizations and individuals who work and live in the District. Taking a nine-question quiz automatically directs you to links for every possible resource available for you. DC homeowner programs range from matching fund savings accounts (just because you live in the District) to lower interest rate first mortgages, and no-interest DPA and closing cost loans that may be deferred for up to 30 years, plus matching fund grants for closing costs. The list is long. Once you've seen your custom resource list, enter your email address, and they'll send you the list with embedded links to the different programs. I'm highlighting two specific program providers here:

DC Housing Finance Agency (DCHFA.org; 202-777-1600). Click on the collapsed menu bar in the upper right corner and select Homeownership, then scroll down to Find a Lender. If you work in a public service capacity connected to DC, click on DC4ME and check out the seven-page list of employers who participate with their mortgage programs.

DC Department of Housing and Community Development (dhcd.dc.gov; 202-442-7200). If you qualify for either the DHCD's DC Open Doors program or Home Purchase Assistance Program, click Find a Lender and work with that lender to see if you qualify for any other programs such as their Employer Assisted Housing Program and a Negotiated Employee Home Purchase Program.

Florida

Florida Housing Finance Corporation (floridahousing.org; 850-488-4197). Click on the Programs tab, select Homebuyer, and take the Homebuyer Loan Program Wizard to see programs you might qualify for. If you're interested in an area that straddles counties, like Melbourne in Brevard County and Saint Cloud in Osceola County, search both. You will have the same purchase price limit—but your income can be higher in Osceola County, where housing prices are lower. It may be worth a half-hour commute to get more house for your money. Florida is keen on people who *work* in their community being able to *live* in their community. Their Hometown Heroes Housing program offers competitive first mortgages, and up to 5% of your first mortgage loan amount for down payment and closing costs. The most recent 12-page list of qualifying occupations includes everything from activity duty military and veterans to firefighters, paramedics, law enforcement, teachers, nurses *and* any profession requiring licensing or certification. Even being *employed* by a licensed facility in roles like childcare instructor, home health aide, veterinarian assistant and massage therapist. And if you're self-employed? You're also included if you work in a listed licensed occupation. Check out Florida's *Opening the Door to Homeownership* downloadable booklet for more details on their programs.

Georgia

Georgia Department of Community Affairs (dca.ga.gov; 404-679-4840). GDCA requires you to contribute at least $1,000 of your own money ($500 if you're a veteran) toward the purchase price of your home through their Georgia Dream program, which is designed to help first time owners and veterans pay their down payment and closing costs. From the website's home page, use the navigation bar in the upper right corner to select Affordable Housing, and then Homeownership. From here, you'll find the program details. If you qualify for a low-down payment first mortgage, a down payment assistance loan may be enough to cover much of your down payment and closing costs. All eligible homebuyers may qualify for the Standard DPA for down payment and closing costs. Folks in first responder, education or healthcare industries, or active military may qualify for the PEN DPA. The CHOICE DPA is offered if anyone in your household is disabled.

Guam

Guam Housing Corporation (guamhousing.org/loan-programs; 671-647-4143). To qualify for any of Guam's programs you must be a US Citizen or Permanent Resident Alien. You cannot have owned a home in the last *five* years and must live in Guam for at least five years before applying. Guam's DPA programs include a closing cost grant through their First-Time Homeowners Assistance Program, and an interest-free second mortgage through their Community Affordable Housing Action Trust. Guam also offers direct first mortgages—if you've been turned down by a conventional lender—through their Regular (Direct) Loan and their Six Percent Loan programs, as well as a Rural Housing Loan program offering 100% financing with a 33–38-year mortgage to low and very low-income residents. With a U.S. military population of approximately 30,000, GHC also helps package VA loans—but only if you're a Native American or a Chamorro Land Trust Recipient.

Hawaii

Hawaii Homeownership Center (hihomeownership.org; 808-523-9500). HHOC Housing works in partnership with HHOC Housing and Land Trust (HHLT) and HHOC Mortgage, a non-profit mortgage broker and lender. All program information is easily accessible from the HHOC main website. The HHLT is an affordable housing pool. They offer below-market price one- or two-bedroom townhomes or condominiums (currently only available in Oahu), where HHLT has the option to buy back when you're ready to sell. This is a great option if you're single, newly married or have young children and want to own a home at an affordable price. HHOC Mortgage (HHOCmortgage.org) works with local lenders and mortgage companies to provide primary mortgages and specialized loans for down payment assistance and closing costs, including deferred or matched contribution loans where you could qualify for $6,000 in deferred assistance for every $1,000 you contribute. Use the drop-down menu for Hawaii's Steps to Homeownership and click the *Own a Home* tab on the right side to find a short list of resources, including home buyer education, individual coaching workshops and coaching for after you buy your home. Taking Homebuyer Education classes requires you to be an HHOC member. Lifetime membership is $60; a 50% membership discount is available to Hawaii State Teachers Association members. Join online or mail your membership check to HHOC. Your HHOC membership entitles you to attend the class, get unlimited Homeownership Coaching and access all their webinar courses.

Idaho

Idaho Housing and Finance Association (idahohousing.com/homebuyers; 855-505-4700). IHFA offers some of the lowest mortgage interest rates in the state, plus down payment and closing cost assistance options. You do *not* need to be a first-time homebuyer, but you do need to meet the debt-to-income ratio and credit score minimums, which depend on the type of first mortgage you're seeking. To determine your eligibility, connect with a lending partner from IHFA's list. Most local banks and credit unions participate in IHFA's programs. You will need to contribute at least .5% of the purchase price unless you're a nurse, teacher, first responder, active military or veteran. The *FinallyHome!* homebuyer's education (finallyhome.org) is mandatory for some loans and strongly recommended for all loans and is offered in English or Spanish. Once you graduate from the class, you'll receive chat and email support and one-on-one counseling.

Illinois

Illinois Housing Development Authority (ihdamortgage.org/homebuyers; 877-456-2656). IHDA provides an incredibly straightforward website for homebuyers and you do *not* need to be an Illinois resident to apply. Your property must be less than five acres. No co-signers are allowed, but you can have a co-borrower who also will claim this house as their primary residence. Start by watching the short video outlining the homebuying process. Then review the current programs under their Active Program Directory. All lenders agree to use the same interest rates, so pick a lender you're comfortable with, who has a good working knowledge of the IHDA programs. A pre-purchase homeowners education course is required for all loans. Local course providers often offer more personalized services along with your course. H.O.M.E. DuPage, for example, offers an intensive eight-hour class and then an additional *free* 150-minute interactive discussion with industry experts who can answer questions about the DPA programs, homeowner insurance, inspections, mortgages and real estate law. You will need to contribute 1% of the sale price or $1,000, whichever is greater, which can be used as the earnest money you provide to get the property under contract, to pay your appraisal fees, or even your pre-paid homeowners insurance. Illinois offers repayable, deferred or forgivable down payment assistance options. Their Smart Buy program offers a chance to get up to $40,000 in student loan relief *and* up to $5,000 in down payment assistance. To qualify for Smart Buy, you must have at least $1,000 (up to $40,000) in current or deferred student loan debt in your name. Any remaining student loan debt above $40,000 must be paid off by you at closing. If you have a co-buyer and you both have student debt, pick whichever one comes closest to $40,000. If your student loans are in default or delinquent, you must bring them current first.

Indiana

Indiana Housing and Community Development Authority (in. gov/ihcda/homebuyers; 317-232-7777). IHCDA offers four specific programs. Have a lender familiar with the programs sort out which one is best for you, as IHCDA's on-line program guides aren't very user friendly. The lender list doesn't highlight any specific experienced loan officers—just the companies. Look for your current bank or credit union on the list, or local banks, to find nearby lenders familiar with the programs for in person conversations. To qualify, in general, you'll need to either be a first-time homebuyer, buy in a target area or be an eligible veteran. A non-refundable $250 reservation fee must be paid once your lender is ready to file your application (after the appraisal is complete). You may be required to take a *Credit Smart* Homebuyer Education Course or *HomeView* course depending on the program. It's not a bad idea to take one or both courses regardless. The IHCDA offers either a deferred or forgivable down payment option. Lender fees for their Step-Down Program are capped at a 1% origination fee and a maximum $1,600 in lender fees, but this loan cannot be combined with any of IHC-DA's down payment assistance programs. Email homeownership@ihcda.in.gov with specific questions.

Iowa

Iowa Finance Authority (iowafinance.com/homeownership; 515-348-6200). The IFA provides a quick eligibility quiz where you enter your income and your purchase price. From that point, you can answer a few more questions, provide your email and IFA narrows down which programs you might be qualified to use. Iowa requires first-time homebuyers to take an online self-paced homebuyer education course, available in English and Spanish. If you lack internet access, you can take an in-person HUD-approved homebuyer education class. Iowa's two mortgage programs both have additional down payment assistance options in the form of either a grant *or* a deferred loan. They also offer a special military grant. Active-duty military, veterans and surviving spouses can qualify. Your property can include up to four living units as long as one unit is your primary residence. For questions about the above programs, call IFA directly, or email homebuyer.inquiry@iowafinance.com. Iowa's Beginning Farmer Loan Program provides mortgage assistance to help you acquire farmland, buildings, machinery, equipment and even breeding livestock, at reduced interest rates, or to improve existing buildings or farmlands. Visit iowafinance.com/beginning-farming-programs for current requirements and loan amounts. A non-refundable $100 application fee is required.

Kansas

Kansas Housing Resources Corporation (kshousingcorp.org/first-time-homebuyer; 785-217-2044). Kansas takes a very personalized approach with first-time homebuyer programs. Scroll down on their website and click on the big orange *Start Your Homebuying Journey Here* box. Fill out their short form with your name and email address and the area where you're interested in buying. Some cities and counties have their own Homebuyer Program, and KHRC specialists will direct you to them if you are house hunting in an area where KHRC's programs aren't used. KHRC's down payment assistance program is offered as a zero-interest deferred loan. At least 1% (and no more than 10%) of the sale price must come from your own funds. This money can be used to pay for your appraisal, property inspection and other up-front closing costs. They also offer a First Time Homebuyer Savings Program. If you haven't been a homeowner or listed on a property title for at least three years, you may be able to open a First-Time Home Buyer Savings Account or Certificate of Deposit at any qualified financial institution. Your deposits can't exceed $24,000 ($48,000 if married filing jointly). Direct your additional program questions to Marilyn Stanley at FTHB@kshousingcorp.org.

Kentucky

Kentucky Housing Corporation (kyhousing.org/homeownership; 502-564-7630). Scroll to the bottom of the KHC webpage to find the Future Homebuyer box. On the right-hand side, you'll see a menu where you can get details about the programs offered and the process. You must be a U.S. citizen, or a national or qualified alien. All detached single-family homes qualify. If you're looking to buy a condo, townhouse or other attached residence, check with your lender to see if the property is eligible. Kentucky offers down payment assistance as a repayable 10-year second mortgage. If you're eligible for a KHC first mortgage, you qualify for this loan. Kentucky also offers an option for refinancing. If your credit score is at least 620 and you've paid 12 months of on-time mortgage payments, you could be eligible. This is helpful if you're finishing a Chapter 13 payment plan and interest rates are lower than your current rate.

Louisiana

Louisiana Housing Corporation (lhc.la.gov/homebuyers; 225-763-8654). LHC offers several low-rate loan programs, mostly for first time homebuyers, as well as single parents or displaced homemakers who owned a house with their former spouse. Their Delta 100 Program is parish specific—you must be buying a single-family home in the Delta Parishes. This program is especially good if you don't have traditional credit anymore but have demonstrated your ability to commit to homeownership in other ways, like building up sufficient cash reserves to show you can pay the mortgage. This program offers 100% financing and up to 3% closing cost assistance. You must personally contribute (no gifts) either 1% of the purchase price or $1,500, whichever is lower. The participating lender for this program is Home Bank (Scott.Cobb@home24bank.com; 225-300-8329). The LHC Mortgage Revenue Bond Loan provides down payment and closing cost assistance which may be deferred or forgivable. LHC's downloadable *Homebuyer's Guide* is a bit outdated, and some links don't work. If you have specific questions, it's best to call them.

Maine

MaineHousing (mainehousing.org; 207-626-4663). Under Featured Programs, click Mortgage Programs and you'll be directed to Maine's First Home Loan Program information and a simple six step path to homeownership. Maine recommends you start by taking the Maine HoMEworks (mainehomeworks.org) homebuyer education class for several reasons. You'll better understand the buying process, gain some tips for managing your money as a homeowner, and figure out which mortgage option suits you best. Like other state programs, income limits apply but are high enough that most Maine residents qualify. MaineHousing mortgages all come with built-in payment protection (through Maine HOPE). If you lose your job, Maine HOPE advances up to four full mortgage payments which then becomes a zero-interest deferred loan. Down payment and closing cost assistance options can also be used for escrow expenses paid before closing. You must contribute at least 1% of the mortgage loan amount toward your purchase, and this money may be a gift. Your home can even be a fixer-upper. Maine offers programs for active-duty military and veterans, even if you've previously owned a home, as well as a First Generation Program if you've never owned a home and never lived in a home owned by biological parents or legal guardians *or* if you've ever been in foster care. Some down payment and closing cost assistance is available with this program if you take both an approved Financial Literacy program *and* a Homebuyer Education Class. You'll still need to contribute 1% of the purchase price; the cost of your classes counts toward that contribution. One extra program Maine offers is a Mobile Home Replacement Initiative. If you live in a pre-1976 mobile home, you could qualify to replace your home with a more energy-efficient one.

Maryland

Maryland Mortgage Program (mmp.maryland.gov). Rather than provide a phone or email contact, the Maryland Mortgage Program (MMP) directs you to approved lenders and real estate agents who are extremely familiar with the program. Start by clicking on the *7 Steps to Purchasing a Home* graphic and you'll be directed to Maryland's Journey to Homeownership page, which walks you through the process and includes the most direct program links. If you have student debt and might qualify for the MMP student-debt homebuyer's program, look for the lenders with a mark in the SmartBuy column. To locate a Housing Opportunity Certified real estate agent, scroll down to the "get connected with a trusted local agent" box and select the county or city where you want to buy. (The counties in the dropdown are *not* alphabetical). MMP offers what they call Dual Track *Product* Lines. One track is for repeat or first-time homebuyers and the other is for first time homebuyers only. All MMP down payment assistance loans are zero interest and deferred. Across the state a comprehensive group of employers, builders and community organizations provide additional loans or grants which can be layered with some MMP down payment loans. Complete lists of participating partners are on the website. Maryland's SmartBuy may be the right option for you if you still have student loan debt that you're either repaying or which is in deferment. You can apply for the SmartBuy program if you have at least $1,000 in student debt. Under this program, MMP pays off student loan debt equal to either 15% of the purchase price or $20,000—whichever is lower. You have to pay off the entire student loan balance for at least one borrower, or not at all. If you're a bit over the $20,000 maximum you can still qualify if you pay off the additional balance before closing. If you have a co-borrower and you both have student loans and the total of *both* are under the

15% of purchase price or $20,000 maximum, you can pay off both of your student loan debt. Every year, 20% of that loan debt is forgiven unless you sell, refinance or move. I used to live in Montgomery County, Maryland and they go above and beyond with their programs. In addition to the generous MMP offers, if you work for certain Montgomery County departments or are a full time employee of the Montgomery County Public School System *and* a member of one of four specific related associations *and* meet the program's current requirements you could be eligible for a forgivable Montgomery Employee DPA Loan (MEDPAL). You do have to contribute 1% of the purchase price.

Massachusetts

Massachusetts MassHousing (masshousing.com; 888-843-6432). Fill out their quick online form to start your homebuying journey. Mortgage loans and down payment assistance programs are available statewide and the repayable or deferred down payment assistance loans can be combined with other local down payment and closing cost programs. Check with the locale where you're looking to buy for all options. MassHousing offers a closing cost credit for veterans and active-duty servicemembers. And if you're interested in a house that needs renovations you may be able use your loan proceeds for your purchase and renovations.

Michigan

Michigan State Housing Development Authority (michigan.gov/MSHDA; 855-646-7432). Michigan's programs are short and sweet. Start with the drop-down menu on the top right and select Homeownership to see available programs. The MI 10K Down Payment Assistance zero-interest deferred loan can be combined with your first mortgage. Michigan offers a specialized program for lower-income buyers which offers loans at a full percentage lower interest rate. And with MSHDA's First-Generation Down Payment Assistance (FirstGenDPA) program you could receive a deferred loan to cover upfront home buying expenses, including your down payment, closing costs and prepaid expenses. You'll need to put in at least 1% of the purchase price from your own cash and must take a face-to-face homebuyer education course.

Minnesota
Minnesota Housing Finance Agency (mnhousing.gov/homeownership; 651-296-7608). If you kept your home after bankruptcy, but your mortgage rates are high and your income falls within program limits, you might be eligible to refinance through MN Housing's Step Up program to make your mortgage more affordable. To easily navigate the MN Housing website, use the drop-down menu on the right of your screen. Select the Homeownership tab, then click the caret symbol to open up links under the tab. Both MN Housing programs offer optional down payment and closing cost loans. The First Generation Homebuyer *Down Payment Assistance Loan* (firstgendpa.org) provides up to 10% of your home's purchase price as a down payment. You could be eligible if you or your parents lost a home through *foreclosure*. You must be a Minnesota resident to qualify for this forgivable loan.

Mississippi
Mississippi Home Corporation (mshomecorp.com, 601-718-4642). MHC only offers down payment and closing cost assistance programs. Click the Homebuyer tab and then *Getting Started*, to walk through the three statewide DPA programs. All three programs can be used by first-time or previous home buyers. Each DPA loan, whether repayable or deferred, can be used for both down payment assistance and closing costs. MHC's HOME4All program provides grant money to lower income U.S. citizens for your

down payment and closing costs, to reduce your mortgage interest or to pay down your mortgage principal. This program has *specific* instructions about how to proceed, so follow their directions carefully to maximize your success. Due to a teacher shortage in parts of Mississippi, the MS Department of Education offers grant money if you agree to teach in a critical shortage area. The grant funds can be combined with any of the other MHC's DPA programs, depending on your income. You must stay employed at that school district for at least three years. Your contribution from your personal funds must be at least 1% of the home's purchase price. And you must provide at least one month's reserve to cover your housing payment, but this amount can be gifted to you. You'll find a complete list of school districts currently offering this program in MHC's printable program flyer. Your homebuyer education class completion certificate is good for *two years*.

Missouri

Missouri Housing Development Commission (mhdc.com; 816-759-6600). Missouri provides easy navigation through their homebuyer programs when you click on the big *Homeownership* box on the front page. First-time homebuyers (or any veterans who served on active duty and were not dishonorably discharged) may qualify for a lower interest rate mortgage that can also be combined with forgivable down payment assistance loans. MHDC's secondary program for both first-time and repeat homebuyers with higher incomes offers the same benefits.

Montana

Montana Department of Commerce Board of Housing (housing. mt.gov/homeownership; 406-841-2700). The left side menu bar links you to various parts of Montana's Homeownership programs. If you're eligible for a Regular Bond Program Loan, two options are available which offer deferred down payment and closing cost assistance. All borrowers contribute a minimum of $1,000 in cash (which can be gifted). For the MBOH Veterans Home Loan Program, you must be a *true* first-time homebuyer, having *never* owned a home before. Montana offers other specialty programs if you meet lower income limits. You may also qualify for down payment assistance from non-profits, local governments or other partnering organizations.

Nebraska

Nebraska Investment Finance Authority (nifa.org; 402-434-3900). NIFA offers a truly helpful, yet somewhat overbearing chat entity known as Quinn the QualBot. If you find Quinn bothersome, click the big burgundy X at the bottom of the chat box. When you enter the NIFA site, a pop-up screen opens with current interest rates for each program. Scroll down and it will close. If you're buying a multi-unit property of 2–4 units, NIFA will include net rental income in your total household income calculations, which may make you ineligible for the program, so check to see if it's financially advantageous before you decide to buy a multi-unit property. NIFA offers programs for first-time and repeat buyers, and an option for active military and qualified veterans (First Home Military). Active-duty personnel must qualify as first-time homebuyers. You can qualify as a repeat buyer if you're buying a home in a target area. You may also qualify as a first-time homebuyer if your home was lost in a divorce and you didn't receive any sales proceeds, or if your previous home was lost in a natural disaster, or you were forced to relocate for your job. You will need to provide your own down payment and closing costs. These funds can be gifted or can come from other down payment assistance programs. Remember Quinn the QualBot? He's the entry point for connecting you with a participating loan officer. If you don't feel the loan officer Quinn selects is a good fit, or if you need assistance finding a participating real estate agent, call NIFA directly.

Nevada

Nevada Housing Division (HomeIsPossibleNV.org; 775-687-2240). Nevada's HIP program's *Get Started* page walks you through their process. All Nevada programs are statewide and available for low- and middle-income residents. HIP makes their process as personal as possible, offering a low-interest 30-year second mortgage to help pay down payment and closing cost assistance, which is available to both first time and repeat homebuyers. You can currently own a home outside Nevada when you close. A zero-interest 30-year version is also available for first-time homebuyers. HIP has previously offered specialty programs for heroes (law enforcement and first responders) as well as for established Nevada public classroom teachers. Sign up to get notified when they launch a new program. Nevada's helpful blog is an added feature, with specific and actionable articles. Several favorite posts offered up options to modify your loan if you're facing foreclosure, and tips from real first-time homebuyers of what you *really* need to know before you buy. Fill out their contact form if you still have questions.

New Hampshire

New Hampshire Housing (NewHampshireHousing.com; 800-649-0470). NHH encourages you to start by building your home buying team. They offer up specific loan officers, approved lender organizations and real estate agents who are advisory partners with NHH, well versed in their programs. And your required Homebuyer Education course is free. You could receive a 30-year zero-interest deferred second mortgage to help you pay your down payment and closing costs. NHH also currently offers first-generation homebuyers up to $10,000 down payment assistance.

(With limited funding, this program could be suspended or ended any time.) Specific face-to-face homebuyer classes from approved providers are required for the first-generation loan. If you prefer buying a fixer-upper, you can add up to an additional $75,000 to your first mortgage to help with repairs and upgrades. This rehab loan can be combined with a DPA loan. Take NHH's free one-hour Rehab class to learn more.

New Jersey

New Jersey Housing and Mortgage Finance Agency (nj.gov/dca/hmfa; 609-278-7400). In NJ, your credit score doesn't matter as much, so they don't set specific credit score limits. Their qualified lenders will evaluate your credit history and where you're at post-bankruptcy, and will let you know what best steps you can take to become "mortgage-ready." I recommend reading the state's detailed homebuying guide, *The Road Home New Jersey*, before you buy your home. Two statewide bond-funded programs exist in New Jersey: the NJHMFA Down Payment Assistance Program and a Police and Firemen Retirement System Mortgage Program. If you qualify, you could receive funds to put toward your down payment and closing costs in the form of a zero-interest, deferred and forgivable loan. If your parents or legal guardians don't currently own a home *and* no one buying with you has owned a home anywhere in the United States in the past three years *or* you were ever in foster care within New Jersey, you could also qualify for additional First Gen down payment assistance. If you're an active member of the NJ Police and Firefighter Retirement System (PFRS) and have one year of creditable service, you may be eligible for a 30-year fixed rate mortgage with a lower interest rate, even if you're not a first-time homebuyer. You may also be able to buy land to build your home. The most you can borrow is 85% of the home's value, but you can also get a second mortgage for the remainder. This program comes with additional costs, so have your lender walk you through your choices.

New Mexico

New Mexico "Housing NM" (housingnm.org/programs/home-buyers; 505-843-6880). New Mexico's statewide programs are supported by revenue bonds through the state's Mortgage Finance Authority, allowing them to offer competitive 30-year fixed rate mortgage rates, plus various down payment assistance loans. HNM's programs can be used for *any* single-family property in New Mexico. Your primary mortgage can be combined with down payment and closing cost loans which may be repayable or forgivable. HNM's 23-page *Housing Homeowner Manual* is a must read before you start the process. HNM also keeps it real with *Getting Started: Six Steps to Savvy Homebuying.* Step 4 walks you through real life scenarios of people who had serious concerns about their eligibility, in case you're thinking *this program can't possibly work for me.* The steps provide down-to-earth, actionable advice. I give four stars to their *Homebuying Terminology* section. I haven't seen real estate terms defined so well in everyday language since *SmartMoney* magazine folded. Homebuyer Education courses are mandatory for all HNM programs. Two course providers have unique down payment assistance programs which may be combined with HNM's programs. These providers are:

- The Santa Fe Housing Trust (housingtrustonline.org, 505-989-3960). You start by reading their instructions, then downloading and completing an application form before setting up an appointment. Their website is short and sweet. If you have unanswered questions, it's best to call them.
- Homewise (homewise.org, frontdesk@homewise.org; 505-983-9473) is a Santa Fe-based non-profit full-service housing agency. They offer lender services, real estate experts and a wide

selection of free financial and homebuyer education classes. Once you've read through everything, use their contact form to write with additional questions.

New York

State of New York Mortgage Agency, SONYMA (hcr.ny.gov/homebuyers; 800-382-4663). SONYMA offers a statewide first-time homebuyer program and many other programs. One unique program is *Give Us Credit/Credit is Due,* which is designed for people who are overcoming past financial hardships or don't have traditional credit. This program looks more at your *savings and income* than at your credit score. Other options include funds for remodeling or repairing your home, up to four units (RemodelNY), with even more funds available if you're buying a vacant home. Both programs require your home to be at least 500 square feet, on five acres or less, and agricultural use is not permitted. All SONYMA programs are eligible for optional down payment assistance, *and* you can also use other grants and subsidies with no limit. SONYMA's website contains extensive information and is well laid out. If you still have questions, SONYMA encourages you to call or fill out their contact form. All SONYMA down payment assistance loans are zero-interest 10-year forgivable loans. The Homes for Veterans program is great if you, your spouse or any co-borrower is active-duty military or a veteran, including service in the National Guard or Reserves. The Graduate to Homeownership program is another stellar add-on available in certain regions of New York. If in the past 48 months you received your associate, bachelor's, master's or doctoral degree you could be eligible for this program *if* you buy a home in one of the designated downtown revitalization programs.

Neighborhood Housing Services of New York City (NHSNYC .org; 212-519-2500). NHSNYC helps first-time homebuyers with low- and moderate-income households. Hover over the Programs and Services Tab and you'll see Homeowner Services, Lending Services and Assistance Programs. You may qualify for a competitive 30-year fixed rate mortgage, and forgivable down payment and closing cost assistance. To see if you qualify, fill out the contact form, and specify which location you want to reach *and* that you're interested in the First-Time Homebuyer Program.

North Carolina

North Carolina Housing Finance Agency (nchfa.com/homebuyers; 919-877-5700). NCHFA's programs are short and sweet, if your credit score is at least 640. Read through all sections of the *Homebuyers* tab *and* read the *Home Matters* Blog. The NC Home Advantage Mortgage is for first-time and repeat homebuyers *and* includes down payment assistance. If you are a first-time homebuyer or military veteran, check out the 1st Home Advantage Down Payment program, as you could be eligible for additional DPA funds. All down payment loans are forgivable after 15 years. Forgiveness starts in year 11 with 20% forgiven annually over five years. You may also be eligible for down payment assistance from NC's Community Homebuying Program or the Self-Help Loan Pool if you buy a home built or rehabbed by Habitat for Humanity. If you still have questions, fill out their contact form.

North Dakota

North Dakota Housing Finance Agency (ndhfa.org; 701-328-8080). Select *Ready to Buy a Home* from the main menu tabs. NDHFA offers four programs for first time or recurring buyers. Additional loans are available if you're buying a home in a target area. North Dakota's specialty program is HomeAccess, with various ways you can qualify: if you are a single parent with at least 50% custody of a dependent child, you or your spouse are a qualified veteran, or if you, your spouse or a dependent living with you is 65 or older or permanently disabled. All North Dakota programs can be paired with one of two down payment loans.

Northern Marianas

Northern Marianas Housing Corporation (nmhcgov.net; 670-234-6866 ext. 9447). To qualify as a first-time homebuyer in the Northern Marianas it must have been more than a *decade* since you've owned a home. NMHC's Mortgage Credit Division offers two forgivable first-time homebuyer programs. Your interest rate, mortgage length and down payment assistance depend on your income. You must reside in the home for at least 10 years before the loan starts becoming forgivable. NMHC is building a catalog of available homes people can purchase through their program, so when you are ready to sell, they may have first right of refusal to buy your home. At NMHC, you'll start with a mandatory pre-qualification interview. Read through the *Applying for a Home Program Loan* page *before* setting up your interview. You must pull together specific financial information for *all* adults who will live in the home and a program manager will review these documents with you during the interview. If you're pre-qualified at the interview, they will give you an application to fill out. Pay close attention to the details. If your application packet is incomplete, they will not accept it. Call them if you have questions.

Ohio

Ohio Housing Finance Agency (myohiohome.org; 614-466-7970). Ohio's site offers an easy in-depth eligibility questionnaire. Click on the blue box and answer the questions; the system will share the programs you're likely eligible to use. Once you finish the quiz, click on What to Expect and read the 20-page *Homebuyer Guide* which offers concrete advice and information. Ohio's income and purchase price limits are quite generous. In municipalities, your property must be below two acres; outside of municipalities, you can buy up to five acres. Ohio's free, required homeowner education includes mandatory one-on-one phone counseling and a course of their own creation, where you receive online access to their printable *Homebuyer Education Guide*. When you're ready you can either take the test and provide your budget information online or print the exam and budget forms and fax in your completed documents. Ohio helps first-time homebuyers get fixed rate 30-year first mortgages and repayable or forgivable down payment assistance loans. Ohio has a wide-ranging Ohio Heroes loan program. The groups that qualify include veterans, active-duty military or reserve and their surviving spouses; police officers, firefighters (including volunteers), EMTs and paramedics; physicians, nurse practitioners, RNs, LPNs and STNAs; and teachers from pre-K through grade 12, plus school administrators and counselors. Ohio's Grants For Grads program offers enticements if you graduated with an associate, bachelor, master, doctorate or other degree from a college or university in the past 48 months and want to make Ohio your home. Ohio also offers enhanced interest savings accounts to help you buy a home. If you're already an Ohio resident and at least 18 you can open an Ohio Homebuyer Plus program and save up to $100,000. Any co-borrower can open their own account and *also* save up to $100,000. Funds must be used within five years of your *first* deposit. Visit tos.ohio.gov/homebuyerplus/fis for a list of participating financial institutions. To help you be a successful homeowner, Ohio also offers Free Homeowner Resources listing over 300 local programs that offer grants and loans for energy assistance (like relief from high air conditioning bills), weatherization and repairs and improvements.

Oklahoma

Oklahoma Housing Finance Agency (ohfa.org/homebuyers; 405-419-8207). Oklahoma starts you off with a required three-minute video. Watch the video, browse OHFA's programs and then connect with a lender. OHFA only offers down payment assistance, so you'll need a lender to set you up with a first mortgage. Down payment assistance may be available as a silent zero-interest second mortgage that you pay in full when you sell your home, refinance, or your first mortgage is paid off. Specialty programs—which allow you to obtain reduced interest rate 30-year first mortgages—are available for teachers (including at public, private and parochial schools), first responders of all types and state employees who are currently employed by an Oklahoma state agency. You are encouraged to call with your questions.

Oregon

Oregon Housing and Community Services (oregon.gov/ohcs/homeownership; 503-986-2000). OHCS offers a unique form of homebuying assistance called Flex Lending. Approved mortgage lenders statewide connect you with the best 30-year fixed rate first mortgage. You can then pair that loan with an OHCS down payment loan. You must have lived in Oregon for a minimum of 12 months before applying. Down payment assistance funds may be repayable, deferred, forgivable or offered as a grant. Homeownership Centers, listed by county, connect you with housing counseling, required homebuyer education courses, home buying savings accounts, and their own down payment assistance opportunities.

Pennsylvania

Pennsylvania Housing Finance Agency (phfa.org/homebuyers; 855-827-3466). Pennsylvania is the fifth most populated state, and their programs reflect their commitment to helping you become a homeowner. PHFA and another organization (which I'll cover in a moment) are the hubs for many Pennsylvania programs. For all PHFA first mortgage programs, your minimum contribution toward your purchase must be $1,000 or 1% of your purchase (whichever is *lower*). Down payment assistance loans may be repayable, deferred or forgivable. If your employer participates in PHFA's Employer Assisted Housing Initiative, you may be eligible for a zero-interest 10-year second mortgage for down payment and closing cost assistance. Check with your company's Human Resources department to see if they participate. Some counseling agencies also help you apply for special or localized programs if you meet their criteria. PHFA encourages you to contact these agencies first, then select a participating lender familiar with all programs you might be eligible to use. Some PHFA partners also offer a series of four free *Financial Education Workshops*. Workshop topics range from "Goals, Assets and Earnings" to "Manage Risks and Protect Your Money." Attending the workshops makes you eligible for free one-on-one counseling sessions (face-to-face or via phone), which you can take in tandem with the workshop series. Another great option is PHFA's no-cost *Building Your Financial House* series of eight monthly sessions. These sessions dive deeper into the four-series topics—and include a case study with real-life examples. Held as live-virtual classes, they are delivered by PHFA's financial education staff from September to May. Attend all eight classes and you'll be entered into a drawing to win a $500 perfect attendance prize. Contact Patricia Washington (pwashington@phfa.org) for details.

Affordable Housing Centers of Pennsylvania (ahcopa.org, 215-765-1221). AHCOPA's First Time Homebuyer Program is where the state really shines, by linking you to *hundreds* of specific, often local, programs. Register for a free First Time Homebuyer Workshop which teaches you how to get financially prepared, how to access available grant funds and what to expect from your loan officer, real estate agent and other professionals. The workshop is available online *and* live so you can get all your questions answered.

The Grants/Down Payment Assistance section provides links to different city and county programs, plus banks that offer funds for first-time home buyers. Here are my favorites from the current list:

- Lubert Individual Development Accounts—First Time Home-buyer Match Savings Program (unitedforimpact.org).
- Chester County First Time Home Buyer Program (housing-partnershipcc.com; 610-518-1522).
- Cumberland County First Time Home Buyer Program (cchra .com; 717-249-1315)
- Delaware County Homeownership First Program (cciphousing .org; 610-876-8663).
- First Front Door (firstfrontdoor.com). Also available in Delaware and West Virginia.
- Montgomery County First Time Homebuyers Program (montgomerycountypa.gov; 610-278-3540.
- Philly First Home and Turn the Key (phdcphila.org/dhcd; 215-686-9749).

Puerto Rico

Puerto Rico Housing Finance Authority (recuperacion.pr.gov; 787-946-0045, ext. 4620). The PRHFA is dedicated to helping the people most essential to Puerto Rico purchase their first homes and is funded by a Community Development Block Grant specifically for disaster recovery. Choose between Spanish and English on the website, then select Citizens and scroll down to Direct Programs to the Citizens. The Homebuyer Assistance Program page contains all the information and links for this program, including lists of Housing Counseling Agencies and Participating Institutions. If you meet the criteria for low and moderate income (LMI) and urgent need (UN) residents *and* you're part of the Critical Recovery Workforce (CRW) you may be eligible for down payment and mortgage subsidy assistance. I mention all these abbreviations because they're heavily used in the program guidelines. The list of employed members of the Critical Recovery Workforce is extensive and you may qualify if you work in these areas: Education, Emergency Management (including Atmospheric Surveillance), Emergency Medical, Firefighters, Healthcare Professionals (including mental health), Infrastructure, Law Enforcement, Supply Chain and even Veterinary/Animal Services (including animal rescue). Review the guidelines for a complete list and then call to confirm if you think your work might be included. You must be a U.S. citizen, non-citizen national or qualified alien and must either be a first-time homebuyer, a single parent or a displaced homemaker. You may even qualify if you're married but don't own a home with your spouse, or if you and others are co-heirs to a home. Every case is considered individually.

Rhode Island

Rhode Island Housing (rihousing.com/buyers; 401-457-1234). RIHousing's first generation homebuyer loans are serviced through the RIHousing Loan Center not through participating lenders. RIHousing offers programs for first-time, repeat buyers and first generation buyers, plus renovation loans for fixer-uppers. Down payment assistance loan options may be repayable, deferred or forgivable.

South Carolina

South Carolina Housing (schousing.sc.gov; 803-254-3886). Almost all SC Housing loans are available statewide. The only program where you absolutely *must* be a first-time homebuyer is the SC Housing Homebuyer program, which can be combined with forgivable down payment assistance. All funding is on a first-come, first-served basis. Once funds are allocated for the year for each program, the program is paused. Most down payment assistance loans are zero-interest deferred and forgivable. SC Housing also offers a special statewide homeownership program which you may qualify for if you're in an approved Public Housing agency Housing Choice Voucher assistance program. For details, contact the HCV administrator at your public housing agency or call 803-896-2211. Two other South Carolina programs of note:

- County of Lexington (lex-co.sc.gov; 803-785-8121) offers a deferred forgivable down payment assistance loan through their Homeownership Assistance Program.
- CommunityWorks Carolina (communityworkscarolina.org) offers a variety of forgivable and non-forgivable down payment assistance programs through specialty programs in select areas or if you work for select employers. Contact Katy Davenport at 864-235-6331 or kdavenport@cwcarolina.org with questions about these programs.

South Dakota

South Dakota Housing (sdhousing.org; 605-773-3181). Click the Ready-to-Buy tab to jump into South Dakota's Homebuyer programs. Loans are available for first-time and repeat buyers with a choice between a Fixed Rate Option (with a lower interest rate 30-year fixed mortgage) or a Fixed Rate Plus Option which adds a zero-interest deferred down payment assistance loan. The Governor's House Program is available if you meet certain income limits, are at least 62, or have disabilities. These two- or three-bedroom homes are grouped together to make them more affordable, accessible and energy-efficient. These homes are less than $100,000 and are newly built so you can personalize them. Call 800-540-4241 to discover Governor's House properties near where you want to live. South Dakota also offers Grants for Grads if you've received your bachelor, master, doctorate or other higher education degree in the past 60 months.

Tennessee

Tennessee Housing Development Authority (thda.org/homebuyers; 615-815-2200). Tennessee offers a short *Handbook for Homebuyers* in both English and Spanish. THDA offers low-interest rate loans through their 30-year fixed interest programs, including First-Time Homebuyers, Repeat Buyers and Homeowners for Heroes, if you are a state or local law enforcement officer, an EMT or paramedic or a firefighter. If you're an active-duty member of the armed services or qualified veteran, you do *not* have to be a first-time homebuyer. All THDA loans can be paired with a down payment assistance loan which is either repayable or forgivable.

Texas

Texas Department of Housing and Community Affairs TDHCA. (800-792-1119; thetexashomebuyerprogram.com). Start with the free *Texas Statewide Homebuyer Education Program* or get familiar with the programs by taking a free two-hour online *Becoming a Homeowner* course. The My First Texas Home program is *only* for first-time homebuyers or veterans, and you *must* be a Texas resident when you file your application. You don't have to be a first-time buyer to be eligible for the My Choice Texas Home program. Both programs offer interesting options that may meet your financial needs for both your primary mortgage and down payment and closing cost assistance.

Texas State Affordable Housing Corporation (TSAHC). (tsahc.org; 877-508-4611). Open the Home Buyers and Renters tab and you'll find links to every bit of TSAHC's programs. Watch the short video of how the TSAHC down payment programs work, then take the Eligibility Quiz to narrow down programs for which you may qualify. TSAHC provides 30-year fixed rate first mortgages, down payment assistance grants and deferred loans. You don't have to be a first-time homeowner to qualify. TSAHC's

Homes for Texas Heroes program has a broad list of hero *professions*. Let your lender know that you *may* qualify, and they'll confirm that for you. Your down payment assistance depends on the type of 30-year mortgage you get and can be deferred, forgivable or a grant.

Utah

Utah Housing Corporation (utahhousingcorp.org/homebuyer; 801-902-8200). Utah offers reduced interest rates on 30-year fixed interest mortgages to first-time homebuyers, single parents and veterans. Utah has specific criteria for qualification after bankruptcy, so ask your lender if you'll qualify. Roommates who pay you rent are allowed, as long as you also occupy the home fulltime. Utah Housing loans can be combined with different down payment assistance options which may be repayable or deferred. Down payment grant funding is available for veterans if you haven't owned a home *in Utah* for the past *seven* years. Additional down payment grant assistance may be available if you work in law enforcement or are a corrections officer. If you're moving to Utah for a job in corrections or law enforcement, the first-time homebuyer requirement is waived, if your home purchase is completed within six months of starting your new job (12 months if you're buying a brand-new home).

Vermont

Vermont Housing Finance Agency (vhfa.org/homebuyers; 802-652-3456). Vermont's programs are for first-time homebuyers and repeat buyers if you're buying in select counties. VHFA down payment assistance is available for first-time homebuyers only, as a deferred loan or as a grant. VHFA also offers a first-generation homebuyer program. You may find other (non-VHFA) Vermont homebuyer grants and down payment assistance helpful. These include the Shared Equity 20% down payment grant offered by NeighborWorks of Western Vermont (nwwvt.org, 800-438-2303), which you can use when buying in Rutland or Bennington County.

Virgin Islands

Virgin Islands Housing Finance Authority (vihfa.gov; 340-777-4432 ext. 2269). Scroll down to the Become a Homeowner Section for program details. To qualify for a VIHFA program, you must have resided in the Territory for a minimum of three years *and* filed your last three annual tax returns in the Virgin Islands. VIHFA's required Home Buyer's Education Program is very comprehensive and designed for your success. They encourage you to attend the class in person and use their free in-person counseling and other courses. VIHFA also offers Post-Purchasing Counseling to help prevent mortgage delinquencies and foreclosures, as well as Financial Fitness Training so you can become more confident about your personal financial decisions. The VIHFA sometimes provides direct lending and other times you'll need to first qualify for a primary mortgage. VIHFA's First-Time Home Buyers Loan can be used to buy a single-family home (which can be prefabricated or manufactured), rehab a fixer-upper, or purchase up to one-half acre of land on which to build your home. VIHFA offers low-interest loans and grants for single-family homes, and some condos and townhouse units. For more details call Ms. Freida Webster, Director of Homeownership at 340-777-4432 ext. 2269.

Virginia

Virginia Housing (virginiahousing.com/homebuyers; 804-782-1986). Start with their free 21-page *Home Loan Options* booklet and check your eligibility with their Lending Wizard. You can be a first-time home buyer *or* a repeat buyer for most 30-year first mortgages. If you're a veteran and sustained a line-of-duty injury that created a disability, you may be eligible for a Granting Freedom grant to pay for home modifications to accommodate your disability. Virginia Housing offers additional down payment and closing cost assistance, including grants. If your credit score is at least 680, you can pay your down payment using a combination of gifts, grants and a down payment loan, if you contribute at least 1% of the purchase price from your own funds.

Virginia Department of Housing and Community Development (dhcd.virginia.com; 804-371-7000). In addition to the Virginia Housing programs, DHCD offers a Homeownership Down Payment Assistance Program (DPA), so long as your bankruptcy discharge occurred more than three years ago. If you have any delinquent federal debts (student loans, tax liens, or SBA loan) you will *not* be eligible for this grant. You must contribute between $500 and 1% of the home purchase price from your personal funds, depending on your income. Visit the website to select a DPA partner in your county to see if you qualify. In addition, depending on your income, you might be eligible to open a Virginia Individual Development Account (VIDA), which provides 10:1 matching funds, up to a total of $10,000. You put in $1,000 and they put in $10,000 which you can use to pay toward your down payment.

Washington State

Washington State Housing Finance Commission (wshfc.org/buyers; 206-464-7139). With WSHFC, you start by taking a five-hour Homebuyer Education Course. Your certificate is good for two years from the date you complete your course. WSHFC's programs offer lower-rate first mortgages and potential down payment assistance. The Covenant Homeownership Program is for first-time homebuyers from qualifying ethnic groups whose family has been in Washington state since before 1968. If you, your parents or grandparents lived in Washington before April 1968, and you're a first-time homebuyer, you may qualify. You must be a pre-1968 resident of Washington state *or* a descendant of one. Contact the free Washington Homeownership Hotline (877-894-4663) to see if you qualify. You must also either be a first-time homebuyer, a single parent, a displaced homemaker or have only owned a residence with no permanent foundation. Washington offers five additional statewide programs and four different specialty programs. Specific down payment assistance (DPA) programs are also offered by Clark County, ARCH East King County, and Bellingham. These programs require you to use specific community organizations for your mandatory housing *counseling* session. You must personally contribute $2,500 or 1% of the purchase price. Up to 25% of that requirement can be gifted to you. For questions about any of the above DPA loans, contact Dietrich Schmitz (206-287-4459). Washington's Beginning Farmer and Ranch Program (wshfc.org/FarmRanch) is set up to make farming affordable. You may qualify if you've never owned and operated a farm or ranch *or* owned one that was less than 30% of your county's median farm size. You and/or your children *must* actively manage and work the farm. You must use a loan officer from Northwest Farm Credit Services. Finally, through the non-profit HomeSight Homeownership Center (homesightwa.org; 206-760-4205), you may qualify for additional deferred down payment assistance when buying in certain areas.

West Virginia

West Virginia Housing Development Fund (wvhdf.com/home-buyers; 304-391-8600). West Virginia keeps things simple. Watch their short *Are You Ready For Homeownership?* video, read their 21-page *First-Time Buyer's Guide* and the *Preparing For Ownership* document. When you're done, call 800-933-8511 to contact an approved loan originator. The Homeownership Program is available for many West Virginia residents, and up to 100% of your home's purchase price can be financed. You must qualify as a first-time homebuyer to buy in certain counties. You can buy a single-family home, townhome, PUD, condominium or a new double-wide manufactured home. Your property can be up to five acres. The Movin' Up Program doesn't require you to be a first-time homebuyer and has no limit on your property size. Both programs can be combined with a repayable down payment assistance loan.

Wisconsin

Wisconsin Housing and Economic Development Authority (wheda.com). The WHEDA website outlines their *Six Steps to a WHEDA Loan* with links to each section of the process. WHEDA also offers a *True Costs of Homeownership* information sheet outlining the costs of buying, owning and maintaining your home. And their *Find a Lender* page includes great questions to ask lenders.

WHEDA offers two first mortgage programs under the WHEDA Advantage label and you *don't* need to be a first-time homebuyer to qualify for either. There's no requirement for you to use your own funds to buy, unless you buy a multi-unit property. In which case you'll need to contribute 3% of the purchase price plus six months of reserve funds to demonstrate you can pay the mortgage. For both programs, you can use a repayable or deferred down payment assistance loan to pay this contribution. Renovation and rehabilitation financing programs are also available. Two Wisconsin cities also offer strong homebuyer assistance:

- Madison (cityofmadison.com/homeloans) offers a variety of deferred down payment and closing cost assistance. Visit the website and request their matrix of down payment programs for the City of Madison and Dane County. Many can be used together.

- Milwaukee (Milwaukee.gov/mhdpa) offers down payment assistance in the form of a forgivable grant for current residents of the City of Milwaukee or if you're interested in rehabilitating and living in a city-owned foreclosed home.

Wyoming

Wyoming Community Development Authority (wyomingcda. com/homebuyers; 307-265-0603). Start with the Homebuyer Checklist and complete their two-part homebuyer education. Your course completion certificate will be good for 18 months. Wyoming offers two first-time homebuyer programs and three mortgage programs for repeat buyers. All programs can be combined with down payment assistance funds. Wyoming is so committed to your success, they offer a free 4-week Financial Foundations course *and* Financial Coaching through the Wyoming Housing Network, to help you raise your credit score. Call 307-233-8518 if you still have questions.

Options for Owner Financing

When you don't have down payment funds or don't qualify for down payment assistance programs, you have three other options. These strategies will work best when the current homeowner isn't strapped for cash and would welcome a steady stream of income from you while you work to qualify for a mortgage. Homeowners who have paid off their mortgage and have already bought their new home may be interested in offering owner financing. My grandparents used this strategy to sell their Indiana farm after they built a Florida retirement home.

Owner financing can be structured in various ways, with different risks for you and for the owner. The first two options below can be especially helpful after bankruptcy.

Interest-only balloon mortgage. Under this arrangement, the seller offers you an interest-only loan for two to five years, with a balloon payment due for the total purchase price at the end of the loan period. The purchase price is set on the day you sign the contract; if the home's value increases during the loan period, you'll have instant equity to use as a down payment when mortgage shopping. When the balloon payment comes due, you'll pay it with a conventional loan to finalize the sale. If you can't get a mortgage loan

---

Pros and Cons of Interest-Only Mortgages

Interest-only mortgages are like stock options. They appear to offer you a lower monthly mortgage payment, but what you're really paying is glorified rent. Your monthly payment doesn't build equity and basically bets on your home value increasing during the 5–10-year interest-only mortgage. Between natural disasters and economic fluctuations, that's a lot of risk.

The primary allure of interest-only loans is to "help" you buy a more expensive home than you can afford by offering you a few years of lower payments. What happens when the loan converts to an adjustable interest rate, or requires you to start paying the principal, or the entire loan balance becomes due (a balloon loan), or your income decreases? Any of these can make it difficult to convert that interest-only loan into a principal-and-interest loan. And here's the rub if you're "fortunate" enough to have an adjustable-interest-rate loan: The first time your lender is allowed to adjust your rate, they can legally raise your interest rate a full 5 percent. If you're currently paying 5 percent interest, your new interest rate could go up to 10 percent—doubling your mortgage payment.

Housing prices in your area could drop for any reason, including economic changes or a natural disaster, leaving you with a mortgage payment on a house worth much less than what you owe—or that no longer exists. Fall behind on your payments and you're back to where you were before your bankruptcy, especially if the lender forecloses. That's the last thing you want to happen. Make sure you know the risks of using an interest-only mortgage after bankruptcy.

by the date the full amount is due, home ownership immediately reverts to the seller and you must vacate the property.

Conventional mortgage owned by the seller. In this case, the home-owner becomes your mortgage holder, and you pay principal and interest to *them*, rather than to a lender, under the same terms and conditions as a bank-held mortgage. The seller earns a steady stream of income from the home, and if you default, the seller can foreclose on the loan and *take back* the property, just as a traditional mortgage company could.

If the owner doesn't want to spend years tracking your mortgage payments, issuing monthly mortgage and annual interest statements, or initiating collections or a foreclosure action in the event of default, the owner can sell the loan to Fannie Mae. To accomplish this (in addition to meeting a few other requirements), have a mortgage lender draw up the papers using standardized forms and take them to the seller. The seller offers you owner-financing, then sells the loan to Fannie Mae and immediately receives payment for their equity.

Two good sites for finding properties for sale with owner financing are landsearch.com and landwatch.com. If you're not interested in owner financing, there is a third option:

Lease/Rent-to-Own. Look for sellers willing to lease the home to you with an option to buy. Delaying your purchase for several years gives you time to qualify for more conventional financing, and you build equity toward the purchase price that you agreed on when you signed the lease, rather than building a pile of rent receipts.

Under this type of arrangement, you generally rent the home for two to three years with an option to buy at lease-end, and an agreed-upon portion of your rent is set aside to create your down payment. A few years of building up a down payment fund can give you time to qualify for more conventional financing. If you move before you exercise your option and finalize your home purchase, unless the lease states otherwise, you forfeit all or a portion of the set-aside funds. So only use this option if you are certain you will be staying in that area.

When you choose this option, the paperwork is critical. You'll need a sales document *and* a lease document, and everything must be up to your state's code, which changes frequently. So have a real estate lawyer with experience in lease-to-own arrangements draw up the contract or at least review it before you sign. The contract should state that you can buy the house at *the lower of* the home's appraised value at the time you exercise your option or at the sale price on the date the lease contract is signed. This way, you won't pay more than the home's fair market value when you exercise your option.

One drawback: your monthly payments aren't reported to any credit bureaus. When you're ready to get a mortgage loan to finalize the purchase, your lender will want definitive proof of your on-time payments. Make sure you have monthly receipts or bank statements for this purpose.

Rent-to-Own Options

A commercial twist on lease options is gaining popularity. Rent-to-own home programs run by big companies are snapping up homes and renting them back with lease options that are *not* consumer-friendly. No matter how tempting the marketing is, I encourage you to steer clear. These programs are designed to financially benefit the company and its shareholders, not you. It's far better to find owner-financed properties.

Best After-Bankruptcy Mortgage Lenders

Mortgage lenders fall into two categories: *A-list* lenders and *BCD* lenders. The worse your credit report looks, the further down the alphabet you get shuttled. That's why it's important to rebuild your credit until you're back on the A or B list *before* financing a home. To find the best mortgage lender for your situation, use a mortgage *broker* who works with many lenders to find your best financing option.

A good mortgage broker will have you fill out a mini loan application to find the best mortgage options for you based on your credit history. Be up front about your bankruptcy so the broker can show lenders why you're a good credit risk. Some brokers will even help you write a letter explaining the circumstances surrounding your bankruptcy. These are the good guys.

And then there are the *other* mortgage brokers—the ones who immediately label you as a *subprime* borrower. These brokers are easy to spot. They scan your credit report and say something like, "Oh, well, I see you have a bankruptcy here. Hmmm. . . . That will make it more difficult to get you approved for a loan. Sure, we can still get you a mortgage, but you're gonna have to pay a higher interest rate, of course, because of this bankruptcy here. . . ."

Don't fall for this ploy. With at least 6 to 12 monthly, on-time post-bankruptcy payments showing on your credit report (or if you reaffirmed a car loan and paid at least the past six monthly payments on time), you should qualify for a fair mortgage interest rate. After two years, you should qualify for the going rate.

If a mortgage broker steers you toward a higher-interest-rate loan, politely but firmly say, "I know I have enough credit references to qualify for the going market rate. Since you're not able to approve a loan at that rate, I don't want to waste any more of your time." Then pick up your papers and walk out the door. Do *not* hesitate or reconsider them. If they are not looking out for your best interests at *this* point, they won't be your advocate during the process.

Online versus Face-to-Face Mortgage Brokers

For convenience, many people prefer to deal with mortgage brokers electronically. After bankruptcy, however, I recommend *against* using an online broker. Online brokers can't look you in the eye and see you are truly ready for a fresh start. As a result, you jump through more hoops and must provide more documentation. Also, lenders who work with online mortgage brokers often sell your mortgage loan to another lender, which can disrupt your on-time payments.

Start your search for a mortgage broker on the NMLS Consumer Access website (nmlsconsumeraccess.org), where you can verify a mortgage broker is licensed and has had no regulatory action taken against them for financial misbehavior. Enter your city and state and filter your search by *company*. Click through the listed companies and check out their websites. You may find that some are locally owned companies, others are branches of larger mortgage companies (not mortgage brokers), and some are branches of larger mortgage brokerage firms. You want a mortgage broker with a solid history in your community. Smaller companies often have lower overhead, so they can charge lower fees.

If the mortgage brokerage doesn't have a website, take a pass. If they do, read up on their services, their people, and their approach to get a feel for how you might like to work with them. Then visit the Better Business Bureau (bbb.org), and search for *mortgage broker* in your city and state and select *all businesses* to find the ones closest to you. Click on a business name to get more information. Verify they've been in business at least 10 years, then check the Reviews and Complaints tabs. If their BBB file doesn't list many reviews, search for the company name and "reviews" online and see what you discover. Then pick your top two favorites and make appointments to visit them.

Buy a Home within a Year of Bankruptcy

If you need to relocate after your bankruptcy or want to buy before your credit is fully restored, you have two options:

1. Take over an existing loan on a property that's worth *less* than the value of the current mortgage. In areas where property values are falling sharply, you may find homeowners who are upside-down on their mortgage, meaning they owe more than their home is worth. When taking over a loan like this, you may not even need a down payment. Instead, you come up with enough money to pay closing costs and bring the defaulted loan current if the owner has missed payments, which could be as little as a few thousand dollars. You will do the homeowner a huge favor by helping them avoid foreclosure or bankruptcy.

2. Get a nonconforming mortgage. Nonconforming mortgages, which don't meet the strict criteria set by government-sponsored loans and are often for amounts higher than the conforming loan limit, are often issued by "BCD" lenders, who (as I mentioned earlier) are more than happy to help you qualify for a mortgage soon after your bankruptcy discharge. If you go this route, expect to pay a minimum down payment of 25 percent plus double-digit interest. I'm not a big fan of nonconforming loans given that nearly all your monthly payments for the first 10 years is interest. Unless rents in your area are higher than a mortgage payment would be and property values are rapidly rising, it's better to wait a year or two and buy with a conventional mortgage. If you decide to go with a nonconforming mortgage,

make sure your contract states that the interest rate is automatically reduced after several years of good payments on your part, or make sure you're guaranteed the opportunity to refinance at a lower interest rate after two years of good payments—with *no prepayment penalty.*

Refinance after Bankruptcy

While I didn't own a home when I declared bankruptcy, you may. When you are ready to refinance, call several different mortgage loan brokers and tell them you're looking for *competitive refinancing rates.* Avoid lenders that specialize in bad-credit mortgage refinancing. You want a mortgage broker who deals with A-list lenders and has *access* to BCD funding sources.

Options for refinancing vary, depending on whether you filed Chapter 7 or Chapter 13. Regardless of what type of bankruptcy you filed, though, you can avoid paying an astronomical interest rate when you refinance your home after bankruptcy *if* you first follow the strategies for rebuilding your credit *before* you apply to refinance.

Let's recap the strategies for when you're looking to refinance after Chapter 7 bankruptcy. Basically, the longer your bankruptcy has been discharged, the better. Refinancing within six months of your discharge will be expensive. Rebuild your credit for six to 12 months to get a reasonable interest rate. You could be considered an A+ borrower within two years, assuming you have no new negative credit information on your credit reports *and* have added certain new positive credit information. Time isn't the only factor that mortgage refinancing companies consider—you must show you've reestablished your credit with at least *two* good credit references in addition to your mortgage. A car loan and a credit card or unsecured loan would be helpful.

Avoid Prepayment Penalties

Subprime lenders often include a prepayment penalty in their contracts. They know, after a few years of paying higher interest, you'll seize the first opportunity to refinance at a more reasonable rate. So, they often include a clause stating that you'll be charged a *penalty* if you pay off their loan early. The penalty is either a fixed percentage, like 3 percent of the outstanding balance, or six months of the interest you would have paid them. If you have a $100,000 balance on your mortgage, a 3 percent prepayment penalty would cost you $3,000. But if the prepayment penalty is interest-based and your loan's interest rate is above 6 percent, you'll pay more to get out of the loan. For example, to get out of a loan with an 8.5 percent interest rate and a prepayment penalty, six months of interest will cost you about $4,200. Even if you get a windfall and want to pay the loan in full, you'd still be required to pay that penalty.

When it comes to prepayment penalties, make the lender *show* you the specific language in the contract saying there's no prepayment penalty. Don't take anyone's word when they say there is no prepayment penalty or rely on their sales pitch and oral guarantee. Read the contract word for word and find exactly where it clearly states *there is no prepayment penalty*. Then initial that spot for added protection before you sign the document.

Most loan applications and contracts now clearly state you won't get a refund of finance charges or interest you have *already* paid, even if you prepay the *remaining* principal or balance of the loan. Don't be alarmed by that language—it's there to prevent confusion about what you do and don't get back when you pay off your loan early.

If you filed Chapter 13, your options for refinancing depend on whether you have completed your repayment plan or are still in repayment, which adds a few restrictions to refinancing. Mortgage lenders and financial services companies that help refinance mortgages when you're currently making payments under a Chapter 13 repayment plan usually offer three options:

1. Work within the terms of your Chapter 13.
2. Use a Chapter 13 buyout to pay off the balance owed under your bankruptcy repayment plan by refinancing your current mortgage. Consumer-friendly lenders won't attempt a buyout loan unless it significantly lowers your monthly payments, you've had a good payment history since you began your bankruptcy repayment plan, *and* you have at least 25% equity in your home.
3. Dismiss your Chapter 13 bankruptcy and roll your outstanding debts into a new mortgage loan amount. Loans that require your bankruptcy to be dismissed are usually offered *only* after you've been in your repayment plan for at least three years.

Your best option depends on your current circumstances, the amount of home equity you have, and the amount of unpaid debt remaining under your Chapter 13 repayment plan. For the most part, you're required to have completed at least one year of your Chapter 13 repayment plan with all payments made on time.

One possible glitch: your current mortgage holder may have reported late payments even though you always paid your trustee on time. To be on the safe side, gather copies of your canceled checks or account statements showing when you made your Chapter 13 payments and share these documents with your mortgage broker. Ask the broker what specific documentation the lender will need from you regarding your Chapter 13 plan. To make sure your refinancing doesn't affect your Chapter 13 bankruptcy protection, it doesn't hurt to ask your bankruptcy attorney if they offer debtors' rights services or can refer you to a debtors' rights attorney.

Have the mortgage broker or lender put in writing whether their solution works *around* your existing Chapter 13 bankruptcy or requires you to *dissolve* your Chapter 13 bankruptcy. You want to know specifically how a dissolution will impact your expenses, so crunch the numbers. Also, make sure the lender clearly states whether their solution uses your home equity to pay outstanding debts currently protected by your Chapter 13 plan. In general, your home equity is protected under bankruptcy, so using it to pay off those debts might *not* be your best option.

Check with your state attorney general's office and the Better Business Bureau to determine whether the potential mortgage lender provides quality services.

Whether you're refinancing after a Chapter 7 bankruptcy or once you've completed your Chapter 13 repayment plan, it pays to have kept your mortgage as current as possible. Mortgage lenders look *most* closely at the most recent 12 months of payment history. Generally, if you have more than four 30-day-late payments and more than a single longer late payment, you'll be matched with a C lender. Even if your payment history in the past year is spottier, there's still hope. Some mortgage brokers work with lenders who include a clause in their contract specifying that your interest rate will be lowered after two years of good payments. As always, if you go this route, get it in writing *in* the contract.

Create Home Where You Are

You know the old saying *Home is where the heart is*? It's so true. We often want to own a house because we think ownership gives us freedom to do whatever we want with *our* property. We forget that, if we have a mortgage, the *bank* actually owns the house, not us. Renting frustrates us because we believe it limits what we can do with our home, or we think paying rent wastes money because we're not building up equity. (Another illusion, as equity quickly disappears when home prices drop.) Elderly homeowners with fully paid homes often lose their home when they can't afford the property taxes (or simply forget to pay them).

The truth is, buying a home may or may not be your smartest financial move right now—*and* you can turn any rental property into a proper home. To truly bounce back from your bankruptcy, you need to be strategic and patient and build up your financial skills. Meanwhile, invest time and energy in creating and enjoying a sense of home wherever you live today.

When I moved to the North Carolina beaches, I was looking for a place to buy but didn't know where exactly I wanted to settle. Instead of rushing to buy a home, I wrote down what I wanted. I wanted beautiful water views from every room, a beautifully decorated living space, and a lush garden. Big requirements for a potential condo or apartment, right? Turns out, no. I found a third-floor condo for rent that overlooked the ocean from the front patio and a thriving salt marsh from the back patio. The front deck was so large I easily added a patio table for four and built a lush container garden that was admired by all who visited. My landlord agreed I could redecorate—including painting and wallpapering as I desired, and I created a warm and inviting home.

As it turns out, I was meant to be there only for a few short years. I relocated to Florida, where I rented a one-bedroom riverfront condo for a year. The housing market was collapsing, and riverfront condos were going for pennies on the dollar, so I signed a purchase agreement to buy a two-bedroom condo in the complex where I rented—for $42,000. I would be borrowing roughly $33,600. The day before closing, the Realtor® called to say they had *good news* for me. They were lowering the interest rate by 2.25 percent on my 30-year mortgage. All I had to do was pay nine points to lock in the new rate. (As noted earlier, a point equals 1 percent of the loan amount.) So, in addition to my $8,400 down payment, they now wanted me to pay another $3,024 *up front* in exchange for a lower interest rate. Mind you, this $3,024 wouldn't reduce my loan amount. It was just an extra closing cost.

I politely declined and said I was good with the original mortgage loan agreement. At that point the broker told me they were no longer offering my original financing deal. I guess they figured out how easy it would be to pay off a $33,600 mortgage in just a few years, rather than 30 years—which meant they would be out a lot of interest. Since I'm not fond of financial professionals who change terms and conditions at the last minute, I walked away from the deal. Be willing to do the same.

Ever since, we've rented comfortable, beautiful homes at affordable market rents while saving up for our retirement home. Our landlords have allowed us to redecorate inside and improve the outside with irrigation systems, paths, gardens, fences, and even artificial turf to replace a shady, muddy lawn. We've added security systems, redecorated bathrooms, and even updated appliances. Some upgrades we've paid for ourselves; others our landlord paid.

When homeownership seems out of reach, creating *home sweet home* may still be possible.

Ponder this question about where you currently live: *what can I do with this place to create what I want in a home?* Then start creating that home where you are. When you do, you will soon find yourself more willing to move toward becoming a homeowner from a place of joy and excitement. You deserve it!

Get the Rental Home You Want

Currently renting an apartment or home? Chances are good your current landlord will never know you declared bankruptcy if they weren't included as a creditor. However, if you're looking to relocate or want to rent somewhere new, you still can—even if your bankruptcy included your current landlord. As always, your first step is to review and update your credit reports (using the strategies in Chapter 2). Then take these steps:

1. Confirm all discharged accounts are correctly reported and don't still show up as delinquent.

2. Get a good secured credit card (using the guidelines from Chapter 9) that reports your payments to the major credit bureaus and doesn't report that it's a secured card. Even three months of a good payment history on this card builds a positive credit reference.

3. Get a letter from your current landlord showing your strong on-time payment history and that you're current on your payments. Even if you've only paid on time since your bankruptcy, it's a positive reference.

4. Check private-party listings for people who rent individual homes, condos, or apartments. CraigsList and Facebook Marketplace are two excellent sources, as are bulletin boards at your local grocery store, library, or coffee shop. If you're interested in renting in a specific apartment complex, stop by and get the property manager or building owner's contact information. Ask friends who live in the complex for a reference. Referrals from people you know—especially if the landlord knows they are longtime tenants with a good payment history—can be helpful. Take every opportunity to directly appeal to the owner.

5. Be honest about your bankruptcy. Most apartment complex and property management rental applications ask if you've ever declared bankruptcy and they'll see your bankruptcy on your credit report, so don't try to hide it. Landlords are focused on *currently* past due or *chronically* late paid accounts. This gives them a sense of whether you're likely to pay your rent on time. Most major apartment complexes automatically screen out potential tenants with two or more derogatory accounts on their credit report.

6. Talk with the landlord or property manager directly. Tour a potential rental in person when possible. Come equipped with

your own personal credit references to help lay a positive foundation before they ever see your credit report. Bring a recent credit report and paystub and a reference letter from your employer. Bring a typed statement with a single-paragraph explanation of why you declared bankruptcy and what steps you've taken since to change your financial situation and stay current on all bills. Don't make excuses; just state the facts.

7. Minimize the landlord's risk with extra offers. Landlords want reliable tenants who will pay their rent on time and will respect their property. Offer to pay an extra month's security deposit as a good-faith gesture. Offer to deposit your rent directly into their checking account or to pay it through auto-pay or using a cash app like Venmo, so they don't have to worry about on-time payments or depositing a check. This will often help you win your case.

Need a Furnished Rental?

New local regulations on rental companies like Airbnb and VRBO have created a strong market for furnished rental properties. In many towns, local governments now require a 30-day minimum rental for properties that aren't owner-occupied. Check local rental groups on Facebook first and reach out to any owners whose properties match your needs. Then search Airbnb or VRBO. Select the location, then any month, and then *monthly* for the length of stay. Flag any properties that fit what you want, then reach out to see if they're interested in signing a year's lease instead of looking for month-to-month tenants. If they're interested, they'll usually require you to sign a standard lease agreement, with a partially refundable security deposit. Since the property is fully furnished, it's likely up to half of your rental deposit will be retained to pay for wear and tear on the furnishings.

Chapter 13

Stop Identity Theft in its Tracks

Today, personal and financial information is routinely hacked. People can easily use your identity to drain your accounts, take out personal loans, and max out credit lines they've established in your name. It can happen to anyone at any time.

Sandra Bullock's 1995 thriller *The Net* foreshadowed cyber character assassination when a computer-savvy criminal swapped an average-Jane's identity with that of an unsavory character in a quest to create world chaos. Two decades later, Jason Bateman and Melissa McCarthy's comedy *Identity Thief* was a slapstick moral tale highlighting the serious consequences of having your financial identity stolen. You're building a solid credit history after bankruptcy, and you shouldn't let anyone—fictional or otherwise—jeopardize your new financial security.

I first experienced the effects of identity theft when I received a letter from the IRS telling me I owed thousands of dollars in unpaid income taxes for the $30,000 I'd supposedly made the previous year. I was 9 years old. Someone had illegally used my Social Security number as an employee and had no taxes withheld from their earnings. My parents sorted out that one. More recently, when federal unemployment benefits were being issued on debit cards, someone applied for benefits in my spouse's name; the IRS now requires an annual PIN when we file our taxes. And last year, my debit card was hacked by someone repeatedly purchasing the same small amount through Walmart's online store. My bank texted to see if I recognized the multiple purchases; at my request, they canceled my debit card.

Even small breaches create inconveniences or wreak havoc you neither need nor deserve, especially when you've worked so hard to restore your credit. That's why I strongly recommend that you implement the advice in this chapter to make yourself bulletproof to identity theft, verify whether your personal or financial information is at risk or has been breached, and swiftly stop identity theft if it happens (and clean up the aftershocks) with a minimum of damage to you and your financial reputation.

Tips for Avoiding Identity Theft

I tend to first see the good in people, *and* I also take simple precautions (like looking out the window *before* opening the front door). Simple actions like crossing at the light and looking both ways before you step off the curb protect you from getting hit when crossing the street. Similar precautions protect your identity.

Online games and quizzes and even seemingly benign questions from a stranger can reveal personal data used to secure your identity. We wind up doing the heavy lifting for bad actors without knowing it. Think of the common security questions used to verify your identity on the phone or online. Asking you to invent funny names using your personal information (like "combine your favorite fruit and the name of your first dog to create your action hero name") or having someone guess something about you are common ways hackers gain access to this secure information.

If you're asked, "When you were a kid, did you ever think you'd grow up to be doing this?" and you respond, "Heck no, I wanted to be a professional soccer player," you've just handed them an answer to your secure information. If you don't believe anyone can get secure information from you in everyday conversations, I encourage you to read *The Truth Detector* by Jack Schafer.

Here are my recommendations to maximize your information's security:

- Only give your Social Security number, mother's maiden name, or account numbers to people for verification purposes when *you've* initiated the contact. If you call a company that outsources their customer service calls and feel uncomfortable giving your information to that representative, call a local branch or the company headquarters instead.

- Take outgoing mail to the post office rather than leaving it in your mailbox. This is especially important if the mail contains bills you're paying with a check. Identity thieves love one-stop-shopping where a single envelope contains your account number, checking account number, *and* your signature (which they can then practice forging).

- Remove mail daily from your mailbox to thwart potential identity thieves. Living in a small town, we have a communal mailbox at the road's edge. Occasionally, the back of the mailbox bank pops open, leaving all mail exposed. If you ever see something like this, immediately call the local post office and they'll quickly come to lock it.

- Place a vacation hold on your mail if you will be gone for more than five business days.

- Pay attention to when monthly bills are supposed to arrive. Call creditors if a bill hasn't arrived within a week of that date.

- Change your personal identification number (PIN) or passwords for all credit card, bank, and other online financial accounts annually. Make your PIN something others would be unlikely to guess.

- Install a good spyware program, antivirus program, and virtual private network (VPN) on your computer to protect yourself from hackers if you use online banking or bill-paying services. Identity thieves now use keylogging spyware to capture keystrokes. Criminals mimic you, log in, and transfer money wherever they desire.

- Keep your Social Security card at home, in your safe or in your safe-deposit box, *not* in your wallet.

- Review all charges, payments, deposits, and withdrawals on your billing statements and financial account statements monthly. Immediately contact the company if anything is incorrect.

- Request your free credit reports as often as possible. Review them carefully to make sure you recognize all accounts and that your balances and payment histories are correct.

- Place an active-duty alert on your credit reports if you're in the military and are called up or deployed. This is a special fraud alert option for military members.

- Shred or burn documents containing personal or financial information. Make it difficult for dumpster-diving thieves to get your information. I prefer burning over shredding, but feel free to shred and then burn your financial documents if you want. New pattern recognition scanning software recovers shredded documents, rebuilding them like a digital jigsaw puzzle in minutes.

- Track every expense in a checkbook register or notebook or by using financial software like Quicken Simplifi or a mobile app like Monefy. Save your receipts so you can double-check them against your bank account statement, or check your account balances, income, and expenses daily on your bank's website.

- Keep copies of all your account numbers, expiration dates, and creditor fraud department phone numbers and customer service numbers in a secure place.

Opt Out of Identity Theft

Your first line of defense against home burglaries is to lock your doors, right? That same commonsense advice protects you from identity theft. Having a direct-mail background, I know how bad apples use direct-mail lists to lure people with *preapproved or pre-screened offers* for credit, insurance, and other financial purchases—which carry the greatest risk for identity theft. Opting out can keep these offers from showing up in your mailbox either for five years or permanently.

To start the process, visit optoutprescreen.com and fill out their electronic form, or call them at 888-567-8688. The site is secure, and you must provide any home and mobile telephone numbers,

---

The Spyware Industry Leader for Decades

My personal favorite spyware program is Spybot Search & Destroy, created by Patrick Kolla-ten Venne in 2000. Patrick was so serious about "spyware busting" that he offered Spybot for free for decades, requesting only a donation if you desired and a prayer for the "most beautiful girl in the world." Spybot has protected my computer for decades and has helped others uncripple their computers. As Spybot became the leading spyware, Patrick and his army of volunteer computer sleuths created Safer Networking (safer-networking.org). You can download their free SpyBot Identity Monitor to search for any personal data breaches or buy their combination spyware plus antivirus software.

Few outstanding antivirus software programs exist, according to my late father-in-law, owner of a computer programming company. He firmly believed Kaspersky (usa.kaspersky.com) was the best antivirus and VPN choice on the market for consumers and business owners, but Kaspersky is currently banned from doing business in the United States, which is why our family uses UltraAV and UltraVPN (ultraantivirus.com) to secure our computers. One subscription secures up to 20 devices.

full name, Social Security number, and date of birth. The information you provide is confidential and is *only* used to process your opt-out request. Once you confirm your information, you will be automatically opted out for five years. The system will generate a form for you to print and mail if you want to *permanently* block these financial offers. If you decide to opt out by phone, tell them you want to opt out permanently and they'll send you the form.

Send the form via certified mail, return receipt requested, so you get the pretty green card back showing the date they received and signed for your request. If you don't receive your mail-in form in a few weeks or you're still being deluged with financial junk mail 30 days after the date they signed for your envelope, call them.

Control Who Sees Your Financial Information

Your next step to protect against identity theft is to control who sees the information in your credit reports. By placing a security freeze (also known as a credit freeze) on your credit reports, no one else can open a credit account in your name.

Why Use a Security Freeze?

A security freeze requires that you take a few extra steps whenever you apply for credit—and the time *is* worth the effort. (A security freeze is also helpful if you find yourself financially strapped and your ego wants you to *urgently* get more credit.) Remember that front door you locked when you left home? On a typical day, you leave home, run errands, and return juggling your baby, baby bag, groceries, and everything else. You get out your keys, unlock the door, and turn the knob before you go in. Normal inconvenience, right? Now imagine it is pouring rain, the baby is wet and cranky, and your phone starts ringing with a call you absolutely must take. With a greater urgency to get inside quicker, you might be a bit miffed about that locked door. But how much worse would you feel if you had left your door unlocked and came home to find your home ransacked?

A credit report security freeze is that locked door. It is inconvenient when you're in a hurry to get approved for credit *and* well worth it to know your identity is safe and sound. When you're rebuilding your credit, the last thing you want is to discover someone has been in your financial house, vandalizing your progress. Many companies like LifeLock™ alert you to identity breaches—but the small print always says they can't monitor everything and that they're not responsible if they miss a breach.

How to Request a Security Freeze

Adding a security freeze costs nothing but a bit of your time. How much time depends on whether you want to do it before or after your identity is stolen. Since a security freeze is a mandatory step if your identity has already been stolen, you might as well do it now to avoid identity theft.

All four credit bureaus make it easy to add a security freeze, but you must contact them individually, as they'll be giving you a secure PIN that can *only* be used with their credit report. You can add a security freeze online or via phone or mail (using their printable form). If you opt to mail the form, send it via certified mail, return receipt requested:

Equifax Security Freeze: 888-378-4329; P.O. Box 105788, Atlanta, GA 30348-5788; equifax.com (select the Credit Report Help tab)

Experian Customer Support: 888-397-3742; P.O. Box 9554, Allen, TX 75013; experian.com (select the Credit Support tab)

Innovis Consumer Assistance: 866-712-4546; P.O. Box 1358, Columbus, OH 43216-1358; innovis.com (select the Personal tab)

TransUnion Service Center: 800-916-8800; P.O. Box 160, Woodlyn, PA 19016; transunion.com (select Customer Support on the main menu bar)

Your first choice, when seeking new credit, should always be a company you *currently* do business with (your bank, creditors, or car or mortgage lender). They can *always* access your credit report, monitor your accounts for suspicious activity, and increase your credit line—without you needing to lift the security freeze. For new creditors, you will need to temporarily lift the security freeze so the lender can access your credit report. You can lift the security freeze temporarily online, via phone, or by mail. While you *can* call or go online to temporarily lift your security freeze, I highly recommend requesting the lift by certified mail, return receipt requested. Your return receipt is proof that you—and not someone else—requested the security freeze be lifted.

When applying for credit, ask the creditor which credit bureau they use to check your credit—that way you only have to lift the security freeze at that credit bureau.

Suspect Identity Theft?

Identity theft truly comes in all shapes and sizes. I once helped a family whose disabled adult son was being sued by an apartment complex for unpaid rent. But he lived at home, so he could not possibly have leased another place. A few phone calls to access the documents quickly uncovered and resolved the crime.

If you've ever lost your wallet, been taken in by a financial phishing scheme, or have reason to believe someone has accessed your financial information, I encourage you to place an *initial fraud alert* on your credit reports. This protects against attempts by others to establish a new account, issue an additional card for an existing account, or increase the credit limit on an account—unless you can prove to the creditor that *you* are requesting the change.

With an initial fraud alert, you give the creditor a specific telephone number from the credit bureau that they *must* call to verify that you are the person requesting the credit. If a potential creditor can't reach the credit bureau to get your authorization, the credit request will be denied. An initial fraud alert report stays on your credit report for one year, as does an active-duty fraud alert if you're being deployed. An extended fraud alert—which is used when you know someone has stolen your identity—stays on your credit report for seven years.

To activate a fraud alert, notify Experian by visiting experian.com and selecting the Credit Support tab. Click the link for Fraud Alert. You'll use the same contact phone number and address as you would for a security freeze but will complete the Fraud Alert form instead. Experian will then notify Equifax and TransUnion for you. You will need to notify Innovis separately at 866-712-0021; P.O. Box 530088, Atlanta, GA 30353-0088. Or visit innovis.com, select the Personal tab, and download the fraud alert form to mail your request via certified mail, return receipt requested.

If someone has tried to steal your identity, after you submit your extended alert, be on the lookout for these four signs that someone is using your financial identity, and report this activity to the police:

1. You receive letters stating you're approved for or denied credit at companies where you have never applied for an account.
2. You see unfamiliar charges or skipped check numbers on your bank or credit card statements.
3. Your Social Security personal earnings and benefit statement shows unknown work history and earnings.
4. A string of unfamiliar, out-of-state charges appear on your statements.

Once the extended fraud alert goes into effect, any business wishing to extend credit to you must verify your identity first before issuing you credit. The creditor may attempt to contact you directly, which could cause delays if you haven't kept your contact information current. If you move or change your phone number, your name, or your marital status, for example, be sure to tell the credit bureaus so they can update your file.

Stop Identity Theft in Its Tracks

Pop quiz: You suddenly find your shirt is on fire. Do you run screaming down the street, or do you stop, drop, and roll? Don't panic if you find your identity has been stolen. Your first actions will determine how much chaos the theft creates. Every time you contact creditors or financial institutions regarding your identity theft, document your conversation. Create a logbook and include the name, date, phone number, email address, time, and details of each communication. Confirm all discussions in writing. Keep copies of all correspondence you send and print out any email correspondence. Send all correspondence via certified mail, return receipt requested, to create a paper trail should you need to defend yourself in court against a creditor that attempts to collect on a fraudulent debt.

To put out the fire, so to speak, take these six steps immediately:

STEP 1.

Put an *extended* fraud alert on your credit report files, which will stay active for seven years. An extended fraud alert protects you from *anyone* establishing a new credit account, adding a card to an existing account, or increasing your credit limit. As with an *initial* fraud alert, the credit bureau provides a unique number that lenders must use to verify that you are the person requesting the credit. If they can't obtain authorization, the credit request will be denied.

STEP 2.

Report the identity theft to local law enforcement. Depending on where you live, police will have you file a police report or a miscellaneous incident report. When you file your report, include anything you know about the dates the theft may have occurred, what accounts may have been opened, and anything you might know or suspect about the alleged thief. Some police agencies only offer "automated online reports." Bypass that process and request a face-to-face meeting with a police officer. Seeing you can help them identify the "fake you" when the person is caught. Filing a face-to-face report also lets you provide additional information that the automated report may overlook.

STEP 3.

File an *ID Theft Affidavit* with the Federal Trade Commission (identitytheft.gov). These documents help prevent you from being financially responsible for any fraudulent activity. This website walks you through the steps to report what happened, with as much detail as you have. The site uses that information to create a personal recovery plan. If you'd prefer, you can create a free account on their website and they will go through the steps with you.

STEP 4.

Send reports and letters and any other supporting documents to creditors or collection agencies that hold the fraudulent accounts. Send these documents via certified mail, return receipt requested, as proof that the account is not your responsibility. Should any judgments be entered against you due to these fraudulent accounts, you'll have proof that you notified creditors and collectors as soon as you became aware of the identity theft.

STEP 5.

Close and reopen all current financial and credit accounts. Call
or write to the security or fraud investigation department at every
company where you have a financial account. Request that they
close your account and open another one with a new account number. Send each letter via certified mail, return receipt requested.
Remember to send *copies*—never originals—of supporting documents, unless they tell you they need an original, signed copy.
Follow up any phone calls with a letter outlining what was discussed in the phone call. Report any fraudulent ATM, debit card,
or stolen/forged check transactions to your bank or credit union.
Ask them to put a stop-payment order on all incoming charges.
Close your checking and savings accounts, and ask your financial
institution to reopen them and issue new account numbers. Get
a new ATM card, account number, and password. Do the same
for any investment accounts you have. Many financial companies
offer fraud alerts on debit and credit card charges and will flag
unusual activity, usually texting or calling you to see whether you
recognize the charges. Sign up for these free services if you don't
already use them.

STEP 6.

Determine where fraudulent bills are going. Contact creditors
with fraudulently opened accounts. Politely direct the creditor
to send you a copy of the account application used to open any
account in your name and to provide the address where they are
sending the credit card or bills. They are required to send you this
application and any other business transaction records relating to
the account in your name, at no charge, within 30 days of your
request. Follow your telephone request with a mailed request,
sent certified, return receipt requested.

Once you have the address where the mail in your name is being sent, give all information to the police. *Do not track the criminal yourself.* Unlike in the movies, many identity thieves are often armed and dangerous criminals. Contact the local postmaster at that zip code and submit a mail forwarding form so that all mail in your name goes to a postal box you set up. This can uncover other accounts that have been opened or applied for in your name. Once a fraudulent account is closed and the identity theft issue has been resolved, request a letter from the creditor stating that they have closed the disputed account and that you are not responsible for the fraudulent debts. This letter will be your best proof if this debt ever reappears on your credit reports or with a collection agency.

Recovering from Identity Theft

Having someone impersonate you and steal your financial information is a personal violation that activates the same adrenaline reaction as if someone entered your home and physically stole something precious—which they have, in a sense. The identity thief attempted to or did hijack your reputation, your integrity, and your money. Creditors don't know whether you are the real you or the fake you. So don't be surprised if they seem hostile or disparage your character as you're recovering from this identity theft. A creditor's perception of you as a criminal doesn't make it so. Stay the course. Be calm and helpful. Help them help you.

You know who you are. Help them see who you are, and don't take it personally. Whoever the identity thief may be, they haven't done this *to you.* They have simply *done* this. The best way to heal is to recognize that this wasn't a personal attack. The thief simply took advantage of a situation they discovered. Recognizing this will help you more quickly and easily recover mentally and emotionally from an identity theft.

SECTION IV

IF YOU FIND YOURSELF
IN OVER YOUR
HEAD AGAIN

Chapter 14

Triage

It's not uncommon for your finances to spin out of control again after bankruptcy, despite your best intentions. Not having cash on hand to do what you want, when you want, can be frustrating. Borrowing money provides instant gratification. Most people start using credit again thinking *this* time will be different. Then something happens.

You carry a balance for a few months to finance an appliance or essential furniture. One day you realize you're charging everyday items, just as you did before your bankruptcy. Bankruptcy was supposed to stop this endless cycle and give you a fresh start, right? Things may already be as bad as they were before your bankruptcy—or headed that way—which is why this section is important, whether you are already stuck in the debt cycle again or want to detour around it.

While helping people break the debt cycle after bankruptcy, I've identified five factors that determine whether someone ends up deep in debt again:

1. **Underearning.** Bringing in less money than your expenses *and* less than you are worth.
2. **Overspending.** Spending more than is coming in and not regularly setting aside small amounts to cover inevitable large expenses.
3. **Undersaving.** Not having enough money set aside from your income to create a cash cushion.

4. **Overcompensating.** Thinking more *things* will make you feel worthy and wealthy.

5. **Underinsuring.** Choosing lower premiums that leave you with higher out-of-pocket medical bills, skipping comprehensive and collision auto insurance, not having a term life insurance policy, and bypassing disability insurance.

Most people who wind up back in debt after bankruptcy didn't have the information I'm sharing here. They didn't have specific guidance to update their credit reports, systematically rebuild their credit in meaningful ways, and keep up with debts they reaffirm or take on after bankruptcy. All these steps are essential to creating a strong financial future.

When you don't update your credit reports to show debts were discharged under bankruptcy, creditors believe you have accounts that are past due or in collection. Frustrated you're not making progress, you may even pay debt collectors for a debt you no longer owe. You pay higher interest rates and higher insurance premiums when you don't *systematically* rebuild your credit in ways that raise your credit score. You may even have jumped at quick credit-rebuilding schemes. Can you hear the train whistle blowing? *All aboard the runaway debt train.*

Armed with the right financial information, you can escape before that debt train pulls out of the station, picks up steam on that tight curve, and speeds off into the night, nonstop to Bankruptcyville.

Finding yourself in debt again can be enraging and scary. Your ego will use this opportunity to trash-talk you endlessly. These thoughts and feelings aren't important. What *is* important is the positive action you take. First, you'll go to urgent care for triage to stop the financial bleeding and stabilize the situation, then head into emergency surgery to improve the immediate health of your income. Then . . . it's time to rehab your expenses.

Triage to Stop Financial Bleeding

Take these six steps to stop the bleeding:

STEP 1.

Switch from *debt management* to *debt repayment*. Here's the difference: When you send in a $200 payment on your credit card balance, then charge $200 that month, you're *managing* your debt as part of the debt cycle. *Repaying* your debt means at the end of the month you pay off your credit card in full using savings you've set aside for that purpose, *not* money you get paid this month.

STEP 2.

Freeze all unnecessary spending, starting with credit cards. First, switch all autopayments to the minimum monthly payment. Second, cancel all monthly nonessential charges that run through your credit cards *or* your bank accounts, and switch essentials like your phone bill to your debit card. You can find these monthly expenses on your most recent statements. Start there and cancel everything you buy on a subscription. Once you've eliminated monthly recurring expenses, look back through all your statements, starting with this month's and next month's statements *from last year*. If it's May, review last year's May and June statements for big *quarterly or annual* expenses on autopay. Cancel any that are non-essential. For essential items, switch them to monthly, even if that means you pay a small fee. If you're itching to use your credit cards, stick them in the freezer in a water-filled plastic bag, where you can't easily access them to add new debt.

STEP 3.

Commit to not borrowing any money from anywhere. When you stop charging, it can be tempting to bridge the gap between your income and your expenses with personal loans from friends and family, cash advances, and payday loans. These are all ways of borrowing against your future income. Don't do it. Also avoid tapping your everyday or retirement savings, and steer clear of buy now, pay later offers. Whether it's a subscription or a new dining room set, do not buy anything unless you have the money to pay for it now.

STEP 4.

Give yourself and your family members a temporary allowance. This may sound odd or controlling, but it can be a lifesaver. Most people spend an enormous amount weekly with no idea of where the money goes. You leave home with $40 and by day's end your money's spent with nothing to show for it. Set a specific time frame for the allowance (60 to 90 days perhaps), with a weekly check-in with family. Journal or check in with a friend if you live alone. Money can carry a lot of emotional baggage, so use that check-in to talk through any feelings that come up as you cut back on your spending. Download for free my *Heal Your Relationship with Money* workbook (rebuildafterbankruptcy.com) that asks 28 questions to help you identify the core beliefs that have created your attitudes about money, debt, and prosperity.

In most families one person will be more financially savvy than the others. Work together as a team and use your strengths. I'm the money person in my family. When big expenses are coming up and we don't want to move money out of savings to pay them, I'll let my family know and remind them of what we do want, based on what we've agreed on: "We've got the annual insurance payment coming out this month," or "With the Grand Canyon trip coming up, we want to make sure we have plenty of cash on hand for all the fun activities we want to do." Then I'll share my recommended action: "So, until this date, we need to spend no more than this amount each week on eating out and other extra expenses." I'll ask if anyone has any questions or objections, and I take time to listen to concerns, questions, and additional information others have about upcoming expenses.

Not getting what we want when we want can push buttons, so it's important to reframe any sense of lack into a sense of purpose, which you can do by remembering this: eliminating expenses now—for a few months—makes it possible to have more of what you want in life, without debt. If you choose not to cut back in the short term, you might get the things you want when you want them, but you'll continue to wrestle with debt. Set up a temporary allowance for up to six months and the result can truly be permanent prosperity.

STEP 5.

Pay essential and important bills. Pay the minimum due for your *secured* debts: your car loan, mortgage or rent, insurance, and essential utilities and living expenses. When I say *essential*, I mean fuel, electric, water, trash, a bare-bones phone bill, and prescriptions. Cable or streaming services, the Amazon Prime account, and mail-order subscriptions are *not* essential.

STEP 6.

Make small good-faith payments on other unsecured debts. Take 25 percent of whatever is left from trimming your expenses and paying essentials and put it into savings. Use the remaining 75 percent to make good-faith payments on your other unsecured debts, even if it's $5 a month. Just because a creditor says you *must* pay a certain amount each month doesn't mean you have to sacrifice your and your family's well-being. Yes, you may fall behind in your payments temporarily. But for debts not reported to the credit bureaus, the most important thing is that you're still paying *something* on them each month. Tell each of your creditors that this is how much you can realistically pay each month right now. Do *not* overextend yourself trying to make the creditor happy. (See Chapter 17 for more on how to talk with your creditors when you're at risk of falling behind on your payments (or already have).

A client who opened a small restaurant supplemented her income as a massage therapist, which she lost temporarily when she broke her wrist. Without her massage income, she fell behind on essential payments to a restaurant supplier, who demanded payment in full before her next delivery. When we ran her numbers, it was clear she could pay for the next shipment COD (cash on delivery), continue generating money to keep her doors open, and pay the supplier the outstanding balance *if* the supplier was willing to accept a monthly payment of 5 percent of that balance until it was paid off. She presented the offer to her supplier, explaining that she wanted to pay them in full *and* that the only way she could do that was to keep the restaurant open and pay the balance as proposed. They appreciated her honesty and accepted the plan, and their working relationship continued for decades.

All that matters is that you're committed to paying your debt in full. Set up your repayment plan for unsecured debts over enough months that it doesn't create undue hardship for you and your family.

Those are your steps to triage the situation and stabilize your finances again. Next, it's time for surgery to improve the immediate health of your income.

Surgery to Fortify Your Income

Have you noticed how the go-to advice from most financial experts for increasing income is to take on a side gig or an extra job? That's hard to do if you're already working two or more jobs, are a single parent, or are caring for aging relatives or someone with special needs. Sure, taking on extra work is a great way to increase your income if you can do it. But thinking outside the box is even better.

A single mom and her four pre-teens made extra money by stuffing envelopes and fulfilling orders for small local companies. When I lived on a houseboat, I rented a spare room from a friend to fulfill my book orders. A family whose goal was for the wife to stay at home with their three young children made up the difference in her lost income by renting one side of their garage to someone who was restoring an antique car and renting a part of their driveway to someone else looking for a spot to park their boat. Renting out a room, a part of your garage, or part of your driveway or yard are easy ways to generate extra income. So is leasing out an extra car. Turo, the vehicle version of Airbnb, lets you rent your car to individual renters.

I get that giving up your privacy by sharing your space is hard—*and* it generates monthly cash to break the debt cycle. When financial times were tough in the old days, widows and other cash-strapped families who owned homes rented out rooms and became boarding houses, providing housing and meals for single people, short-term travelers, or those who couldn't afford to rent and furnish their own home.

Home-sharing options like Airbnb and VRBO aren't always the best option financially when you're looking to rent out a part of your home because of the fees they collect. Local universities, hospitals, and midsize companies often need monthly rentals for visiting professors, medical professionals, or executives and consultants who don't want to live in a hotel. Call the public affairs office of universities and hospitals and the human resources department of corporations near you to see whether they need short-term rentals in your area.

Think outside the box and focus on your goal. As a fledging writer in Manhattan, I rented the upper room in a loft owned by a young couple who had just had a baby. They had a long-term plan for their home and were willing to sacrifice privacy for a few years so they could pay off their mortgage early. In addition to me, they had a tenant who commuted from his family home upstate. He arrived at the loft on Monday after work and left on Friday morning. Another tenant was a professional photographer who traveled often. She had standing contracts with *Soap Opera Digest* and *Food & Wine* magazines, and when she was home, she used the main room for photo shoots. Upon going downstairs, I'd often find scantily clad actors lounging in the living room, or a kitchen full of tantalizing food with notes like *Don't eat the strawberries!* As it turns out, that glossy sheen you see in magazine photos is courtesy of a generous spray of WD-40.

Rehab Your Expenses for More Income

Paring expenses and freeing up trapped money makes your income go further. Implement the following strategies on a regular basis for the best results:

STEP 1.

Sell items you can do without. Start with big-ticket items, like a boat, classic car, or motorcycle. Yes, they may have sentimental value, but more importantly, they have practical value. They represent trapped money you could use to reset your finances. You can always replace the items once you're back on track again, as Thomas

Jefferson did. An avid book collector, Jefferson sold his entire library in 1815 to pay off his personal debt and keep his farm running without having to sell off his slaves and break up families—a common practice at the time. By the time of his death in 1826, he'd built up a new library containing thousands of books.

Freeing up trapped money is one way to add to your income. Reducing your costs tied to expensive items you own but rarely use is another. To determine whether selling a big-ticket item is worth it to you, calculate what the item costs you to own versus what it would cost to rent it for the same number of days you use it. Let's say you have a boat. Write down how many days you spent *on* the boat in the past 12 months. Don't include the days you spent cleaning, etc.—only the days you *used* the boat. Then write down how much money you've spent on the boat in the past 12 months. Include all monthly payments, insurance, repairs, dock fees, and supplies. Finally, calculate how many hours you spent maintaining the boat, then multiply that number by an hourly rate for your time. These numbers tell you how much you've paid to own the boat in the past year. Make a few calls to see what it would cost to rent a boat for the number of days you used yours. If it's less expensive to rent, sell the boat. You can always buy another one.

Sell big-ticket items now and get the best price you can while *you* control the transaction; don't wait until you're desperate to sell. Word of mouth, bulletin boards, local newspaper ads, Craigslist, Facebook Marketplace, and specialized consignment stores are great ways to sell large and small items. Garage sales can also generate extra money. Go through all your possessions to find books, DVDs, CDs, videotapes, extra electronic equipment, appliances, collectibles, clothes, sports equipment, tools, and other items you can sell. Bonus: you'll declutter your home in the process.

Pace yourself. Start with larger items, then focus on one category (like books), one room or one shelf, box, or drawer at a time.

Converting your first batch of clutter into cold, hard cash may motivate you to continue. If people ask why you're purging items, just say, "I figured someone else would enjoy having them more than I'm enjoying them now." Down the road, with your finances under control, you can again buy any items you still want—for cash.

STEP 2.

Track expenses weekly for a full month. Remember the story I shared earlier about the family whose daughter learned the power of being able to shape her future through the financial choices she makes now? That power can be yours too—by learning how you and your family spend money. Put a shoebox on the kitchen counter for a month. Get or create receipts for everything you buy and put those receipts into the shoebox. Ask your family to do the same. If you use a vending machine at work, immediately write "Soda, $2.50" and the date on a scrap of paper, then stick it in your wallet or your pocket. When you get home, empty your homemade receipts into the shoebox. At the end of each week or month, add up all expenses for that period. Divide the expenses into categories so you can see exactly where your money went. Review your choices and confirm you're spending your money *exactly* the way you want to. Information gives you the power to make different decisions and frees up money to pay debts or to create what you really want in life.

STEP 3.

Examine where you overspend on essentials. Some necessities should *not* be scrimped on, like life insurance, if you have a family you want to take care of should you die unexpectedly. At the same time, there's no reason to overpay. For instance, premiums on term life insurance are much lower than premiums on an insurance policy that has a cash value (such as whole life, variable life, or universal life insurance). Buying term life insurance means you can get a larger amount of life insurance for less. You may find it helpful to replace your cash-value life insurance with a 15–20-year term life insurance policy. Many outstanding insurance companies sell term life insurance without charging a commission. Apply for the new insurance and, once you're accepted, cash out or cancel any former policy. To cancel, either visit the insurance company's website for instructions, or write to your former insurance company and ask them to send you cancellation forms *and* forms for the return of any cash value. Send your letter via certified mail, return receipt requested. You should hear back within two to three weeks. If you don't, call your insurance agent or the company directly. Once you receive any cash value owed to you, use that money to prepay your new premiums, put it toward your most pressing bill, or add it to your savings.

The Insurance Information Institute (iii.org) is my go-to place for information on choosing life insurance. They can help you figure out what coverage you need and understand what's important in an insurance company's rating. They provide helpful videos, articles, and data on life insurance.

Another excellent resource is Term4Sale (term4sale.com), an unbiased life insurance search engine. Fill out their eight-question form for instant results based on your answers. Search for a plan with a 15–20-year term (they're usually renewable), guaranteed to age 70 or higher, with a minimum life company rating (A.M. Best rating) of A or better (this includes A+ and A++). Once you click the Compare Now button, you'll get a list of results and will see a Health Analyzer button on the left side. Clicking that will take you to a 10-question form, which you can complete to see how likely it is you'll get the quoted rate.

Another good site is SelectQuote (selectquote.com), which helps you compare quotes from a highly selective group of insurance companies and connects you with a live insurance agent.

STEP 4.

Set up a budget based on how you want your existing money to work for you. Once you've figured out what your essential monthly expenses are, it's time to do something with that information. You can do what budget counselors do—create and implement a budget plan—*if* you can approach your money situation objectively, communicate and negotiate *unemotionally* with your creditors, and stick with your plan without being accountable to anyone other than yourself (and your family).

You're not alone if you can't separate emotionally from your situation or stick to a budget. Most people lack this ability, regardless of how much money they have. For decades, budget counselor Judy Lawrence has worked with clients from all financial walks of life. She once had an heiress client who received over a million dollars a year from a trust fund—and couldn't make ends meet. Judy got her to work within a budget of $20,000 a month, and she was able to save, donate, *and* build her art collection. No matter how rich you are, you'll never have enough without a solid plan outlining how you will use your money and without healing the core beliefs, like unworthiness, that keep you from feeling financially secure.

I once had a client who believed she'd feel worthy once she had a million dollars in the bank. When she reached her financial goal and discovered her self-worth hadn't changed, she thought the magic number might be $2 million. Then $4 million. When she reached $9 million and still didn't feel it was enough, she contacted me.

Most of us haven't learned how to make our money work *for* us. Instead, we're constantly trying to cram our expenses into an unrealistic budget. For a really good do-it-yourself program, I recommend getting a copy of *The Budget Kit: The Common Cents Money Management Workbook* by Judy Lawrence. The workbook is simple and straightforward, and it prepares you for expected *and* unexpected expenses throughout the year. If you're computer-savvy, Judy also offers the worksheets from the book as Excel spreadsheets so you can easily input your information, make changes, and run through "what if" scenarios to your heart's content. (The book is free if you hire Judy for a budgeting session; you'll find her contact information in the Resources section at the end of the book.)

Many nonprofit organizations, including HUD-approved organizations (those approved by the Department of Housing and Urban Development) offer free budget counseling. The programs highlighted in the "State and Territory Housing Authority" section (Chapter 12) offer excellent online or in-person budgeting courses for free or for a modest fee (usually under $60). And some offer incredible free courses, videos, and articles. Others offer debt management or debt repayment programs, in which they help you consolidate your debt into one monthly payment, which includes the program's small monthly fee. Although the quality of service and the cost varies by organization and location, you can generally find good budgeting help. You'll find more details on budget and credit counseling in Chapter 15.

Falling Behind on Reaffirmed Debt

If you're having a hard time keeping up with reaffirmation payments and can no longer cancel the agreement, first determine what financial changes you can make to catch up.

Once you've exhausted other options, you may have to surrender the reaffirmed item. If that's the case, call the creditor to see whether they will take back the item in exchange for complete forgiveness of the debt. It's highly unlikely, but it *is* worth asking. If the creditor won't take back the item, see if you can sell it and work out a repayment agreement with the creditor for the balance of the debt. Once you sell the item and pay a good chunk of the debt, ask the creditor to spread out the remaining balance so that your monthly payment is half of what it was under the reaffirmation agreement. Don't worry if the creditor balks. Stick to your guns and let them know that this lower amount is all you can pay each month and keep sending them that amount with or without an agreement. You have the power in this situation, not the creditor.

Another option is to let the creditor repossess the item. They'll sell it at auction and charge you for the balance owed. This is a last resort; a repossession will show up as a big black post-bankruptcy mark on your credit reports, so exhaust all other options first. As a rule, you will get more money selling the item yourself and applying that money to paying off the debt.

You may wind up with a small black mark on your credit report from falling behind on your payments under the reaffirmation agreement. It's not ideal to have a couple of 30-day-late or 60-day-late notations on your credit report after bankruptcy. But it would be far worse to have a 120-day-late notation, a history of 30-day-late payments, or a repossession. Cut your losses, get rid of the item, and repay the debt on a schedule you can afford.

Selling an Upside-Down Car

Believe it or not, you can sell your car when you *owe* more than the car is worth. First, find a buyer, negotiate a price, and make sure the buyer is approved for financing if they're not paying cash. Next, meet with or call your lender. Tell them you have a buyer and let the lender know how much the buyer is willing to pay. If there's a shortfall, ask your lender if they'll accept the purchase amount as a huge payment on your loan and then issue you a personal loan for the remaining balance, with lower monthly payments until you've paid the full amount.

Having a buyer pay $20,000 on a 6 percent car loan could save *you* thousands of dollars in interest. But why would your *lender* accept this agreement? Because they'll avoid the cost of repossession if you're unable to pay your car loan. Don't worry if the first person you talk to can't help you. Keep asking to speak to the next person up the ladder until you connect with a person who has the authority to work with you. Smaller banks and private finance companies may be more willing to work with you. Some larger lenders may balk at helping you since the remaining amount you owe would no longer be secured by the car. See if they'll take something else as collateral. The answer is always no if you don't ask.

Chapter 15

Financial Counseling

Sometimes having a third party act as a go-between helps if you need to work out a debt repayment plan with your creditors. If a friend or family member has a healthy relationship with their own money and can stay unemotional, you can give creditors permission to talk with that person. Alternatively, using a budget or credit counselor could be a good option to help you work through your financial issues, which *may* include helping you create a debt repayment plan that fits your family's income and creates financial stability.

Let's look at how to find a reputable counseling agency and a counselor who is a good fit for you. Then I'll share what you can expect while working with a financial counselor.

Finding a Reputable Budget or Credit Counselor

Some financial counseling agencies receive bad press, often for good reason. Most credit counseling agencies help both you and your creditors. Credit card issuers like Visa, Mastercard, Discover, and American Express pay credit counseling agencies to help you pay your bills. The creditor is assured they'll receive monthly payments on your debt—in some amount. You get a break on your interest and avoid having a serious black mark on your credit after bankruptcy. The financial counseling agency is the middleman, making it all happen. Some people like independent financial counselors because they're not receiving payments from creditors to offset their expenses; the fee charged by these professionals will usually be higher than if you work with a middleman.

I recommend working with agencies that belong to the National Foundation for Credit Counseling (nfcc.org). NFCC has been around for 75 years, and member organizations gain accreditation by requiring certification training for *all* credit counselors in their organization. Member organizations must also adhere to a strict code of ethics.

Your best bet for finding an NFCC member is to start with the credit counseling services in your state, which are provided through your housing authority's website. Although the NFCC offers a 24-hour automated phone line and an online *We'll Contact You* form, the selected agency they refer you to may not be a good fit.

The Financial Counseling Association of America (FCAA) also offers a search engine that connects you to a single counseling agency, but FCAA members aren't required to be accredited or certified. I believe it's better to select a counseling agency on your own to ensure it suits you. Contact different agencies and tell them you're looking for *household budgeting help*.

Many NFCC member organizations offer online and phone support as well as in-person counseling, with varied hours that often include evenings and weekends. If the agency you contact isn't a good fit in terms of availability, ask for a referral from them for an agency that's open during the hours you need to meet.

Many good independent counseling services are *not* NFCC members. Whether or not they offer debt management repayment programs, they have no governing body to protect your rights and ensure the counselor you're working with is trained and/or certified. If you're thinking of hiring an independent agency, thoroughly vet them using the criteria above and ask for references from past clients.

Some offices of larger credit counseling services are more *consumer*-friendly while others are more *creditor*-friendly. Shop around to find an organization willing to work on your behalf.

Choose the Best Budget or Credit Counselor for You

Choosing the best financial counselor is like choosing the best credit card—there is no one best counselor for everyone. The best counselor for *you* depends on your needs. Individual financial coaches work well if you want hands-on guidance, but they will also expect you to be actively involved in repairing your finances. Get clear on what you want help with and on what will be required of you.

For instance, people I counseled were required to commit to not adding *any* new debt, one day at a time. You had to actively change your thinking about debt and money, explore and expand your financial knowledge and beliefs, replace negative thoughts and actions about money with more positive ones, and set concrete, attainable goals on what you wanted to do, be, and experience in life (using my GoalGetting strategy in Chapter 7).

Criteria for a Good Credit Counselor

Ask to meet with an experienced credit counselor who has been with the agency for at least *five* years, even if the agency is an NFCC member. Newly hired credit counselors at NFCC member agencies receive a few weeks of training and follow an experienced counselor around. After their initial orientation, counselors begin the certification process, which takes 18 months. During that time, the credit counselor is tested on material covering counseling psychology, consumer rights, and collection practices. As a result, a new counselor may not have experience with or knowledge about your particular problem. Your financial future is too important to use an inexperienced counselor. When you meet with the counselor for your free or low-cost (usually $20–$50) budget counseling session, get all answers to these questions *in writing*:

1. Which of my creditors have worked with you in the past to reduce payments or freeze or lower interest and fees? Not all creditors willingly negotiate with credit counselors. If most or all your creditors *are* willing to negotiate, a repayment plan may be in your best interest. If most of your creditors *won't* work with the credit counselor, a repayment plan won't be as helpful.

2. How can I pay my monthly payment? Most agencies use autopay, so that your monthly payment is withdrawn directly from your bank account. Autopayments ensure your payments will be on time and will make it easier for you to stick with a repayment plan, because you don't have to think about it once autopay is set up. But if you prefer to pay in other ways (certified check, money order, cash), ask whether those options are available. You can also ask to pay a portion weekly or every other week to match your paydays, so the full payment arrives on time, if that kind of arrangement works for you.

3. *When* will my creditors be paid? Some counseling services send money to creditors on a specific date each month, which can cause your creditors to be paid after their due dates. Ask if the counseling service works with your creditors to either change your due dates or set up your payment schedule based on when you get paid. The best services will work around your bills' due dates *and* when you get paid.

4. How can I see the progress I'm making on my debt repayment plan? You should be able to regularly see how much of your payment goes to debt repayment, to interest, and to the agency for its services. Most larger credit counseling services provide 24/7 online access to your account. Others send monthly reports via mail or email. After you've made three to six months of payments, request a copy of your credit reports from annualcreditreport.com to verify the creditors are reporting your accounts the way the counselor said they would.

5. Do I have to include *all* debts in the repayment plan or only some? Accounts that have low balances or that are current don't need to be listed in the repayment plan, unless you want them to be. Don't let a credit counselor strong-arm you into putting all your debts into the repayment plan unless you believe it's the only way you'll get them paid off. Each debt included in the plan will cost you a monthly fee that you could put toward your debt balance or into savings.

6. Will I always deal with *you* or at least get a live person on the phone when I call during regular business hours? You'll also want to find out how long it takes for them to return phone calls. Make sure you're comfortable both with their answers and with any other people on your team. After your free budget counseling session, call your counselor once or twice with any questions you have about the budget paperwork to ensure your questions are easily answered and your phone calls are promptly returned.

7. What will my monthly payments be, and how much of that will go toward debt repayment and how much goes toward fees? Generally, expect to pay between $20 and $50 in setup fees, and $5 *a month* for each creditor. If you're paying much more than that, the counselor isn't helping.

What to Expect When You Use a Budget or Credit Counselor

Call the financial counselor to make an appointment. Bring paperwork with you showing your assets, debts, expenses, and income. Bring the statements, bills, and receipts they ask you to bring. The counselor should conduct an in-depth interview with you to help you set up a household budget, separating your needs from your wants. Helping set up a detailed spending plan should be their primary focus. If they immediately pitch you on their credit counseling services or a debt repayment plan, they may be more interested in making money off your debts than helping you create a workable financial plan.

This first budget counseling session may be all you'll need. Or you may want to continue working with the counselor to organize repaying your debts through their repayment program or a program you create for yourself. Credit counselors are *only* helpful when you have income left after paying your essential expenses, which can be used to pay your creditors. Even part-time income may be enough to get you started.

Do *not* make any payments to or sign any papers with a debt repayment organization until *after* they've given you the specific amount you'll pay under their plan. Ask every question you have and make certain you understand the answers—and get them in writing. Explore all your options and then pick the one you believe will work best for you.

If you decide to continue working with your budget counselor to set up a repayment plan, they will negotiate with your creditors on the terms of the agreement. Your credit counselor should be able to get your creditors to immediately freeze or reduce their interest rate—or do so *after* you've made three to six on-time payments.

Larger creditors like Bank of America and Citi—which often negotiate lower interest rates only when you use a credit counseling service—are more likely to lower or freeze your interest rate immediately. Most agencies also will try to get creditors to accept smaller payments from you and lower or eliminate late payment and overlimit penalties. Some can get creditors to update your account status on your credit reports, and sometimes a credit counselor can stop creditor phone calls to you.

Basically, a debt repayment plan gives you a way to pay off your debts within a set period, ensuring your creditors get back what they lent you, usually with lower interest rates. Most programs require monthly payments equal to about 3 percent of your debt, usually over 36 months, as with Chapter 13 bankruptcy. For $10,000 in debt, 3 percent would be $300, so you would pay approximately $10,800 over the course of three years. Under a repayment plan, the agency will pay your creditors directly, dividing your monthly payment among them. Stick with the program and your debts could be paid off within three years.

Creditors generally only report to the credit bureaus that you're in a repayment plan if you're paying less than your normal minimum monthly payment *or* if your payments under the plan are paid late. Check with the Better Business Bureau for complaints about an agency's payment history. After three to six months of repayment through a good credit counselor, your credit report should show your payments as current.

In general, it is better to show you paid your account with budgeting help than to show you were consistently late or to wind up with a post-bankruptcy charge-off on your credit report.

Once You Finish Your Debt Repayment Plan

Once you finish the repayment program, your accounts will be adjusted to show your account was paid in full. Once you complete your repayment program, request your credit reports again. Use the strategies in Chapter 2 to verify all accounts paid under the repayment program are reported accurately and update them to show your credit history in the best light possible. It's not uncommon for credit reports to show you're still in a debt repayment or debt management program. Other times, your credit reports will show you still have past-due bills, even after you've paid those bills.

How to Make More Than You Spend

Declaring bankruptcy and getting debt relief is empowering. But these actions don't do any good if you still spend more than you bring in. You'll eventually find yourself back in debt—caught in the vicious debt cycle. To break this cycle, I recommend using a money manager and expense tracker app like Monefy and following the strategies outlined in these books:

- *How to Get Out of Debt, Stay Out of Debt and Live Prosperously* by Jerrold Mundis
- *Money Drunk/Money Sober: 90 Days to Financial Freedom* by Julia Cameron and Mark Bryan
- *The Budget Kit: The Common Cents Money Management Workbook* by Judy Lawrence
- *When Money Is the Drug: The Compulsion for Credit, Cash and Chronic Debt* by Donna Boundy

---

Chapter 16

12 Steps to Financial Freedom

If the way you handle money day-to-day keeps you from digging your way out of debt, you may be a compulsive or habitual over-spender or compulsive gambler. While people fall into these patterns for various reasons, at their core these issues aren't really about money—they're about coping with deeper underlying struggles, but the "solution" just deepens your debt. 12 Step programs like Debtors Anonymous and Gamblers Anonymous are great programs. But how do you know if you really have a problem?

Conquer Habitual Overspending

If you think you might be a compulsive or habitual over-spender, Debtors Anonymous can help. DA offers support and guidance to help you overcome barriers to your financial recovery. You do not need to be in debt to be a DA member; the only requirement is a willingness to not incur any unsecured debt *today*. People are drawn to DA for many reasons: business failures, a pattern of bouncing checks, excessive student loans, shopping therapy, unpaid taxes, gambling, real estate losses, even messy divorces.

DA is founded on the principle that financial solvency—building up to a positive net worth—starts with taking responsibility for your debts *and* for your actions that created the debts. A good DA meeting can help you repay your creditors in a positive way, help you set up a budget or spending plan, and help you work with what you *have* without getting stressed or financially strapped trying to pay the squeakiest wheel. People in DA focus on their habits and build friendships with others in a debt-free space where you can work through your money issues. They've either been there before or are going through the same thing.

As supportive as Debtors Anonymous groups can be, be forewarned: some factions frown on bankruptcy. This attitude mostly was born of weariness from seeing people show up in debt up to their eyeballs just a few years after they declared bankruptcy. But don't let that deter you from getting the support you need. Over the past three decades, a growing tribe of people have joined DA right after bankruptcy—and remain solvent.

At debtorsanonymous.org you can find a complete list of meetings, both virtual and in person. Virtual meetings are held via video, phone, or email. If you're on the fence about attending a meeting, I recommend listening to a few speakers who share their experiences through audio recordings, which you can find on the Fellowship Podcasts page under Fellowship Services.

Break Up with Your Debt

You're not alone if you spend money to make yourself feel better, out of fear of doing without, as a way of expressing your love, or to be *accepted* by others. Starting today, change the *emotional* aspect of your spending habits a little at a time. When you crave the quick fix of spending money to feel better, stop. Slow down, take deep breaths, go for a walk, garden, putter around the house, take a hot bath, journal, dance, cry, work out, beat up your pillow, or phone a friend who is also breaking up with their debt. Repeat a simple mantra such as *I am safe, and I am loved.*

Clear Out the Clutter

Take time to clear out some clutter in your life. In the process, you may find something you forgot you owned, which is almost as good as going out and buying something new! Studies show that clutter and debt are often connected in our lives. That's why my colleague Janet L. Hall and I wrote *30 Days to Eliminate Clutter and Debt* (G&D Media, 2024; clutteranddebt.com). This book combines debt reduction, organizing, time management, and prosperity principles so you can make the inner changes that bring your clutter and debt under control.

Bet on Yourself with Help from Gamblers Anonymous

Like compulsive or habitual overspending, compulsive gambling can derail your financial security. The U.S. Department of Public Health estimates that 28 million American adults suffer from compulsive gambling—a serious illness that creates financial and emotional problems.

Gambling takes many forms. It could be obsessively playing the lottery, investing large sums of money in risky ventures, or continually starting up new businesses with the dream of striking it rich. Basically, it's any action you take with the hope of getting a big payoff to fix a financial issue or to feel better. If you like betting, whether or not you think it's a problem for you, honestly answer the following 20 questions, adapted from Gamblers Anonymous (GA):

1. Do you ever take time off work to go gambling or to recuperate from gambling?
2. Has gambling made your home life unhappy?
3. Has gambling affected your reputation?

4. Have you ever felt bad after gambling?
5. Do you ever gamble to get money to pay debts or solve financial difficulties?
6. Does gambling decrease your ambition or your efficiency?
7. After losing, do you feel you must return as soon as possible so you can win back your losses?
8. After a win, do you have a strong urge to win more?
9. Do you often gamble until your last dollar is gone?
10. Do you ever borrow money to finance your gambling or to pay for essentials you couldn't buy because you gambled away your money?
11. Have you ever sold or pawned anything to gamble?
12. Are you reluctant to use "gambling money" for normal expenditures?
13. Does gambling make you careless about your or your family's well-being?
14. Do you ever gamble longer than you had planned?
15. Have you ever gambled to escape worry or trouble?
16. Have you ever considered committing an illegal act to finance your gambling?
17. Does gambling make it harder to sleep?
18. When you have an argument, disappointment, or frustration, do you get an urge to gamble to make yourself feel better?
19. Do you ever have an urge to celebrate good fortune by gambling?
20. Have you ever considered suicide because of your gambling?

How did you do? Most compulsive gamblers will answer yes to at least seven of these questions.

If you think you may have a gambling problem, I encourage you to contact Gamblers Anonymous. This free 12-step support program is open to anyone who wants to stop gambling. For meetings in your area, call 909-931-9056 or visit gamblersanonymous.org. GA offers a searchable online directory of in-person, virtual, and phone meetings, plus emergency hotlines if you need or want to talk immediately to someone in your area.

Chapter 17

Avoid Falling Back into Debt

Staying solvent can be easy, even if a financial crunch hits down the road. Follow these three steps the minute you know your financial situation is about to change and you'll keep moving forward:

STEP 1.
Find out what you owe every person or business—to the penny. Your next step is to break that total amount into manageable chunks that will help you get up to date on your bills. Stay calm about the amount you owe. It is just a number. Some creditors will accept payments much smaller than your required monthly amount until you regain your financial footing. Sending even a $5 or $10 payment monthly shows each creditor that you are actively trying to catch up.

STEP 2.
Create a pared down budget for your daily living expenses. Then determine how much money you have beyond the essentials and how much you can realistically pay each creditor monthly. Also let your creditors know how long you believe it will be before you can resume your regular payment schedule. Give yourself a minimum of six months.

STEP 3.
Communicate with everyone you owe, preferably by phone or in person. Write down what you want to say and then call or meet

with your creditor. Explain your situation calmly. Tell them you're creating a repayment plan and want to keep them informed. Tell them you completely understand if they need to charge you late fees and that you know the effect that being late can have on your credit score, but you want to continue paying them something and hope they won't cancel your account or turn you over to collections as long as you make these lower payments.

Talk with Creditors before Missing or Delaying Payment

Your creditors will be more likely to help you if *you* contact them before they reach out because your payment is late. If talking to your creditors sends you into a panic, ask a friend or relative who is even-tempered and a good negotiator to be your spokesperson, with you present. That way the creditor knows you've authorized this person to talk to them. Then share what amount you will be able to pay each month.

Most creditors know that working out a revised payment plan is often in their best interest. Not every large creditor has flexibility, but it's worth asking. A woman once called Citi to create a plan for her credit card. She politely stuck to her guns about how much she could pay each month and created a win-win situation for both her and her creditor. When you call larger creditors, ask about their hardship program and explain how much you will now be sending each month. They don't have to agree with what you're doing for you to make these changes in your payments. You'd like them to work with you to lower your payment and/or reduce your interest rate, but the most important part of this process is that you're setting up a repayment plan that you can stick with.

Write down the name of the person you talk to, the date and time, and what you agreed to do. You may or may not be successful with the first person you talk to. Do not be discouraged! Although you would love for your creditor to say "Yes!" to your repayment plan, it's not always possible. Faced with a choice of *no* money or *some* money, however, most creditors will work with you. And every creditor will accept any amount you're able to pay. Never get emotional and never agree to pay the creditor more than you know you can pay each month. Once you break an agreement with a creditor, they are much less likely to work with you on a repayment plan.

Let's say you think you *could* afford to repay $50, but that might put you in a pinch. Instead offer $25. Say, "I know I can pay you $25 a month." If they ask for $50, simply say, "I'd like to agree to $50 a month, but that's just not realistic. I don't want to disappoint you if I can't come up with that amount monthly. I can commit to $25 a month and will send extra money whenever I can." Let your creditors know up front that your word is important to you. It strengthens your credibility.

Whether or not your creditor agrees to your reduced payment plan, write a follow-up letter to the person you spoke with to confirm what you'll be paying. Write to the correspondence address for the company—it's listed on your statement (often in the fine print). Keep a copy of the letter for your records. Send the letter via certified mail, return receipt requested, so you have proof the letter was received. Set up your payments via autopay so you don't miss one. As an extra step, consider opening a separate bank account somewhere you don't regularly bank. Put only your repayment funds into this account. This way the money you've promised these creditors is always available.

If you're uncomfortable asking for help from your creditors over the phone, send them the letter on the following page via certified mail, return receipt requested, to the correspondence address on your bill. Send your letter as soon as you know your financial situation will change (or as soon as you can once you've missed a payment). This letter will help you get caught up with most creditors without damaging your newly reborn credit rating.

You may need to take one more step if any creditors won't work with you or continually hound you with telephone calls. If that is the case, send them the letter on page 288 via certified mail, return receipt requested.

If you have to send this second letter include a copy of your original letter to the creditor that discusses your suggested repayment plan. Once the creditor has signed for the letter, you are then in a position to sue them if they attempt to contact you, or anyone else, by phone to talk about your debt. Every time a creditor violates your rights by attempting to contact you over the phone, you can sue them for a minimum of $1,000. Once a creditor realizes that you know your rights and won't be harassed, they'll be more likely to work out a repayment plan with you that you can afford.

I was once negotiating a $10,000 American Express bill for a client. Amex said they would tell me on Monday if they'd accept the $3,000 my client had offered as payment in full. They then proceeded to make collection calls on Friday, Saturday, and Sunday, leaving messages on my client's home, work, and cell phones—even though they knew I had power of attorney. When they called me on Monday to accept the $3,000 offer, I explained that, sadly, we had a dilemma. They had violated my client's rights with their collection attempts, and he was eligible to sue them for $1,000 for each of those nine calls—meaning they would have to pay *him* $9,000. I told the creditor I needed them to tell me what they wanted to do: did they want to pay the client $9,000, or did they want to accept $1,000 as payment in full? The Amex representative took a deep breath, sighed, and replied, "I'll send the paperwork right now accepting $1,000 as payment in full."

[Date]
[Creditor]
[Address]
[City, State, Zip]

Re: [Your account number]

Dear Sir/Madam:

My financial situation has changed unexpectedly because [I was laid off, lost my job, had a medical crisis, was divorced, experienced a natural disaster, etc.]. I cannot currently make the minimum payments required on this account and am asking for your assistance in getting this bill paid. I have a solid payment history with your company [note if you're currently behind], and I want to keep my good credit with you. I see two possible solutions to this problem, and I have listed them in the order that would work best for me.

1. I would like to request a 60-day deferral, allowing me to skip two payments. [If your account is already behind, ask for a 90-day deferral.] I trust you will re-age the account so it remains current and that my skipped payments will not be reported as past due.

OR

2. I would like to request that the interest be frozen and the minimum payment be cut in half for the next 12 months. This would give me enough time to adjust my budget so I can then begin repaying my account at its regular payment amount and interest rate one year from now.

I apologize for the inconvenience, but I hope you can help me get through this difficult time. Please send me your written reply and call me within the next 10 days to let me know which option is best for you, so I can budget the payment amount. You can reach me at [your phone number]. The best time to call is [time]. Thank you again.

Sincerely,
[Your name]

[Date]
[Creditor]
[Address]
[City, State, Zip]

Re: [Your account number]

Dear Sir/Madam:

I have attempted to work out a repayment plan with you to repay my debt, without my having to declare bankruptcy or default on this debt entirely. To date, you have been unwilling to work with me to make this repayment plan a possibility. Instead, you continue to make harassing phone calls demanding repayment of this debt.

I am writing to let you know that it is inconvenient for you to phone me at home, at work, or via my cell phone, or to contact anyone associated with me, whether they be neighbors, co-workers, or anyone else who does not hold a power of attorney for me. As of the date you receive this letter, all further contact with me must be in writing to my billing address. No other contact should be made by you to me or to anyone I know regarding this debt.

As you know, any future calls from you will be a violation of my rights as a consumer, and I will exercise my rights to their fullest extent, including bringing suit against you for violation of the Fair Debt Collection Practices Act.

As I have told you in the past, my financial situation has changed unexpectedly because [I was laid off, lost my job, had a medical crisis, was divorced, experienced a natural disaster, etc.]. I cannot currently make the minimum payments required on this account and am asking for your assistance in getting this bill paid using the repayment plan I have worked out.

I trust that you will work with me, in writing, to develop a repayment plan that will allow this debt to be successfully repaid. Thank you again.

Sincerely,
[Your name]

Past-Due Credit Card Bills

Usually, credit card companies will *not* close your account if you continue to make some payment and are not charging anything new—but they will report your late payments and may lower your credit limit to match your current balance. And if you can't pay at all, they will eventually suspend or close your account while adding late-payment fees and additional interest monthly. This is why I recommend using a good *secured* credit card (see Chapter 9).

Your credit score will be affected less if you close the account at your request the minute you realize you're going to be late paying. Cut up or shred your card and send the company the following letter of explanation (see page 290), stating that you are closing the account. This way, you don't put a post-bankruptcy black mark on your credit report.

If you run into a problem getting a creditor to close your account (and use your security deposit to pay off all or a portion of your balance), send a letter to Division of Financial Practices, Bureau of Consumer Protection, Federal Trade Commission, 600 Pennsylvania Avenue, NW, Washington, DC 20580, together with a copy of the original letter you sent to the creditor.

Tell the FTC that the creditor has not closed your account as requested and ask them to intervene on your behalf. As always, send your letters certified, return receipt requested. I'd recommend also reporting the creditor's activity using the FTC online reporting system at reportfraud.ftc.gov.

[Date]
[Creditor]
[Address]
[City, State, Zip]

Re: [Your account number]

Dear Sir/Madam:

My financial situation has changed unexpectedly because [I was laid off, lost my job, had a medical crisis, was divorced, experienced a natural disaster, etc.].

I request that you close the above-referenced account immediately at my request [and use my secured savings deposit to pay off (or pay down) the balance on the account]. I will continue to make payments on the account until it is paid in full.

I look forward to being a customer of yours in the future. For now, however, I must ask you to close this account.

Thank you for your prompt attention to this matter.

Sincerely,
[Your name]

About to Fall Behind on Your Mortgage?

A year after I bought my first home and started renovations, I was laid off from my job. Between unemployment and my savings, I was able to pay my mortgage for six months. The first month that I knew I wouldn't be able to make my mortgage payment, I called my mortgage lender, who suggested I call the Department of Housing and Urban Development (HUD). I had an FHA loan and HUD is the mortgage insurer for FHA loans, which means HUD insures FHA loans against nonpayment. The first thing the HUD representative said to me was, "I wish you'd called us right after you got laid off instead of using up your savings to pay your mortgage."

Because I had an FHA loan, I was eligible for HUD assignment, which is now called *special forbearance*. Some forbearance programs are short term, ranging from three months to a year. Others can extend up to three years. Your monthly payments under a forbearance could range from zero to a small portion of your current monthly mortgage payment.

Mortgage Forbearance

Once you know your financial situation is changing (due to job loss, extended illness or injury, drastic family situation, natural disaster, etc.), call your lender *immediately* and ask to be connected to the mortgage assistance, mortgage loss mitigation, or loan counseling department. When you reach a loan counselor, say, "I want to apply for forbearance or mortgage modification assistance."

Your loan counselor will ask you to provide current financial information. Rather than give this information over the phone, ask them to send you the form so you can gather your financial paperwork to give them a complete answer. Some lenders have downloadable forms. Make it your top priority to get this information to your lender. Your lender will review your financial information and figure out what solution is best for your situation.

You may qualify for a reduction or suspension of your monthly mortgage payment. Once you've missed three regular mortgage payments, your lender will review your case for forbearance. While your case is being reviewed, your lender *cannot* move to foreclose.

You will be asked to fill out a financial statement detailing your income, expenses, and various debts. List *everyone* you owe money to so your lender gets the total picture of your income and expenses. You must provide a copy of your last tax return *and* your estimated income for the current year. Your lender uses this information to calculate what your payments will be for the forbearance period and will send you a formal forbearance agreement, usually as two copies. Sign both copies, file one, and return the other via certified mail, return receipt requested. Follow the payment plan *exactly* and make all monthly payments on time.

While you're being considered for forbearance, your lender may call you monthly to verify you're living in the home. You lose your right to forbearance if you move out. Living in your home minimizes your lender's risk of loss from damage to your home, so use these check-ins as a chance to thank your lender for working with you to save your home.

With a HUD forbearance program, don't be alarmed if you are initially turned down. A high percentage of requests are turned down once or twice. Follow the appeals process listed on the back of the papers you receive if this happens. I was fortunate. My forbearance application was submitted during a federal government furlough. When the government got back to business, they realized appeals would create more work for them and my application was approved on the first try. Don't give up if you get turned down. Work with your loan counselor to walk you through your next steps.

Use your time while in the repayment plan to build savings and catch up on other essential bills. Implement every strategy I've outlined so you're financially secure before your forbearance ends. When your forbearance period expires, you must start making your regular mortgage payments again under the terms of your forbearance exit strategy.

Mortgage Forbearance Exit Strategies

At the end of your forbearance period, your mortgage lender will likely offer one of several *exit strategies* for getting your mortgage caught up. Make sure you get an agreement for your exit strategy *in writing*. Possible exit strategies include the following:

Balloon payment. This is a lump-sum payment you make for the amount deferred during the forbearance period. This is the last option I would recommend. If you don't have the lump sum available, the lender can then start foreclosure proceedings on your house.

Repayment plan. This plan adds an extra amount to your regular monthly payment (but your new payment can be no more than 150 percent of your original payment). This is a good option only if your income has increased significantly *or* your expenses have decreased enough to offset the increased mortgage payment.

Payment deferral. This option is one of the better ones. The unpaid amount of the mortgage payments you missed during your forbearance period would be deferred until your 30-year mortgage period ends or until you pay off the loan, whichever comes first. This deferral is usually set up in the form of a promissory note.

Loan modification. The best option, in my mind, is when the mortgage lender modifies the loan in a way that doesn't cause additional hardship for you. They may tack on your missed mortgage amounts to the back end of your mortgage, turning your 30-year mortgage into a 33-year mortgage. Or they may lower your interest rate or forgive all or a part of the unpaid principal from those missed payments.

Mortgage Modification

A different kind of mortgage modification—one that avoids forbearance—is available if you've already recovered from your financial issue or are currently paying your mortgage but struggling to catch up on past-due mortgage payments. This modification will roll your outstanding mortgage payments into the remaining balance, instantly bringing your loan current.

In some cases, if you've missed at least four payments *and* you can now pay your regular mortgage payment, your mortgage insurance company may pay your lender the past-due amount on your behalf. You then sign a promissory note from your mortgage company for this amount. Unlike a second mortgage, this promissory note is interest-free. You repay the note either when you sell your home or when you finish paying your first mortgage, whichever comes first.

Working with Your Mortgage Insurance Company

Contact your mortgage insurance company if you have a challenge communicating with your mortgage lender for any reason, including if the lender is trying to force a certain exit strategy on you that you know will fail—the result being that your lender will likely wind up owning your home, equity and all.

Your mortgage insurer is likely either HUD (if you have an FHA loan) or one of the other large private mortgage insurance (PMI) companies. You pay for this insurance as part of your monthly mortgage payment whenever your down payment is less than 20 percent of your purchase price. Unlike other insurance that protects *you*, mortgage insurance protects *your lender* from loss if you suffer financial hardship or are otherwise unable to pay your mortgage.

If your lender forecloses on your loan, your PMI will pay a foreclosure claim to the lender to offset the lender's losses. This amount is usually much more than the sum of your missed mortgage payments, so PMI insurers often find it cheaper to advance your lender the money to cover your missed payments—if it's likely you'll be able to make payments again soon.

Even if you're upside-down on your mortgage, owing more than your home is worth, and needing to sell, PMI may come to your rescue by doing a pre-foreclosure sale. This involves the PMI issuer pay-

---

Your Lender Reselling Your Loan?

By law, if your mortgage lender resells your loan to another lender or mortgage servicing company while you're in a hardship program, the new lender *must* honor the terms of the agreement set up under HUD. Some lenders may try bullying you into believing they can foreclose on the loan or demand immediate full repayment of the money tacked onto the loan. Should this happen, *immediately* contact your mortgage insurance company.

Calmly outline the situation and ask what steps you should take. If you made all required payments under the forbearance agreement and the new lender violates the original forbearance agreement, you may have the right to sue the new lender to protect your home from foreclosure. Contact a debtor's rights attorney if your new lender doesn't honor the terms of your agreement.

---

ing all or a part of your remaining mortgage, so you won't owe your lender money once your home is sold. Before you decide to use this strategy, I strongly recommend you first call your local housing counseling agency or consult an experienced real estate and tax attorney. If you don't follow a specific set of procedures for a pre-foreclosure sale, you could wind up with "phantom income" being reported to the IRS—requiring you to pay income tax on the forgiven amount.

For help locating your PMI insurer's name and contact information, call your mortgage lender and ask them for the information. If your lender hesitates, politely state, "I pay the premiums on this insurance, so I am entitled to this information. It would be easiest to get it from you, but if it's too much trouble, I can call the state banking regulator or commissioner and let them know you're unable to give me this information." That should get you the information you want. If it doesn't, visit consumerfinance.gov and search for *banking regulator*. Once you know who you pay for mortgage insurance, reach out to them directly. Here are the six top mortgage insurers (listed alphabetically) and their contact information:

- **Arch Mortgage Insurance Company:** 877-642-4642; they only accept phone calls
- **Enact (Genworth) Homeowners Assistance Team:** 800-455-0871; hoa@enactmi.com
- **Essent Guaranty:** 877-569-6577; lossmitigation@essent.us
- **MGIC (Mortgage Guaranty Insurance Corporation):** 800-424-6442; customer_service@mgic.com
- **National Mortgage Insurance:** 855-530-6642; defaultreporting@nationalmi.com
- **Radian Guaranty Corporation:** 877-723-4261; customercare@radian.com

Options to Prevent Falling Behind on Mortgage Payments Again

Once you're back on track with your mortgage payments, explore your options for ensuring you don't fall behind again. Those options may include selling your home. Choosing to get out from under a large mortgage can be relieving, as a client struggling to make his Chapter 13 payments discovered. The bulk of his plan payment was his mortgage, which he had fallen behind on prior to

---

What if Your Lender and Mortgage Insurer Can't Help?

If your lender or mortgage insurance company say they can't assist you, call 800-569-4287 (202-708-1455 TTY). This direct line connects you with the nearest HUD-approved housing counseling agency. Many states have additional private and community organizations and programs that can help, even if you have a conventional or VA loan. A housing counseling agency can often help you receive this assistance before you lose your home.

his bankruptcy. Reviewing his finances, he realized he could ease his stress *if* he turned the house over to the lender. He didn't have much equity in the house and wouldn't have seen much profit from a sale. He co-owned his late parents' vacant home with his sister, which despite being listed for months, had no viable buyers. So he came up with a win-win situation. He relinquished his home to the lender, moved into his late parents' house, and began to pay his sister market rent for her *half* of the house—all of which made his monthly Chapter 13 payment more reasonable. The reduced stress made him much more productive and present at home and work.

Other Past-Due Bills

These five types of bills usually offer payment extensions without damaging your credit report:

1. **Utilities.** Your local utility companies may be willing to work out a short-term payment schedule. Call them the minute you know your payment will be late. Don't put it off! Utilities won't generally show up on your credit reports. However, if you are more than 90 days late or your service is interrupted, they may refer you to a collection agency, which *will* show up on your credit reports. Be proactive and work out a payment schedule the minute you fall behind. Otherwise, you may need to pay the total balance in full *and* put up a security deposit for future service.

2. **Medical bills.** Most medical bills are no longer reported to credit bureaus, including collection accounts for less than $500. Ask your medical provider to hold off on turning your account over for collection as long as you're paying something each month. Even a $5 monthly payment may show your creditor you're making a good-faith effort to pay your debt.

3. **Gasoline cards.** There is a *huge* difference between a company's *gas card* and the new Mastercard and Visa *credit cards* being issued by gasoline companies. Gas cards—which you can use only to buy gas and sometimes pay for minor garage services—*do not* usually report your payment history unless your account falls delinquent by 90 days or more and has been turned over to collection. Cards with a Visa or Mastercard logo, however, *are* credit cards, and your monthly payment history will be reported. For a gas card, you can usually work out a modified payment schedule to catch up if you fall behind, but you may not be allowed to make any new charges. Follow the same instructions outlined earlier for your utility bills and pay cash for your gasoline purchases until your gas card balance is paid off.

4. **Car payments.** Many lenders will let you skip one payment during the life of the car loan and will tack it on to the back of the loan period. If you're going to be late or know you'll miss a payment, call the lender before they call you and ask if you can skip a month on your car payment. You'll have much better luck working out arrangements *before* your payment is late. *Use this strategy as a last resort.* Your lender will charge you a processing fee, which is usually 25 percent of your monthly payment. If their fee is any higher, find a way to make a partial car payment. Then simply add an extra $50 or $100 to your regular monthly payment until you're caught up. You'll still incur late payment fees until you've fully paid the missing payment, but it won't cost you nearly as much.

5. **Student loans.** Student loans are a bit trickier and are discussed in more detail in Chapter 4. If you're having financial difficulty because you've been laid off or lost your job, your best bet is to seek a six- or 12-month *unemployment* deferment. A deferment doesn't necessarily bring your past-due payments up to date, so if you need help catching up, talk with your lender.

Some lenders willingly entertain individual options, especially if you propose a repayment plan. Decades ago, I lost my job, and my student loan lender gave me a six-month deferment on my $50 monthly payment. I had already missed one payment, so at the end of my deferment, I arranged to send monthly payments of $60 for five months until I was current again. You can easily do the same. You could even offer to pay *half* of your student loan payment for six months, then the full payment once your finances improve.

Chapter 18

Another Bankruptcy Looms

When we don't know how to live without credit (aka debt), even our bankruptcy can cause more problems than it solves. Changing financial circumstances may make it impossible to pay our debts. Sometimes this happens through our own actions—or inactions— and sometimes not. Either way, what should you do when facing the hard decision of a possible repeat bankruptcy?

Three Steps When Considering a Repeat Bankruptcy

First, read the strategies in Chapter 14 for getting back on your financial feet. These actions can help you make more informed choices for you and your family based on your current situation. Focus on the quick and easy changes you can make to pare expenses or boost income. And keep in mind that the adage that "it takes money to make money" isn't always true. Your attempts to increase your income should *not* include any big start-up expenses that require you to take on more debt or pose the risk of financial loss.

Only you know which actions you are willing to take. Are you willing to initiate a three- or six-month family spending pause, set individual and family allowances, freeze gift giving, tighten your belt, and funnel all income toward catching up and paying down bills? Look at where the edge of your comfort zone is, then declare you are making your financial future a priority and push just a bit beyond that point.

You may feel embarrassed to declare bankruptcy twice, but you're not alone. Bankruptcy protection laws exist to help you get back on your feet. Yet, even after your bankruptcy you may have made mistakes. Maybe you didn't learn better ways to handle your income and expenses. Maybe you needed a financial attitude adjustment and didn't get it. Maybe you were impatient and jumped back into debt, prompted by creditor advertisements designed to convince you that their product would help you rebuild your credit *quickly*. This time, though, you're taking steps toward permanent change. Honor whatever choices brought you to this moment. Stop beating yourself up or blaming others. Simply ask, "What am I going to do about it now?"

Second, determine whether you're eligible to file for bankruptcy again. If you're not, focus your attention on paying priority bills: housing, transportation, food, essential utilities, medicine, and insurance. Where can you cut back on those expenses until you get back on track again? Stop paying unsecured creditors until you build a cash reserve to protect yourself and your family. Make sure you meet your basic needs—and be ruthlessly honest about what is *truly* a basic need.

Third, check with an attorney to see whether Chapter 13 bankruptcy is an option for you if you previously filed for Chapter 7 or already completed Chapter 13. You may be eligible to file for Chapter 13 if your Chapter 7 bankruptcy was filed at least four years ago. If you declared Chapter 7 bankruptcy less than eight years ago and have fallen behind on your mortgage, car payment, alimony, child support, or taxes, you may need to declare Chapter 13 bankruptcy this time. Unlike your Chapter 7 bankruptcy, Chapter 13 lets you set up a repayment plan for your creditors to prevent or postpone a foreclosure or vehicle repossession.

In general, to qualify for a Chapter 7 bankruptcy, your annual household income (based on your average income during the six months before you file) must be below the *median household income* for your state, depending on the number of people in your household. The 2025 median household income for one person in a household varies from a low of $29,153 in Puerto Rico to a high of $85,663 in the District of Columbia. Ask your lawyer whether you qualify to file for Chapter 7 or visit bestcase.com/resources to calculate your annual household income yourself.

Scroll down to click on their calculators, then on the left side of your screen select Quick Median Income Test. Follow the instructions and use their dropdown menu to enter your income from the past six months, deposit by deposit, to calculate your average pretax income. If you've lost your job and your income is near the limit, each month you can wait until you file will help you to qualify for Chapter 7. Waiting a full six months before filing for bankruptcy will give you a much lower current monthly income than if you were to file right after losing your job.

If your average income for the six months prior to filing is *higher* than the median, you could still be eligible to file for Chapter 7 bankruptcy if you meet the *means test*, which is designed to determine how much disposable income you have every month

---

Is Chapter 20 an Option?

Filing under Chapter 7 to discharge what debts you can and then filing under Chapter 13 to set up a payment plan to repay the remaining debt is commonly referred to by bankruptcy attorneys as *filing Chapter 20*. There's no such thing as Chapter 20, of course, but this two-step approach to bankruptcy is a common technique if a creditor has pressured you to reaffirm a debt that would have been dischargeable, or you find yourself with a variety of secured and unsecured debt.

based on IRS national standards rather than your actual costs. In any case, get a free consultation with a bankruptcy attorney and explore your options.

Pay attention to any rules around using state exemptions versus national exemptions. In general, you must have been a state resident for at least two years to use any state exemptions and must have lived in-state for three-and-a-half years before you can use the homestead exemption (unless you sold a home in another state and used the proceeds to buy your current home).

While some people can easily file their own bankruptcy paperwork, I think it's worth having an attorney prepare—or at least review—your paperwork. Bankruptcy law has some complicated twists and turns. Don't let your bankruptcy petition get tossed out because you overlooked something vital in the current bankruptcy laws.

Declaring bankruptcy can help you get your finances under control if no other option is available. It will all be okay. If you find yourself waking up at night or unable to sleep or concentrate because of anxiety and worries about having to declare bankruptcy again, get still for a minute. Take a few deep breaths and slowly repeat *I am doing the right thing. I am doing what is best for me, my family, and our future.*

Still in Repayment for a Chapter 13 Bankruptcy?

Only 25 percent of people who declare Chapter 13 ever finish their repayment plans, so don't be discouraged if you fall behind. To get back on track, first, look at any effortless ways to generate income so you can quickly pay off a larger debt in your Chapter 13 (like your car loan), which might make your repayment plan more affordable. Brainstorm ideas and think outside the box. Review the strategies in Chapter 14, which include renting out a spare room, garage, or driveway space. Sell extra television sets, stereos, small kitchen appliances, electronic or sports equipment, collections, or other rarely used items.

Yes, it's convenient to have multiple televisions or a KitchenAid stand mixer along with handheld and stick blenders, but no, they are *not essential*. Could you live without this $400 mixer or the extra television? Absolutely. Swap *convenience* for increased *financial security*. Use the sale proceeds to give yourself some financial breathing room. It's easy to free up trapped cash—and you can eventually replace the items again, as Thomas Jefferson did (see Chapter 14).

Be patient and take one step at a time. Brainstorm other ways to free up money each month. Engage the whole family. Include both small, easy tasks (like turning off lights and unplugging computers when not in use) and bigger, more challenging ones, especially any you resist. Some moves will save you thousands while others might save you only $16. The choice is yours: how fast do you want to improve your financial life and lower your stress? Make a full list of what you *could* do. Next, underline items you would be *willing* to do. Finally, circle items you *will* do right now.

Additional Steps to Take if Filing Bankruptcy Again

You'll need to pay for and complete both the mandatory *prefiling* credit counseling course and an approved *predischarge* debtor education course before your bankruptcy can be discharged. You will need to submit your prefiling counseling completion certificate with your bankruptcy papers.

If filing bankruptcy appears to be your best option *and you're a homeowner*, seek credit counseling immediately so you can meet

---

When All Else Fails . . .

You have three choices if you simply cannot keep up with your Chapter 13 repayment plan:

1. Have your attorney approach your trustee about possibly extending your payment period to five years (if it's not already five years) or revising your existing repayment plan with lower payments.
2. Have your Chapter 13 dismissed and file a new plan with lower payments. Your ability to dismiss and refile will depend on certain circumstances, so talk with your attorney.
3. Convert your Chapter 13 to Chapter 7. If you are currently in a Chapter 13 repayment plan and can't keep up with your Chapter 13 payments, check with your attorney to determine whether you qualify to declare Chapter 7 bankruptcy. The drawback is that some secured debts may not be dischargeable under Chapter 7. You will have to either surrender secured items or reaffirm the debts with the creditors—which may include your home.

---

the prefiling bankruptcy certification requirement and start the bankruptcy filing before you risk losing your home.

The U.S. Trustee Program determines which credit counseling agencies are approved to provide prefiling course certificates and which debtor education providers are approved to provide pre-discharge course certificates. Depending on which nonprofit agency or provider you select, you may complete your courses online, via phone, or in person. Your bankruptcy *cannot be discharged* until you file this second certificate with the bankruptcy court, showing you have completed the predischarge financial education course. Some debtor education course providers will submit a copy of your predischarge certificate to the court for you.

To find an approved agency or provider, visit uscourts.gov. Click the About Bankruptcy quick link and select Credit Counseling and Debtor Education on the left sidebar. This opens a page where you can select credit counseling agencies or debtor education providers, depending on which course you need. Prices vary widely for the same certificate program. You can pay as little as $14.95 for your credit counseling course at Summit Financial Education (summitfe.org) and $7.95 for your debtor education course (at bankruptcydebtoreducation.com). The credit counseling course takes about an hour; set aside two hours for your debtor education course.

Once you have your prefiling course certificate, contact two or three bankruptcy attorneys—including your original attorney if you wish—to explore your options.

When looking for a good attorney, first check for any board-certified bankruptcy attorneys in your area. Certified attorneys invest hundreds of hours in extra training. They also generally have years of experience, have passed a comprehensive exam on consumer bankruptcy issues, and meet the highest legal and ethical standards.

The American Bankruptcy Institute's American Board of Certification (abcworld.org) lists certified consumer bankruptcy attorneys. Fill out their form with your state and city (or nearest large city) to search in your area. Add *Consumer Bankruptcy* in the Select Certification Type bar to narrow your search. Another resource for finding good local bankruptcy attorneys is the National Association of Consumer Bankruptcy Attorneys (nacba.org). NACBA has a fancier search engine that allows you to select a mileage radius before entering your zip code to help you find nearby attorneys. Scroll down to Find an Attorney and read the instructions before clicking on NACBA Member Database.

Once you have hired an attorney, contact all your creditors and tell them you're declaring bankruptcy. Simply say, "I'm retaining a bankruptcy attorney, who will contact you as soon as my paper-

---

Debts You Can't Discharge

If filing bankruptcy looks like it might be necessary, make sure to avoid:
- incurring any debt of $600 or more within 90 days of filing;
- taking out any cash advance or payday loans totaling $1,000 or more per creditor, within 70 days of filing; and
- borrowing from friends, family members, and others you're close to, within one year of filing.

---

work is filled out." This will stop creditor phone calls to you. And your lawyer will appreciate not fielding calls from creditors until your bankruptcy paperwork is ready.

Once your bankruptcy is discharged, start at the beginning of this book, follow the recommended strategies, and give yourself the gift of a true second chance at financial security.

SECTION V

FROM SURVIVING
TO THRIVING

Chapter 19

Create Financial Balance and Security

In her book, *Rich AF*, Vivian Tu shares her belief that creating true *wealth* comes from advocating for your true *worth*. She declares that elevating yourself above your current level of financial security happens by increasing your earning power. I say *yes, and . . .* what you *do* with your income also matters.

Every choice you make will either empower you or disempower you. Your choices bring you closer to your goals or kick them farther down the road. Even the smallest choices can have long-lasting results. The one-size-fits-all advice most financial professionals provide about what actions to take to improve your financial position simply doesn't work for most of us. That's why I'm sharing everyday strategies you and everyone else can use to create a positive net worth—and steadily generate increased income. It starts by harnessing every bit of value from your life choices.

Get Top Value from Your Debt Repayment

By now, you've followed the DebtBuster strategy from Chapter 4, creating a "set it and forget it" way to pay off any debts not listed on your bankruptcy. Rather than using the *snowball method* favored by penny-pinching financial experts, I suggest another option that

incorporates Tu's advice. Once you pay off one debt, use that payment amount to invest in *yourself* in ways that help you build a positive net worth.

For example, deposit that amount every month into a savings
account, preferably one with a higher interest rate and without
online access or a debit card. Consider this account the cornerstone
of your positive net worth. From this cornerstone you're going to
build a strong financial foundation. Don't dismiss any deposit as
too small to save. Don't get cranky on me if this slow and steady
approach isn't producing results as quickly as you'd like. This strategy is the little-known stepping stone for creating lasting wealth.
Bear with me.

A habitual, systematic strategy to increase your net worth while
paying down and paying off debts creates a win-win situation. Having that money accessible in your pocket each month so you can
buy more things now may *seem* rewarding. It might be tempting
to use that money as a small down payment on something you can
finance.

I have another suggestion. Use this time to create a balanced
financial foundation on which to build a strong financial future
and have what you want. If you absolutely must have fun money,
add it to your budget, using no more than 20 percent of the amount
you're now putting in savings.

Yes, this strategy will extend the time until you are debt-free.
But in my decades of helping people rebuild after bankruptcy, I've
found that people who focus purely on being debt-free will often
reach their goal, only to wind up back in debt again, having to borrow to buy things because they don't have any savings. Focusing on
being debt-free is *not* your best goal. Neither is focusing solely on
raising your credit score. Your best goal is to create a positive net
worth. Focus on reaching a point where what you *own* is worth
more than what you *owe*. With this focus, once your debts reach

zero, you will find yourself debt-free with savings and investments. The question is, what investments offer you the lowest risk and highest return?

Get Top Value for Yourself

You are your best investment. Let me share a quick story. After a North Carolina man attended my workshop on knowing your true worth, he asked his boss for a raise. The boss made a counteroffer. Rather than give him an outright raise, the boss offered to pay for him to attend Wake Forest's part-time MBA program—including all travel costs. Within a few years, he earned his MBA and nearly doubled his income. His boss willingly invested in him to acquire advanced skills; the man invested in *himself* by saying yes and doing the work. Knowledge *is* power.

Look at the goals you set for yourself in Chapter 7. Circle all the goals that will help you generate income. What goals do you have for increasing your skills and knowledge and generating additional income? Read a book, take a class, get certified, go back to school, apprentice to master a skill, or ask someone if you can take them out to lunch to pick their brain for knowledge in areas where you feel you're lacking. Improve your communication skills, your financial knowledge. Invest in knowledge, skills, and tools or equipment that enable you to make more money (and no, I'm *not* encouraging you to buy a printing press and plates for counterfeiting!).

Thanks to the internet, gathering knowledge and skills for pretty much everything is easy—often for free or for little cost. What do you want to learn? What skills do you wish you had? What do you wish you knew how to do? My late friend Daria Finn often declared, "You can learn anything you want to from reading a book"—or, these days, by watching a video. She wanted to become a photographer, so she read a book and became an official photographer for racing events. She wanted to become a race car driver, so she read a book and started racing—and winning. She wanted to write plays, so she read a book and became a playwright, producing plays featuring well-known actors like Olympia Dukakis.

Websites like Academic Earth, Alison, CodeAcademy, Coursera, LifeHack Academy, MasterClass, Open Culture, Open Yale Courses, OpenLearn, Udemy, and YouTube Creator offer free and low-cost courses to help you build personal skills (including anger management, communication, and productivity) *and* learn pretty much everything from art to zoology, from coding to welding. You can even earn certificates or diplomas. ClassCentral is a great place to start. They compile information on all OpenCourseWare providers and the courses they offer.

Get Top Value by Helping Others

My family owns a landscape company and has bought smaller companies whose owners became our employees. Our company would offer to logo their truck and lease the vehicle from them, with the lease payments directly covering their car payment and insurance. In 2020, one longtime employee wanted to sell his now-logoed 2006 truck so he could buy a personal vehicle. I bought his truck for cash, and the landscape company has leased it from me since then. I recouped my purchase price within the first year of lease payments.

Many small businesses need additional equipment, trucks, and trailers and may not have the cash flow to buy even used equipment. Your ability to buy and then lease vehicles and equipment to them benefits both of you. Make sure the lease is drafted to ensure that the company is responsible for everything—including paying for your vehicle's insurance, maintenance, and repairs.

Get Top Value for Things You Buy

I'm a big believer in investing in companies whose products I use regularly and that pay cash dividends at least quarterly. My first stock purchases were Bristol Myers Squibb and Merck (who made my asthma inhalers and my regular medications) as well as Procter & Gamble (now P&G) and Clorox, because they made most household products I used. I rounded out my investments with Wendy's (my then-favorite fast-food chain) and Waste Management (the company that collected my trash). When we buy products from solid companies, our money enriches the company *and* the stockholders. So, it only makes sense for us to benefit from the company's growth.

Teens Pick Winning Stocks

When I worked as an editor of financial newsletters for Phillips Publishing (now InvestorPlace), the company's owner asked me to coach a Junior Achievement team in a stock-picking contest using a fictional $10,000. I shared my investment strategy, teaching them to pick investments based on their purchasing habits and what they observed from real-life trends.

Which movies did their younger siblings watch repeatedly? Which toy company (Hasbro or Mattel) produced the toys for those movies? And which burger chain (Burger King or McDonald's) offered those toys in their kids' meals? Do most teen boys prefer boxers or briefs? Which brand (Hanes® or Fruit of the Loom®) made the best? What makeup brands do teen girls gravitate toward? By focusing on consumer sentiment, they discovered the real-life potential in their stock picks. At the end of the Junior Achievement contest, my team's portfolio had the biggest gains.

Stocks

Investing in individual stocks can be expensive and risky. An easy way to minimize the cost and risk, is to buy shares of a good growth and income mutual fund that invests in companies whose products and services you use. Or you can buy stock directly from financially healthy companies whose products and services you use; look for those that pay dividends *and* allow you to automatically reinvest your dividend income to buy additional shares or fractions of shares. I'll talk about this more in a minute.

Mutual Funds

An inexpensive way to invest in your favorite companies is to buy shares in a solid growth and income mutual fund, which holds a variety of investments selected by the fund manager. The best mutual funds have a long history of positive performance and don't charge you a service fee or "load" to invest your money. Look for a *no-load mutual fund*, which won't charge you to move money in *or* out. It's a bonus if the fund waives or lowers their initial investment minimum if you're willing to make automatic payments—which can be as little as $50. For instance, American Century's minimum is $2,500 for nonretirement accounts. But if you sign up for a monthly automatic investment of $100 or more, you can open your account with just $500.

While at Phillips Publishing, I edited Jay Schabacker's *Mutual Fund Investing* newsletter. Jay had a four-pronged safety-first investing approach. He believed you should know how to invest the right way, know yourself, know the funds, and know the market. He wrote *Winning in Mutual Funds* (1994, AMACOM), which is a classic for learning how to understand and invest in mutual funds. I highly recommend reading (at the very least) the first 100 pages. The book includes two questionnaires that identify your investor risk profile and your knowledge of investments. Your answers will help you pick the type of mutual fund that will enable you to sleep well. In the rest of the book, Jay outlines the best companies that offered mutual funds in 1994 and highlights his Schabacker's 100 All-Stars. His favorite companies and mutual funds—American Century Investments (formerly Twentieth Century), Fidelity, T. Rowe Price, and Vanguard—*still* lead the industry 30 years later.

You can invest in a low-cost index fund that follows a specific market index (e.g., the S&P 500), or you can invest in an actively managed fund, where the fund manager picks the investments and determines when to buy and sell. Look at both the fund's long-term growth rate *and* its dividends, which you can opt to reinvest so they automatically increase the fund shares you own. The names of most of these funds will include *Growth and Income*, *Equity Income*, or something similar.

I personally look for mutual fund investments that have above-average performance and below-average risk going back decades. I want my funds to cost me as little as possible while providing the same dividend and growth approach I take with my stock investments. A good, balanced fund usually holds some cash, bonds, and stocks. Holdings among funds often overlap, so if you're thinking of investing in more than one fund, look at each fund's top holdings to confirm they're unique, because investing in one company that appears in two separate funds comes with double the fees.

At your request, most mutual fund companies will provide a referral to a financial advisor to discuss your investment goals and desires and get professional assistance with your investments. Or, if you're comfortable investing on your own, do the research, read the fund prospectus to make sure the fund meets your needs, and go for it. The initial investment minimums for many mutual funds range from $1,000 to $3,500. You can download applications for most fund families online. Fill out the application and mail it in. Sign up for their automatic investment plan and commit to having

$50 a month or more sent to them from your savings account so your investment continues to grow.

After a year of investing just $50 to $100 a month, you'll have put $600 to $1,200 into a steadily growing investment that over the years can provide an average annual return of 8 percent or more.

Direct Purchase and Dividend Reinvestment Plans

When you find a financially solid company whose products and services you use, see if they offer a dividend reinvestment plan (DRIP, or DRP) and a direct purchase plan (DPP). The most important criteria once you select a stable stock that offers a DRIP is that the company has a long history of stock price growth *and* paying dividends. Often companies with DRIPs require you to own at least one share of stock before enrolling in their direct purchase plan, and many let you buy your first share of stock directly from the company through their DPP. If the company doesn't offer this option, you can usually purchase an initial share through a discount broker like Charles Schwab, Fidelity Brokerage, or E*TRADE. Be sure the broker registers the stock in *your name* so you can enroll in the company's DRIP.

These programs are usually handled through the company's transfer agent. One such transfer agent, Computershare, created the DirectStock program (computershare.com/directstock) where all transactions are done online, and you can filter your choices to show you only companies that offer direct stock purchase plans. Type in the company name or stock symbol to see the minimum investment amount if you're not already a shareholder, any reduction in that minimum if you're committing to automatic monthly purchases, plus all the fees that are charged for that company's DRIP.

Do your homework and check all companies with a trusted financial advisor if you're not a skilled investor. This topic is a bit more in-depth than can be covered here. One of the longest-running and most well-regarded DRIP advisors is Charles B. Carlson, who for 34 years has written the monthly *DRIP Investor* newsletter and the *Directory of DRIPs* which is updated annually (horizonpublishing.com).

Get Top Value for Your Current Big Debts

The next advanced strategy is prepaying your largest debts to reduce the amount of interest (and penalties) you pay. I'm talking about your car loans, mortgage, tax debt, and student loans. You'll save the most if you pay down the principal on the longest loan first or the one with the highest interest rate. You'll find a great calculator for loan payoffs at loan-calculators.org. For your car, use loan-calculators.org/auto-loan-payoff. Paying an extra $150 monthly on the principal for a 6 percent car loan could save you approximately $26 per month in interest.

But look at the savings you reap for a mortgage. Let's say you have a 6.5 percent 30-year mortgage of $300,000. Your monthly payment will be just about $1,900. For the first 15 years, roughly 80 to 85 percent of that payment will be interest. You'll pay on average only $350 monthly on the principal. At the end of 30 years, when you've paid the loan off, you'll have paid $382,633.47 of interest—and a total of $682,633.47 on a $300,000 loan over 360 months. But what if you make your regular payment *and* add an extra $100 to $200 to your principal payment each month?

With an extra $100 monthly, you'll pay off your loan four years early and save yourself $60,000 in interest; an extra $200 monthly pays off your loan seven years early and saves you $103,000 in interest. I can't think of any other investment that gives you that kind of return! If an extra monthly payment isn't in your budget, apply your tax refund or other unexpected income as individual principal payments during the year. Use the loan-calculators.org/extra-payments calculator to play with your numbers. Even if you stay in your house only for a few years, those extra principal payments increase your home equity.

Be sure to specify that your extra payment is for *principal*—this is especially important if you're paying extra on your mortgage or on a *student* loan (see Chapter 4). I recommend setting up your own mortgage payment plan—rather than signing up for a 15-year mortgage, biweekly mortgage, or automatic extra payment plan that locks you in to pay that extra amount each month. Better to keep control over your extra payments yourself. If you ever need that extra $100 for something else for one month, you have the flexibility to put your money where you desire.

For tax debt, I recommend getting the advice of a good tax attorney on the best way to proceed in paying down those debts.

Get Top Value for Your Expenses

When financially strapped clients tell me what they really want, many say something like, "I wish I had enough money so I didn't have to think about the cost of things. I want to be able to buy what I want, knowing I can afford it." If you're a homeowner, prepaying your mortgage will help you achieve this sense of financial security faster, but it's certainly not the *only* way to annually add thousands of dollars to your earning power.

It's interesting how many people say they would *feel financially secure* if they had a million dollars. The truth is, if you worked for 40 years and never made more than $25,000 annually, you will have earned a million dollars. Technically, this means almost all of us have had a million dollars at some point. So why do we still not feel rich or financially secure? I believe it's because we don't value our hard work and—more importantly—we don't value our *expenses*.

When my son started working at 16, I taught him to equate whatever he wanted to buy with how many hours he would have to work—the labor hours he'd invest in order to earn the money—to pay for the item. When he pondered a $235 clothing purchase, we did the math together. At his hourly wage of $18, this purchase would require a labor investment of 13 hours before taxes—more like 15 hours after taxes. He then determined whether it was worth it *to him* to work for 15 hours to buy a new outfit. He's learned to prioritize his purchases based on the value he gets from them.

Understanding the value of our everyday expenses, whether they're for essentials or fun items, lets us better see where we're leaking money like a cracked garden hose attached to a faulty faucet leaks water. The key is to strip away extra expenses without stripping away the value they bring to your life.

Value investing is something I learned from Richard Band, author of the *Profitable Investing* newsletter. As his editor, I attended an annual Las Vegas investment conference with him, where he demonstrated how to play slot machines using value-investing techniques. He had me start with a $10 roll of quarters. He told me to find a three-reel (mechanical preferred) slot machine with nine fixed paylines, meaning all lines are active on every spin. He said to find a machine that took up to three quarters a play, with smaller jackpots where your spin had a higher opportunity to break even (meaning you didn't lose your money on that spin). It's like the fourth foul ball you keep hitting without it being a strike against you.

Richard had me methodically increase and decrease the number of coins I played and told me not to touch my winnings. I played one quarter, then two quarters, then three quarters, then two quarters and then one quarter, no matter what the outcome of the spin. Once my 40 quarters had all been played, I scooped the winnings into my plastic bucket and cashed out. Without fail, I came away with at least $33. My half hour of entertainment came with the bonus of tripling my money. By being methodical in my slot machine play, I got top value for my time and money.

We can apply the same value-investing principles to reduce the financial risk of our main expenses that siphon off our million-dollar earnings. The most common areas in which we pickpocket ourselves are entertainment, club or box subscriptions, content subscriptions and memberships, food, car maintenance, and energy use. These expenses are discussed below. For each area, list all purchases you've made in the past 12 months. Start with last month to see current monthly expenses and work your way back.

Entertainment/Travel

In person or online, we often have many recurring or one-off entertainment purchases: subscription channels, pay-per-view, movies, concerts, sporting events. Review your list and see which expenses provide true value for your money and which don't. Which do you want to stop, reduce, or keep? Where can you create better value for your money and still have what you want? Do you want to pay a premium for commercial-free streaming services, or would you rather put that money toward building your net worth? As you go through this process, notice how many times you catch yourself saying, "It's only an extra $5!"

Many people defensively dig in their heels, not interested in *scrimping and saving*. That's the ego's way of keeping you stuck in some seriously negative thinking. If you've got 20 things you're paying an extra $5 for, that's $100 a month that's *not* staying in your pocket. Imagine someone taking $1,200 a year out of your pocket as an entertainment "convenience" fee. How quickly would you put a stop to that?

If you're partial to specific on-demand streaming services or want to bundle what you watch, look for a single television provider that carries the channels you enjoy. Bundled television providers charge $70 to $160 as a base charge, plus other monthly fees. Review your options at cabletv.com by entering your zip code, then scrolling down to see the available TV providers. If live TV is more your thing, cnet.com offers an annual list of best live TV streaming services with sporting events, including Sling, Hulu, YouTube TV, and DIRECTV.

Compare these packages and prices against services and channels with commercials. For instance, Netflix offers three tiers: standard with ads ($7.99), standard ($17.99), and premium ($24.99). Going with the plan with ads will save you between $120 and $204 a year compared with the other two options. You can watch TV and movies for free with channels like Sling Freestream, Tubi, and Plex; other channels are available at a reduced monthly rate. Increase the value of your time when commercials come on—triage email, exercise, do household tasks, or engage with your family. In the *olden days* when my family had a console television with no remote, we used commercial breaks as an opportunity to do our chores, with one spotter in the living room to yell, "It's back on!"

Want to watch a special event? Many channels offer free trial periods. With others, you can sign up for the channel, pay for a single month, and then cancel after watching the event. A football-loving friend visited me recently and wanted to watch the playoffs. I snagged a $7.99 Paramount+ subscription, we watched both games that evening, and then I canceled the subscription.

If you prefer DVDs over streaming, you can borrow movies for free or at a low cost through your local library or through dvdinbox.com. This rent-by-mail subscription service picks up where Netflix left off when they eliminated their DVD subscribe-by-mail service. Monthly options range from $9.99 to $29.99. The $19.99 standard tier allows you to check out two DVDs at a time, offers unlimited monthly rentals, and has hundreds of thousands of available movies.

I once had a heavenly job as a nationally syndicated movie review columnist, which included free tickets to first-run movies. If you love movies (or plays), check which local theaters offer discount or rewards cards that provide deals on tickets and concessions, plus special matinee pricing. Perks vary by theater. Some offer discounts if you're a student or senior or willing to wait a few weeks to catch the latest releases. Others offer 25 to 50 percent savings if you attend on specific (low attendance) days of the week or before 4 p.m. or 6 p.m. Sources like Fandango also offer perks across movie chains.

For other live events including sports, concerts, and fun activities, discount companies like Groupon and LivingSocial (owned by Groupon) can enhance the value of your entertainment expenses. For ocean or river cruises, discount sites like CruiseCritic and CruiseDirect offer incredible bargains, including last-minute deals on three- or four-night cruises for under $300.

Club/Box Subscriptions

These days, subscription box options are endless—ranging from clothing, baking, pet, crafts, meals, snacks, makeup, manly items, and kid stuff to home décor, jewelry, shaving clubs, and survival gear. And that doesn't even include the variety of fashion rental boxes like Rent the Runway, where monthly subscriptions run into hundreds of dollars. List all these monthly charges and assess the value you receive from these expenses. If you're not opening all the boxes or have a stockpile of their products, cancel or pause your subscriptions.

Content Subscriptions and Memberships

Online and physical subscriptions, memberships, and services may cost only a few dollars each month, but they add up. List every recurring charge you pay for magazines, newspapers, newsletters, audiobooks, gaming, lifestyle and education platforms, and so on.

Include physical and electronic subscriptions. How often do you read or use the content you're buying or act on what you read? Circle items on your list that you read cover to cover or use every month. Chances are, these are the ones that provide true value to you. If you find magazines on the coffee table that are still wrapped in plastic two months after they came in the mail, cancel your subscription right away and get your money back. Those $9.95 (or more) subscriptions add up! Instead, pick up individual issues you really want to read, or read issues at the library or online through OverDrive's free Libby app.

Food

Our food purchases can seriously impact the value we get from our money. Dining out means no cooking and no cleaning, but it's also expensive—especially if you do it often. No need to brown-bag everything, unless that's your thing. Simply start by tracking the amount you spend eating out (snacks, coffee stops, carryout, dine-in restaurants). At the same time, save and review your grocery receipts for a month or two. Specifically look for the amount you spend on prepared food. Then look for ways you can easily reduce the cost of what you already enjoy eating. With a $65 Costco membership, for example, you can substantially reduce your food costs, especially if you buy frozen vegetables or prepared foods. Or, instead of buying a box of frozen burritos, what if you made a batch and froze them?

Brainstorm ways to increase the value of your food purchases. For instance, each month when I'm on a writing retreat, I cook the same six dishes in rotation: meatloaf, barbequed brisket, carnitas, chili, chicken masala, and shrimp and grits. Leftovers get frozen as one or two servings so I can thaw, heat, and eat them when I'm too busy or too tired to cook. In my younger days, while editing a biweekly Baltimore newspaper, my food expenses rose significantly. I lived an hour from work, so cooking at home when on deadline wasn't feasible. A friend who lived near the paper was working on her doctorate, and we hatched a plan to keep us both well fed while using our time and money wisely. We made weekly menus. She bought the groceries, and I'd cook enough at her house every few days for us both to have several dinners and lunches.

Challenge yourself to trim your food costs by 10 percent this month. Journal the actions you take, and plan your food splurges so they seamlessly add value to your life. My weekly double bison burger from 5 Star Burgers, for instance, is non-negotiable!

Car Maintenance

Most of us have heard how, as car owners, we need to top off our fluids, check our filters, keep the tires properly inflated, get regular oil changes, and keep up with the specified periodic maintenance. Makes sense with the cost of buying a car. But we often neglect the whole list and do barebones maintenance or wait until a tiny gremlin of a problem becomes a monster. So I'll offer a cautionary tale. A Southern colleague of mine would buy a car every few years, for the most interesting reason. The only thing he ever did with his car was fill up the gas tank. He never had *any* maintenance done. Eventually, the day would come when the car simply stopped while he was driving—usually in a very dramatic way, often on a highway. He would gather his belongings, flag down a car or call a tow truck, and have the vehicle towed away. Then he'd turn around and buy another car.

No one had taught him what a car required. I, on the other hand, still drive the very first new car I bought. It's a classic and is in great shape because I keep it well maintained, even going the extra step to include a Mopar® additive at every oil change. The dealership constantly offers me opportunities to trade up. The attention and effort needed to maintain an old car may seem excessive, but when the head of the maintenance department follows you out of the service bay and says, "If this were my car, I'd never sell it"—you're getting good value from your vehicle.

Energy Use

Review how much you spend on heat, air conditioning, and electricity to see where you can increase your value. I'm not talking about piling on extra layers in winter or sweating it out in the summer—unless that's your thing. Instead, assess how and when you use energy. Take note of *timed-rate* use for your electricity or gas, where your utility provider lowers or raises their rates at different times of the day. Identify which small appliances and electronics create big energy drains when they're turned off but still plugged in (known as *phantom load*). Set the temperature up or down when no one is home or swap out your thermostat for a programmable one so it's at a comfortable temperature when you arrive home.

Chapter 20

Daily Actions to Stay on Track

Fully armed with the strategies we've covered throughout this book, you've created a solid plan for cleaning up your credit reports, paying off any remaining debt, transforming old financial habits and thought patterns, and bouncing back from bankruptcy with (mostly) ease and grace.

Some days you will feel like you're spinning your wheels. Some weeks your progress will be so slow that watching paint dry would be more exciting. And occasionally, roadblocks will pop up. To stay on top of your finances, focus on these four strategies every day.

Mind Your Money

Knowledge is power. On any given day, I know exactly (to the penny) how much money I have. My entire family knows how much money we each have, including cash on hand, checking account balances, savings, and investments. We know what comes in and what goes out—and when upcoming expenses and income will occur. Why do I take 10 to 15 minutes daily to gather and share this information? I once heard a co-worker tell her boss, "Your lack of planning doesn't constitute an emergency on my part." That was her way of telling him that she couldn't run around putting together his proposal at the last minute when he hadn't given her the needed information in a timely manner. The same goes for our finances.

If we don't mind our money, we wind up spending time and energy (and sometimes money) on triaging our financial situation. For example, a client came to me with nine different investment accounts. For two weeks, she monitored her finances for each account every day—before deciding to take my advice and consolidate them, which saved her an enormous amount of time and eliminated duplicate fees that were reducing her returns.

Checking accounts daily, we can instantly spot errors—overcharges, errors in deposit amounts, payment for items not received, or an account that has been compromised. Nearly half of all people don't even look at their bank statements, much less check their finances daily. Minding our money daily shows us what expenses need to come out of our accounts, when money will be deposited, or if we need to transfer money from savings to cover an expense.

Ten minutes is all it takes to look up everything and write balances on a single sheet of paper. On the right side, about a quarter of the way in, I draw a straight line down the page. In this space, I note upcoming expenses or actions, so we are *always* aware of our current financial position. We do this for our personal *and* business accounts. Do this for yourself and stop spending energy worrying about potential overdraft charges or a bounced check or expending time and energy moving money to avoid fees and penalties.

Be Financially Honorable

Being scared to talk about money, or even to *look* at your finances, slows your financial recovery. Being out of integrity with your finances or any financial transaction does the same. Fear is the enemy that keeps us stuck in old patterns. Ask questions and speak your microscopic truth—being truly transparent about your thoughts, feelings and actions, even when it's scary.

We all carry around old beliefs, habits, and ingrained financial patterns. One way to examine yours is to download my free workbook, *Heal Your Relationship with Money: An Adventure in Dissolving Financial Conflicts & Creating the Life You Desire.* (rebuildafterbankruptcy.com) In going through this interactive workbook, you'll make seven commitments to yourself based on your answers to 28 questions, which I developed with an organizational psychologist. Your deeply honest answers will give you insights that increase your comfort around financial issues. I encourage spouses and other family members to fill out their own workbook, after which you can all discuss your answers together. Learning how and why the key people in your life make certain financial choices can dissolve long-term arguments about money!

Pay Bills Early

Surprisingly, many people only vaguely know when their payments are due. Mail or manually pay bills online and you risk paying late, resulting in fees and penalties. And if the late payment is for a credit card, your interest rate could rise sky-high for months. Confirm each creditor's policy for applying your payments and you'll avoid these consequences.

Set up autopayments for the minimum amount due, then pay any additional amount you desire during the month. When using an online bill-paying service, pay attention to the fine print of their agreement. Your online payment may not *be posted* to your creditor's account until 7 to 10 days *after* the day the bill-paying service sends out your payment (your payout date). Set your payout date far enough in advance to avoid late payment penalties.

Consciously Choose Expenses

Bouncing back from bankruptcy isn't about paring your expenses to the smallest amount possible. It's about living a fuller life by determining the true *value* of each expense. The cost of an expense is *not* the same as its true value. Let me explain.

You know the saying "time equals money"? Let's say you want to free up a few hours weekly to take a class or pursue a hobby or side gig to increase your earning power. Where will you find the time? You look through your calendar and realize you spend eight hours weekly cleaning your house. If you hire a cleaning service to come every other week, you can increase the value of *your time* by up to 32 hours a month. What would it cost to hire a cleaning service to come every other week? At $200 a month ($100 a visit), that cleaning service costs you $6.25 per freed hour.

Here's an example of making a small change that has a big impact. I *love* my morning coffee with cream. Years ago, I realized my Starbucks habit was pickpocketing me—stealing a minimum of $150 monthly. My coffee habit was costing me more than my two-pack-a-day smoking habit ever did, *and* I had other places I wanted to put that $150 each month. So, I bought one of those stovetop espresso makers (about $30) and a 22 oz. tub of my favorite Café Bustelo espresso (under $20), which makes a month's worth of coffee. Let's say that, including the cost of cream, my monthly *cost* is $30. The *value* of making my espresso at home: $120 a month (the amount I save by foregoing Starbucks). I still stop at Starbucks when I'm taking a road trip—or hanker for their sous vide egg bites.

Why spend money you don't have to if you can give yourself the same or a better life experience by doing something different with your money? Examine all your expenses, and calculate the true value for each.

*   *   *

Above all else, remember you are not alone. We empower each other to make good financial decisions with our positive actions. Added together, our collective choices create financial freedom instead of keeping us slaves to Mastercard and other creditors.

The highest compliment readers give me is when they tell me they wish they'd had a copy of this book before they declared bankruptcy. If you have a loved one who is having financial troubles, please share this book with them before things get worse. I encourage you to take advantage of the free resources on my website, paulalangguthryan.com, and my YouTube channel, @BounceBackFrom. Or subscribe to my low-cost Substack newsletter *You Can't Eat Your Credit Score for Lunch!*

For Further Reading

I've hand-selected these resources (listed alphabetically) as ones I believe are the most helpful for creating true financial freedom after your bankruptcy:

30 Days to Eliminate Clutter and Debt: Your Inner Guide to Order and Financial Security; Paula Langguth Ryan and Janet L. Hall (G&D Media, 2024). Clutter and debt are often intertwined. Use this book to uncover and dissolve your inner beliefs and old stories so you can gain control of both your clutter and your debt.

Chapter 13 Bankruptcy: Keep Your Property and Repay Debts Over Time, 16th Edition; Cara O'Neill (Nolo, 2022). If you're still making payments under your Chapter 13 bankruptcy and want more information and strategies for navigating your repayment plan, you'll find answers here. If you need to file again and your attorney recommends either a Chapter 13 or a Chapter 20 bankruptcy (a Chapter 7 followed by a Chapter 13), this book outlines your options for paying off undischarged debts without creditors hounding you.

Cold Hard Truth on Men, Women and Money: 50 Common Money Mistakes and How to Fix Them; Kevin O'Leary (Gallery Books, 2013). Ever wish you had a financially successful mentor and all-around good person who would put their arm around your shoulder and give it to you straight by sharing a lifetime of solid advice on entrepreneurship, business, money, and life? Kevin is that guy. Use this book to fill your head with everything you *never* learned about money, and give yourself an advantage as you bounce back.

Directory of Dividend Reinvestment Plans (DRIPs); Charles B. Carlson (Horizon Publishing, 2025). Horizon Publishing also puts out the monthly *DRIP Investor* newsletter and offers the *Dividend Reinvestment Starter Guide.* Carlson's directory and newsletter bring to life the power of using direct purchase and dividend reinvestment programs to build your own targeted growth and income stock portfolio.

Earn What You Deserve: How to Stop Underearning and Start Thriving; Jerrold Mundis (Bantam, 1996). One of Jerrold's lesser-known financial books, this one deserves your attention if you want to "live long and prosper" yet constantly self-sabotage your efforts. Contains outstanding tools to fundamentally shift your attitudes about money, yourself, *and* yourself in relationship with money.

Get Good With Money: 10 Simple Steps to Becoming Financially Whole; Tiffany Aliche (Rodale, 2021). This book approaches financial ups and downs as part of being human. Imagine your bestie sharing her financial journey and all the steps and skills that will right your financial ship, or keep it off the rocks. A great resource for laying a strong common sense foundation for generational wealth.

How to File for Chapter 7 Bankruptcy, 23rd Edition; Cara O'Neill (Nolo, 2023). This is the book to read whether you're in the middle of your bankruptcy, haven't filed yet, are filing on your own, may have to file again, or just want to know all the details involved in the process as you're moving through it.

How to Get Out of Debt, Stay Out of Debt and Live Prosperously; Jerrold Mundis (Bantam, 2003). This step-by-step guide to eliminate remaining debt and stay away from new debt is an unofficial a Debtors Anonymous resource. Don't be put off by the decidedly "anti-bankruptcy" tone. I firmly believe that freeing yourself from the burden of your debt and then using this book to keep you from backsliding can make success more likely.

Money Drunk/Money Sober: 90 Days to Financial Freedom; Julia Cameron and Mark Bryan (Ballantine, 1992). This book, from the author of *The Artist's Way* and a counselor, pulls the curtain back on financial dysfunction. A great book if you're ready to identify and transform lifelong (and generational) money habits. Their 90-day step-by-step plan for financial freedom is solid and easy to implement.

Open Your Mind to Receive; Catherine Ponder (DeVorss, 1983). Are you great at giving but suck at receiving? Read this book to discover how to accept what's offered *and* become fully aligned with your inner goals. Releasing attitudes and beliefs that keep you stuck is a key component.

Rich AF: The Winning Money Mindset That Will Change Your Life; Vivian Tu (Penguin, 2023). Are you ready to accept that knowledge is power and that a budget is a discovery tool? This book demonstrates how to unlock intentional earnings, spending, and saving. Includes great interactive exercises for recognizing (and embracing) your true value.

The Art of Tithing: Harness the Power of Giving Thanks & Create Lasting Inner and Outer Wealth; Paula Langguth Ryan (G&D Media, 2021). Studies show that gratitude leads to increased wealth. And many people believe tithing—giving away 10 percent of what you receive to where you're spiritually fed—expands your gratitude level. This book's gradual approach to tithing will guide you through your fears around lack, wealth, poverty, trust issues, and everything in between.

The Budget Kit: The Common Cents Money Management Workbook, 6th Edition; Judy Lawrence (Judy Lawrence, 2014; moneytracker.com). This is the book to get if you prefer crunching numbers on paper. Lawrence's approach is nonjudgmental; it's *all* about the numbers. This is the best tool I've found for plotting out how and when money moves in and out of your life—and where and how you want to spend it.

The New Bankruptcy: Will It Work for You?, 10th Edition; Cara O'Neill (Nolo, 2023). If a repeat bankruptcy may be necessary, read this book, which outlines what type of bankruptcy would be best given whatever is going on in your world financially right now.

Trump: How to Get Rich; Donald J. Trump and Meredith McIver (Ballentine, 2004). Ever wish you had a mentor who would share brief, straightforward, actionable advice on how to approach your financial life? Whether you're looking to build, manage, and grow a business, want to excel at your job, become a better negotiator, or teach your children about money, this book is must-read.

When Money Is the Drug: The Compulsion for Credit, Cash and Chronic Debt; Donna Boundy (Harper Collins, 1993). When the way you handle money conflicts with how you *want* to handle money, read this book. How we handle money is also reflected in how we handle our time and energy. This book explains the different compulsions and addictions around money, offering concrete examples *and* actionable advice for when you or someone you love has a compulsive money pattern.

Your Home Loan Toolkit: A Step-by-Step Guide; Consumer Financial Protection Bureau (CFPB). Want to know *exactly* what happens financially when you're buying a home, where your money is going, and where you can save money in the process? This easy-to-follow interactive booklet is a must-read. Download a free copy at cfpb.gov/owning-a-home.

Your Money or Your Life: 9 Steps to Transforming Your Relationship with Money and Achieving Financial Independence; Vicki Robin and Joe Dominguez (Penguin, 2018). This book helps visual learners follow the money—as you earn more, save more, and spend less. Become aware and conscious of what comes in and goes out, and how much energy you spend on both, while getting laser-focused on your goals and dreams.

Acknowledgments

Every book is a team effort. This book, over the past thirty years, even more so. Please know that even if your name doesn't appear here your contribution is appreciated and acknowledged.

This book was made possible by Gilles Dana, who encouraged me to write this new edition. His steadfast patience, support and belief in my work keeps me writing.

Attorney Herb Beskin for being one of the first attorneys to recognize the importance of a book about recovering from bankruptcy, by an author who had "been there, done that."

The incomparable Terri Porter, owner of Creative Ink, for her incredible skills as a substantive editor and for helping me reorganize the book so it meets readers where they are in the process. Just like in college, I pitched, you caught, and we hit this book out of the ballpark.

The outstanding and tireless team at G&D Media, including Evan Litzenblatt, Ellen Goldberg, Richard Smoley, David S. Reinhardt, Meghan Day Healey, and Tyler Herrick.

Kabby Kabakoff and Collin Ungerleider at Kabby Sound Studios for their outstanding work in creating a beautiful audio version of this book—and for turning a week spent by myself in a soundproof room into a fun and precious experience.

My readers and clients who willingly shared their rocky roads and their soaring successes.

And most of all, my family, Sandy and Cooper. Your love and encouragement—even through my long absences—kept me going when my ego wanted to throw in the towel. I love you, and I'm coming home.

Index

identity theft (*cont.*)
  Social Security number and, 239,
    241, 242, 243–44
  spyware and, 241–42, 243
  stopping, 248–51
  tips for avoiding, 240–42
  virtual private networks (VPNs),
    241–42, 243
Identity Thief (2013 film), 239
Illinois Housing Development
  Authority, 195–96
income
  fortifying, 261–62, 303–4
  investing in yourself and, 312,
    313–14, 331
  rehabbing expenses for more,
    262–67, 303–4
  selling unneeded items, 262–64,
    304
income taxes
  annual PINs and, 239
  business car leases and, 156
  DebtBuster strategy and, 64
  as discharged debts, 46–47, 60
  FORM 1099-C, Cancellation of
    Debt, 46–47
  "phantom income" in pre-
    foreclosure sales, 295
  submission in mortgage
    application, 183
  tax liens on credit reports, 33
  tax relief strategy, 59
  tips for paying down tax debt, 320
  as undischarged debts, 59–60, 64
  on withdrawals from retirement
    accounts, 181
Independent Community Banks of
  America, 135
Indiana Housing and Community
  Development Authority,
  196–97

Innovis, 25
  fraud alerts/security freezes, 245,
    247
  Innovis Consumer Assistance,
    245
  ordering credit reports, 28
  secured credit cards reporting to,
    131
insurance
  as cause of overextension, 256
  comprehensive/collision, 147, 149
  credit card fraudulent charge
    protection, 118
  for credit card issuers, 114, 138
  credit score and, 174
  mortgage insurance, 290–91,
    294–97
  preapproved/prescreened offers,
    121, 244–45
  term life insurance, 264–65
Insurance Information Institute, 265
intentions
  in healing relationship with
    money, 81–85
  turning into goals, 82
Intercontinental Hotels Group
  (IHG), 170–71
interest-only mortgages, 225–26
interest rates
  on car loans, 142, 151–56
  credit score and, 150, 151–54
  credit unions and, 151
  impact of late payments on, 330
  on mortgages, 178, 225–26,
    228–29, 230–31
  refinancing after bankruptcy,
    231–34
  renegotiating, 276
  on secured credit cards, 133
  subprime lenders and, *see*
    subprime lenders

About the Author

Once bankrupt herself, Paula Langguth Ryan is the only consumer to testify before the National Bankruptcy Review Commission. Internationally renowned as a communications and conflict resolution expert for Compassionate Mediators, she helps people resolve conflicts around their finances, family and faith.

She is the author of many books, including *30 Days to Eliminate Clutter and Debt*, *The Art of Tithing*, and *Manifest the Perfect Mate*, and the former host of the daily Conflict Free Zone radio show and the What Would Paula Say? television series. Today, Paula offers pithy advice through her two Substack publications: You Can't Eat Your Credit Score for Lunch, and I Come in Peace . . . Or Do I?

Paula and her family divide their time between Colorado and New Mexico.

www.ingramcontent.com/pod-product-compliance
Lightning Source LLC
Chambersburg PA
CBHW071320210326
41597CB00015B/1287